Midwest

TOP 10

GARDEN GUIDE

By Bonnie Blodgett and the Editors of Sunset Books

MENLO PARK · CALIFORNIA

SUNSET BOOKS, INC.

VICE PRESIDENT, GENERAL MANAGER: Richard A. Smeby

VICE PRESIDENT, EDITORIAL DIRECTOR: Bob Doyle

PRODUCTION DIRECTOR: Lory Day

DIRECTOR OF OPERATIONS: Rosann Sutherland

RETAIL SALES DEVELOPMENT MANAGER: Linda Barker

EXECUTIVE EDITOR: Bridget Biscotti Bradley

ART DIRECTOR: Vasken Guiragossian

STAFF FOR THIS BOOK:

MANAGING EDITOR: Bonnie Monte

WRITER: Bonnie Blodgett

SUNSET BOOKS SENIOR EDITOR: Marianne Lipanovich

COPY EDITOR: Julie Harris

RESEARCH: Lynne Steiner

ART DIRECTOR: Vasken Guiragossian

PHOTO EDITOR: Dede Lee

PROOFREADER: Joan Beth Erickson

PREPRESS COORDINATOR: Danielle Javier

INDEXER: Susan Miller

DESIGN & PRODUCTION: Maureen Spuhler

ILLUSTRATORS: Lois Lovejoy, Erin O'Toole

MAP DESIGN AND CARTOGRAPHY:

Reineck & Reineck, San Francisco

COVER: Purple coneflower (*Echinacea purpurea*)
photograph by Greg Ryan/Sally Beyer.

10 9 8 7 6 5 4

First printing January 2004
Copyright © 2004 Sunset Publishing Corporation,
Menlo Park, CA 94025.

Library of Congress Control Number: 2003109783.
ISBN 0-376-03530-7.

Printed in the United States.

For additional copies of *Midwest Top 10 Garden Guide*
or any other Sunset book, call 1-800-526-5111 or visit
our web site at **www.sunsetbooks.com**.

PHOTOGRAPHERS:

BOB BAUER: 240, 241; PHILIPPE BONDUEL/G.P.L.: 160; MARION BRENNER: 208; PATRICIA J. BRUNO/POSITIVE IMAGES: 82R; GAY BUMGARNER: 10BL, 32, 35, 39TR, 43T, 79MR, 143T, 249L, 249R, 253; GAY BUMGARNER/ POSITIVE IMAGES: 1, 8TR, 11, 12TL, 12TR, 157B, 250, 262BM; ROB CARDILLO: 245; BRIAN CARTER/G.P.L.: 215M, DAVID CAVAGNARO: 4, 5, 9, 17, 28, 36L, 39TL, 39B, 41BL, 45BL, 46, 50L, 50R, 54, 57BL, 59, 60, 69T, 70, 72, 76, 87R, 89, 94, 95, 98, 99B, 100T, 114, 117, 120T, 122, 125R, 131, 138, 139, 142TL, 145B, 148, 149T, 149B, 150, 153B, 155TL, 164M, 165, 167B, 169B, 173, 176, 177T, 178, 181M, 181B, 186TL, 186M, 189T, 189B, 191B, 193T, 193B, 194, 195, 199T, 203B, 204, 209BR, 214, 216, 234, 254, 256BL; GEOFF DANN/G.P.L.: 107B; CLAIRE DAVIES/G.P.L.: 63T; JANET DAVIS: 31T, 43B, 69B, 71T, 74, 75T, 79BR, 82L, 91L, 106B, 119T, 119M, 119B, 123, 127TR, 143B, 170, 177B, 209TR, 235, 264; R. TODD DAVIS: 6T, 10T, 14, 24T, 34M, 37T, 37B, 38, 51T, 55, 61T, 97T, 109, 127L, 128M, 134, 144, 145M, 152, 155BR, 221B, 222TL, 246M, 255; CHRISTOPHER FAIRWEATHER/G.P.L.: 91R; DEREK FELL: 65BR, 155TR; GARDEN WORLD IMAGES/HARRY SMITH: 64; DAVID GOLDBERG: 34TL, 58TL, 80TL; JOHN GLOVER/G.P.L.: 85L; JOHN GLOVER/POSITIVE IMAGES: 205B, 211B; MARCUS HARPUR: 219T; SUNNIVA HARTE/G.P.L.: 147; MARIJKE HEUFF/ G.P.L.: 24B; SAXON HOLT: 65L, 110, 206, 223, 226, 227, 229, 231, 236, 238; JERRY HOWARD/POSITIVE IMAGES: 10BR, 203T, 256T; ANDREW LAWSON: 19, 41BR, 45BML, 45BR, 53B, 63B, 67T, 69TM, 73B, 83B, 88, 93T, 97B, 105, 106T, 111T, 132, 151T, 163, 171T, 212, 219B, 258, 263BL; ALLAN MANDELL: 52, 96, 199B, 209TL, 259; MAYER/LE SCANFF/G.P.L.: 51B, 126, 159T; CLIVE NICHOLS/G.P.L.: 29; JERRY PAVIA: 18, 20, 45BMR, 47M, 48, 49T, 56, 61BM, 65TR, 66, 77, 78R, 84, 85R, 86, 107T, 121, 124, 127BR, 129, 133, 136, 137T, 140, 141, 146, 154, 168, 172, 175, 187, 192, 201, 213, 220, 224L, 225T, 225BL, 228, 230, 232, 233, 239, 242, 243T, 256BR, 257, 263BR; BEN PHILLIPS/POSITIVE IMAGES: 22T, 53T, 75B, 78L, 130, 166, 181T, 182, 197T, 197B, 217; NORMAN A. PLATE: 200TL; DIANE A. PRATT/POSITIVE IMAGES: 49B, 153T, 156; LAURA QUATROCHI: 6BL, 73T, 157T, 167T, 171B, 179B, 183, 185B; ANNE REILLY/ POSITIVE IMAGES: 83T; HOWARD RICE/G.P.L.: 161, 174, 185T, 210, 211T; CHERYL R. RICHTER: 7, 8TL, 21, 25, 31B, 33, 40, 41BM, 47T, 47B, 61BL, 67B, 68, 79TR, 99T, 104M, 111B, 112, 116, 118, 120B, 135, 137B, 145T, 151B, 180, 188, 191T, 200M, 215T, 262BL, 262TR; SUSAN A. ROTH: 221M, 225BR, 237T, 243B; GREG RYAN/SALLY BEYER: 6BR, 61BR, 215B, 247; JS SIRA/G.P.L.: 102, 103B, 113, 115; PAM SPAULDING/POSITIVE IMAGES: 41TL, 41TM, 44, 71B, 103T, 108, 169T; LYNN M. STEINER: 41TR, 62, 69BM, 80M, 93B, 125L, 179T, 190, 196, 198, 207L, 224R, 244, 251, 252, 260, 261; FRIEDRICH STRAUSS/G.P.L.: 158, 184; RON SUTHERLAND/G.P.L.: 90; ANTHONY TESSELAAR: 237B; MICHAEL S. THOMPSON: 207R, 222M; JESSIE WALKER: 13, 26, 36R, 58M, 81, 92, 142M, 202, 221T, 248; TOM WOODWARD: 104TL, 128TL, 164TL, 246TL; CYNTHIA WOODYARD: 42, 57BR, 57T, 57BM, 87L, 100B, 101, 159B, 162, 205T, 218

GARDEN DESIGN CREDITS:

JANET & ROLF HAGEN: 259; JOY LARKOM: 185T; LES JARDINS DE BELLEVUE, FRANCE: 51B

compacted. Getting the soil right is always a challenge, no matter where you live. What really gets to us midwestern gardeners is the weather. Some years it seems like we have only two seasons: summer and winter. In addition to temperature extremes, colliding pressure systems produce violent thunderstorms, and sometimes a funnel cloud will dip down from the heavens and take out everything in its path. High winds are common even when the weather's fine. All this turbulence is owing to our wide-open spaces as well as our position on the map, thousands of miles from the moderating influence of ocean currents that move warm air north along the coasts from tropical regions. We're landlocked. For this reason, we often joke that we can't wait for climate change. But the truth is, "warming" just means that our turbulent weather is getting more so, with drought one year, floods the next. Fragile plants don't have a chance.

But there are plenty of tough, reliable plants that *will* perform in our harsh climate. Not surprisingly, many of them are descended from plants that originally took hold on the prairies after the Ice Age. These survivors adapted

BELOW: *A bold, prairie-style border features variegated eulalia grass, purple coneflower, and yellow black-eyed Susan.* OPPOSITE PAGE, TOP: *Daylilies (upper right) and yarrow are drought tolerant, long blooming, cold-hardy perennials that don't mind our region's clay soil.* BOTTOM, LEFT TO RIGHT: *Black-eyed Susan and purple coneflower.*

to long dry spells, horrific storms, intense heat, and bitter cold—and contributed to the ecosystem that produced our vaunted topsoil.

LEARNING THE HARD WAY

It was my first garden that introduced me to the perils of trying to grow plants outdoors in Minnesota—or anywhere in the Midwest for that matter—without sufficient knowledge. One sweltering June morning when I was a teenager and my parents were away, I decided to make a cutting garden. I found a trowel in the garage and set about turning my mother's tiny, crescent-shaped flower bed into a 12-foot square. The ground was so hard it took me all day to excavate to a depth of 2 inches. I planted the seeds, ran Popsicle sticks through the seed packets to mark each variety, then

waited for rain. It never came. By mid-July my garden was as defeated as a dry riverbed. When I looked at it, I saw not the riot of color I'd dreamed about, but an old woman's face, wizened and reproachful, with ugly hairs sprouting up in her deep, jagged wrinkles (nastier weeds I'd never imagined). I pulled up a few stunted delphiniums (how was I to know they're notoriously tricky plants?) and cursed the weather.

I didn't pick up a trowel again until, 15 years later, my husband and I bought an old house in the city. The shady backyard was full of weeds, but this patch of dirt seemed to thrive on neglect. The oak and elm leaves had been allowed to decompose right where they fell, feeding the worms, which fed the dirt, which fed the vegetation, which attracted

FAR LEFT: *East meets Midwest in a shady water garden featuring tall ornamental grasses.* ABOVE: *A old-fashioned gazebo enjoys the cheerful company of roses and daisies, early summer staples in the heartland.* ABOVE RIGHT: *Fall-planted tulips and daffodil bulbs spring to life in April and May under an eastern redbud.*

other forms of wildlife to live, eat, reproduce, and die, much as the fertile topsoil was formed on the grassy plains of yesteryear. As my spade slid easily between the weeds, I was conscious of something transformative taking place deep in my soul. I'd never felt so alive.

I can't say the same for the hosta plants my neighbor had donated to the cause. Left overnight in his wheelbarrow, they were shriveled and browning from lack of water when I planted them hurriedly and then left them for dead. I was dumbfounded to find them fully recovered within a few hours. A soil test supplied an explanation for their amazing comeback. My

soil was rich but not too heavy, so it was able to absorb and retain moisture. I learned it was also mostly alkaline—or "sweet," as the English say—meaning that it had a neutral-to-high pH because it contained more lime than acid. This is typical of soil near the Mississippi River bluffs and throughout much of the Midwest. While hostas aren't too picky about pH, many plants require a sweet soil, among them clematis. Rhododendrons won't tolerate it, but something more to their liking showed up under shrubs and pine trees with highly acid leaves and needles.

Inspired, I pulled weeds and laid a small brick patio under some pines, surrounding it with rhododendrons and azaleas bred for super cold-hardiness at the University of Minnesota. I experimented with shade-tolerant grass-seed

9

mixtures and ground covers, adding impatiens and begonias for color. For a sunny corner, I splurged on a nearly mature dwarf crabapple tree. I leaned a trellis against its trunk and trained a clematis to grow up it. I wasn't even tempted to try delphiniums. Why spend hours spraying and staking a needy plant when so many others are just as pretty and don't need

ABOVE: *Tall trees filter light to a blend of shade-tolerant grasses and ground covers in a tranquil woodland backyard.* BELOW: *Pink tulips* (LEFT) *and giant allium* (RIGHT). OPPOSITE PAGE: *A path winds through masses of zinnias, globe amaranth and other heat-loving annuals.*

special treatment? Instead I planted phlox and coneflower—two reliable midwestern garden staples—in the filtered sunlight below the crabapple tree and decided to test the limits of a hardy geranium said to tolerate some shade. It obliged, flowering for most of June and July. By summer's end I had a lovely garden. I'd learned how to work with the soil I had and, even more important, how to choose the right plants for my climate and sun exposure. Some

of them are featured in this book, which is intended to spare you my own rather steep learning curve.

GETTING OFF TO A GOOD START

I'd like to help you get it right the first time, beginning with your plant list. This book includes plant recommendations in 11 categories: long-blooming perennials for sun and shade, shrubs with great form and foliage, grasses that warm up the winter landscape, trees for every size garden, evergreen conifers for year-round interest, herbs and vegetables that look as good as they taste, floriferous annuals, spectacular bulbs, roses that never get sick, low-maintenance lawns and ground covers, and vigorous vines that won't run amok. Believe it or not, even with the entire plant

kingdom pared down to six to ten plants in each category, you'll still have too many choices. To further ease the selection process, I've included companion planting suggestions so you'll know what plants look good together and have common growing requirements. Plan on buying one to five plants in each category this year and adding more as your garden and your confidence grow.

There will be plenty of debate over why this or that plant didn't make the cut—that's part of the fun of list making—but I can assure you that all the plants that did make it are proven performers throughout the Midwest, and that's saying a lot. It's a big place. We're talking about an area that includes Minnesota, whose 10,000 lakes are frozen half the year; Missouri, where winters are mild but summers scorching; hilly

FAR LEFT: *A variegated dogwood is framed in an arbor festooned with cold-hardy, sun-loving clematis and roses.* NEAR LEFT: *A bench nestles into a three-season garden of flowers, evergreens, and ornamental grasses.* ABOVE: *Summer-blooming pink and red hollyhocks, yellow ligularia, pink and white cleomes, and tall grasses line a path.*

Indiana; and the desolate Dakotas. We're talking about dry plains and wetlands and river valleys—all with widely varying pH and soil structure. What common attributes make the plants on my lists suitable for such a diverse region? I gave high marks for hardiness, drought tolerance, and pest resistance, and gold stars for good manners.

CREATING A GARDEN

Some of you will use this book as a surefire shortcut to a beautiful, low-maintenance landscape. The Top 10 lists will make your trips to the garden center a lot easier. Instead of falling for whatever looks pretty at the moment, you'll be able to combine plants that won't clash with each other or overwhelm your space or die of thirst or freeze to death. Your planting scheme will take care of itself and give you years and years of armchair enjoyment.

For others, this book will be the start of something big. Buoyed by the success you have growing the plants suggested here, you'll want to experiment with different varieties (more temperamental perhaps, but you'll thrill to the challenge). Pretty soon you'll know just where to look to find out about bloom times, space requirements, and a plant's preferred pH. You'll know how to tell if a plant will like your garden or if it won't. You'll learn to shrug off mistakes, even relish them. You'll think of gardening as a voyage of discovery. I do. Welcome aboard.

Seasonal Chores

I admit I'm not much of a planner. All the more reason to keep a garden calendar handy. My season-by-season overview of garden activities tells when—and how—to do everything from sowing seeds in early spring to storing tools for the winter.

Early Spring

REMOVE MULCH from perennial beds as soon as temperatures are consistently well above freezing. Transfer biodegradable mulches such as dead leaves to your compost heap, if you have one. If you don't compost, bag the materials and take them to a municipal composting site. Empty the bags at the site and keep them for reuse.

DIVIDE overcrowded perennials when new shoots have poked up through the soil. Early spring (or fall) is a good time for dividing most perennials, including mid- to late-summer bloomers such as daylilies, delphiniums, phlox, daisies, irises, asters, and rudbeckia. Wait to divide early-spring bloomers until after they've finished flowering. Peonies, Siberian irises, and other plants with fleshy roots should be divided in fall. See "How to Divide Perennials," on page 16.

START SEEDS INDOORS under lights. Some annuals and vegetables need this head start to produce flowers or fruit in a

HOW TO DIVIDE PERENNIALS

If you noticed during the growing season that some of your perennials were dying out at the center, flowering less, or tending to flop over, they are probably overcrowded and need to be divided.

1 Choose a cool, overcast day and, working with one clump at a time, dig up the entire root ball.

2 Remove excess soil from the root ball so you can see what you're doing. Use your fingers for small, delicate plants. For larger ones, shake or hose off as much of the soil as possible.

3 For most perennials you'll need a knife or sharp spade to cut off divisions. For plants like hostas that form big clumps, use the two-fork method: shove the garden forks back to back into the top of the root ball and pry the clump apart.

4 Replant the divisions immediately and water them well.

timely fashion, especially in colder regions of the Midwest. Another short-season tip: Chose early-maturing varieties, like 'Early Girl' and 'Celebrity' tomatoes, for example, to protect your crop from Jack Frost.

PREPARE VEGETABLE BEDS by removing all weeds, using a hoe for shallow-rooted weeds and a hand weeder for deep-rooted weeds like dandelions.

SOW SEEDS OF LETTUCES and other cool-weather crops, such as peas, carrots, beets, spinach, and cabbage, directly in the garden.

SOW BEAN AND CORN SEEDS in midspring.

PLANT NURSERY POTS OR SEEDS of cold-tolerant pansies in outdoor containers.

PRUNE AND FEED ROSES. To prune shrub roses, first cut out dead or crossing canes, then prune the remaining branches back by a half to a third. To prune climbing roses, cut all old wood and all but four or five of the strongest young canes. Pruning out older canes focuses the plant's energy on growing taller young canes, which produce the flowers. (See "How to Prune a Climbing Rose," at right.) Fertilize after pruning with a controlled-release plant food.

CUT DOWN any plants you left standing to provide winter interest—such as ornamental grasses or perennial stalks and seed heads—and dispose of them in the compost heap.

For early lettuce, sow seeds as soon as the ground is workable.

HOW TO PRUNE A CLIMBING ROSE

Let a climbing rose grow unpruned for the first 2 to 3 years, which will give it time to become established. Remove only dead, damaged, or diseased shoots during this time. In subsequent years, follow the steps below:

1 Remove the old and obviously unproductive canes—the ones that produced no strong growth the previous year (shown in blue in the top illustration).

2 On the remaining canes, cut back to two or three buds all the side branches that flowered during the last year (marked in the lower illustration); this will encourage new blooms all along the canes.

17

REMOVE ANY DISEASED PLANT debris from beds but do not compost this material. Dispose of it with trash or burn.

APPLY CRABGRASS PREVENTER and fertilizer to your lawn.

YOU CAN START A NEW LAWN or repair an existing one now, but fall is a better time (see page 28).

Rhododendrons need an acidic soil.

FERTILIZE TREES AND SHRUBS. Use an acidifying fertilizer for rhododendrons, azaleas, evergreens, and blueberries.

PRUNE FRUIT TREES before buds swell, removing decaying or crossing branches. If you want a large fruit crop, prune to create an open center so sun can penetrate the canopy. For strictly ornamental trees, prune to the tree's natural shape.

LOOK FOR DAMAGE resulting from freeze-thaw cycles. Plants, especially young ones, may

HOW TO PLANT A BARE-ROOT SHRUB

1 Make a firm cone of soil in the planting hole. Spread the roots over the cone, positioning the plant at the same depth as (or slightly higher than) it was in the growing field. Use a shovel handle or yardstick to check the depth.

2 Hold the plant upright as you firm soil around its roots. When backfilling is almost complete, add water. This settles the soil around the roots, eliminating any air pockets. If the plant settles below the level of the surrounding soil,

pump it up and down while the soil is saturated to raise it to the proper level.

3 Finish filling the hole with soil, then water again. Take care not to overwater while the plant is still dormant, since soggy soil may inhibit the formation of new roots. When the growing season begins, build up a ridge of soil around the planting site to form a basin that will keep water from running off; water the plant whenever the top 2 inches of soil is dry.

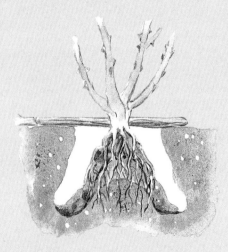
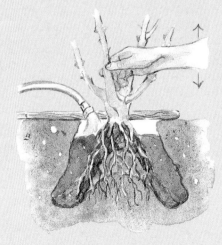
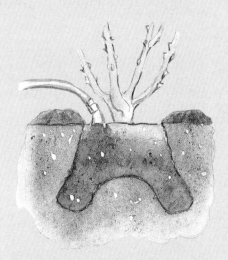

have been heaved out of the soil. Shove the uprooted plants back into the ground and tamp the soil lightly with your foot.

ON WARM DAYS BRING OUT ANY HOUSEPLANTS you wish to keep outdoors for the summer. Keep them outside for 2 hours the first day, then add an hour or so every day to acclimate them to full-time outdoor living.

PLANT TREES AND SHRUBS as soon as the soil can be worked but before buds have swelled or broken open. Bare-root plants are less expensive and will adapt more quickly to their new site than plants sold in containers, but you must plant them immediately and make sure the roots don't dry out. Plants that don't tolerate bare-root transplanting (rhododendrons, azaleas, and some conifers, for example) may be sold with roots and soil encased in burlap ("balled-and-burlapped"). Be sure to carefully remove as much of the burlap as you can before planting. Then follow the instructions given in steps 2 and 3 for planting a tree or shrub sold in a container on page 30.

RIGHT: *Forsythia in bloom is a sure sign of spring in the Midwest.*

Late Spring

DIVIDE EARLY SPRING–BLOOMING PERENNIALS such as primroses if they show signs of overcrowding. See "How to Divide Perennials," on page 16.

STAKE AND DISBUD PEONIES. Stake peonies using a tomato ring or cage to support stems that will soon be heavy with blooms. When buds appear, remove all but one bud per stem. This focuses the plant's energy on making larger flowers.

STAKE PERENNIALS that have a tendency to fall over later in the season. Use a grid-type stake for bushy plants with weak stems, like phlox. Hollyhocks, lilies, delphiniums, and other tall plants with heavy blooms can be tied to bamboo stakes. (See "How to Stake Various Plants," on page 23.) Another tip: Plant tall, skinny plants next to sturdier ones that they can lean on for support.

FERTILIZE PERENNIALS with a controlled-release fertilizer. Or try this organic formulation: Mix 1 tablespoon fish emulsion and $1/2$ teaspoon seaweed or kelp in a gallon of water. Use the mixture to irrigate the root zones and spray foliage every few weeks during growing season.

PREPARE BEDS for vegetables and annuals if you haven't already, or if you've worked only beds for cold-weather vegetables (see page 16).

LEFT: *Removing smaller peony buds makes for showstopping flowers.* RIGHT: *Spring in the Midwest turns lawns emerald green, setting off tulips and fruit trees in bloom.*

THIN SEEDLINGS you started indoors. Transplant seedlings to the garden.

SOW SEEDS FOR ANNUALS and warm-season vegetables such as corn, beans, and squash directly in the garden if you haven't already. Thin the seedlings soon after they've sprouted.

TO KEEP WEED SEEDS from germinating in flower beds, apply an organic weed-germination preventer. Remember that it will also prevent desirable plants from self-sowing.

PLANT SUMMER-FLOWERING PERENNIALS AND ANNUALS in the garden as soon as the ground is warm and workable

and there's no danger of a late frost. Pinch back the tops of young plants to encourage bushier growth.

PLANT SUMMER-FLOWERING BULBOUS PLANTS (dahlias, gladiolus, lilies, cannas, tuberous begonias), including those you've overwintered indoors. Place stakes or wire cages for tall plants that will need support.

SNAP OFF SPENT FLOWERS of spring bulbs, but allow the leaves to wither naturally before cutting them off. This gives them time to store energy for next year's blooms.

BRING OUT GERANIUMS (pelargoniums) you've overwintered indoors and plant them in clean containers with fresh soil.

AERATE THE LAWN if necessary by removing small chunks of turf using an aerating tool. This gets more oxygen to the roots so lawn grasses don't suffocate in compacted soil.

ABOVE: Tuberous begonia plants (and tubers stored over the winter) can be planted outdoors in late spring. RIGHT: An acid soil will make hydrangea flowers turn blue.

TO PREVENT WEEDS in your lawn, apply broad-leafed weed killer as dandelions and other broad-leafed plants leaf out.

CHECK YOUR LAWN MOWER to be sure the blades are sharp. Dull blades damage grass. If necessary, have them sharpened at the hardware store or mower repair shop. Set blades at 2½ inches to avoid cutting the grass too low, which causes it to dry out more quickly, encouraging weeds.

MOW FREQUENTLY to promote lush growth, at least once a week in spring and early summer, and leave clippings on the grass. They'll decompose quickly, replacing lost nitrogen.

PRUNE EARLY-FLOWERING SHRUBS such as forsythia after they've finished blooming. Cut one-third of each shub's branches to the ground, then cut the shrubs back to a third of their previous height. Lilacs should be lightly pruned after flowering and fertilized; add lime if soil is acidic.

HOW TO STAKE VARIOUS PLANTS

Support thin-stemmed, bushy perennials with a grid-style stake (upper left) or stakes and string (bottom left). Tie tall plants to a bamboo stake (right).

REMOVE SUCKER GROWTH on fruit trees immediately. Also remove suckers at root level on roses that have been grafted for cold-hardiness. (Unchecked sucker growth can cause the cold-hardy root stock to overpower the more desirable improved species grafted onto it.)

ADD ALUMINUM SULFATE to the soil around the base of any blue-flowering hydrangeas to keep them from turning pink instead. (For pink flowers add lime.)

PINCH NEW "CANDLES" off pines to curb growth.

Early Summer

PLANT SEEDS OR SEEDLINGS of annual herbs that thrive in warm weather, such as basil, cilantro, and dill. Deadhead regularly so they keep producing fresh foliage and don't go to seed.

KEEP BARE SPOTS BETWEEN PLANTS WEEDED until plants fill in. Dig deep-rooted weeds like dandelions with a hand weeder or trowel. Use a hoe to pull up weeds with shallow roots.

SOW SEEDS for Halloween pumpkins now.

Perennial hardy geraniums (ABOVE) *are at their peak of bloom in early summer. Plant warm-weather herbs such as dill* (RIGHT) *now for a bumper crop.*

PLANT ANNUALS if you haven't already. Pinch back the tops of young plants to encourage bushier growth.

LIGHTLY PRUNE ROSES after they've bloomed, removing any dead or crossing canes and removing any suckers from grafted roses. Make sure climbing roses are securely fastened to their supports.

KEEP CONTAINER PLANTS WELL WATERED AND FERTILIZED. You may need to water plants daily in dry weather. Watering leaches nutrients from the soil, so fertilize at least once a week unless you've applied a controlled-release fertilizer.

PINCH BACK ANNUALS whenever the plants get leggy, to stimulate growth of side shoots. Deadhead to promote flowering (so plants don't focus energy on seed production).

PINCH BACK CHRYSANTHEMUMS for fuller growth and more blooms.

REMOVE FOLIAGE FROM SPRING BULBS after the leaves fade.

CUT BACK EARLY-BLOOMING PERENNIALS. After flowers are spent, shear perennials such as catmint, hardy geraniums, and dianthus back to one-third their size to promote growth of fresh leaves and flowers.

Curving rows of vegetables alternate with annual salvia in a kitchen garden. Keep weeds and pests in check throughout the growing season.

CHANGE WATER IN BIRDBATHS regularly to keep mosquito larvae from hatching.

CHECK PLANTS FOR SIGNS OF IRON DEFICIENCY (chlorosis). Yellow leaves with deep green veins may be an indicator. Spray leaves with a foliar spray containing iron or zinc. If the leaves turn green after this treatment, your diagnosis was correct. If plant does not improve, however, the problem may be a virus. Remove any infected plant from your garden to prevent the virus from spreading.

CONTINUE THINNING vegetable seedlings.

WATCH FOR PEST DAMAGE to foliage as temperatures climb. Control four-lined plant bug *(Poecilocapsus lineatus),* aphids, mites, and other harmful insects with insecticidal soap. Spray liberally. Apply again after rain.

COUNTER SLUGS AND SNAILS. Use bait or saucers of beer among your hostas and other plants that slugs love. Attracted by the beer, the slugs will crawl into the saucers and drown.

PRUNE SUCKERS and water spouts from all fruit trees.

KEEP PULLING UP WEEDS before they go to seed.

SHEAR OR PINCH BACK evergreen conifers.

Late Summer

WATER YOUR GARDEN WEEKLY (if it doesn't rain), for about an hour, to encourage roots to probe deep for moisture and nutrients. Conserve water by using soaker hoses and collected rain water. Water in early morning, if possible. Evening sprinkling can cause fungal problems.

CONTINUE PINCHING AND DEADHEADING flowering plants.

KEEP UP THE WAR ON WEEDS. Don't let them go to seed.

REJUVENATE YOUR CONTAINERS by planting heat-loving plants like celosia, marigolds, portulaca, vinca, and zinnias.

CUT FLOWERS FOR BOUQUETS to bring indoors (and to encourage plants to rebloom).

encourage plants to put on fresh growth. Discontinue shearing in early fall.

PRUNE SUMMER-BLOOMING SHRUBS, like potentillas and hydrangeas, for shape after they've flowered.

REMAIN VIGILANT IN FIGHTING SLUGS, other pests, and diseases. Treat powdery mildew (zinnias, phlox, and bee balm are especially susceptible) when temperatures are below 85°F/29°C by spraying the leaves with this home remedy: 1 tablespoon each of baking soda and quality horticultural oil to 1 gallon of water.

DIG UP AND DIVIDE bearded irises in August after they go dormant. See "How to Divide Perennials," on page 16.

SOW SEEDS FOR COOL-SEASON CROPS, such as lettuce, for fall harvest.

DO NOT FERTILIZE IN HOT, DRY WEATHER. Plants struggling to retain moisture will be stressed if forced to grow. Lawns in super-dry heat will go dormant and turn brown but will green up as weather cools.

SHEAR LATE-BLOOMERS such as purple coneflower, rudbeckia, and phlox after they've finished flowering. This will keep your garden looking tidy and

Fall

PLANT COLD-HARDY PANSIES, chrysanthemums, and flowering cabbages for late-season color. Cover hardy mums that are not well established with a winter mulch in late fall.

DIVIDE PERENNIALS with fleshy roots, such as peonies, oriental poppies, and Siberian irises, if they show signs of overcrowding. Most other perennials can be divided now as well, as long as there's a good month left before the first killing frost so that roots have enough time to get established before plants go dormant. See "How to Divide Perennials," on page 16.

STOP FERTILIZING TREES and shrubs.

START A NEW LAWN or repair an existing one. September is the best time for either. Use a rotary tiller to prepare the soil and work in organic matter before laying sod or seeding a new lawn. Repair dead patches by removing the dead grass, loosening the soil surface, and spreading seed and fertilizer over it. Cover the seed with a thin layer of compost and a light mulch of grass clippings to protect the seed from birds and to keep it moist.

CUT DOWN SPENT PERENNIALS that are looking ratty. Leave those with good fall color and attractive seed heads until spring if you wish. Many ornamental grasses look beautiful in winter as well.

RAKE YOUR LAWN (fallen leaves make excellent compost) and fertilize it with a controlled-release 3-1-2 fertilizer. Now's the time to add lime if soil is acidic (lawn grasses prefer a neutral pH).

HARVEST FALL CROPS such as corn, tomatoes, and herbs, and lettuces sown in late summer.

ABOVE: *After maples' brilliant autumn foliage drops from the trees, the leaves will make excellent compost.* OPPOSITE PAGE: *Left unpruned, the dried stalks and seed heads of purple coneflower, Russian sage, rudbeckia, and feather reed grass will add winter interest.*

APPLY A THIN LAYER OF MULCH around perennials to keep them warmer longer. Once the ground is frozen, add a thick layer of mulch to keep soil temperatures even, which helps prevent plants from being uprooted in a freeze-thaw cycle. This is especially important for new plantings whose roots are not yet well established. Fallen leaves and straw are good materials to use for mulching.

MARK THE POSITIONS of perennials with durable tags so you won't disturb their roots when you plant bulbs in late fall or work in the garden in spring. (Some perennials don't emerge until early summer.)

PLANT SPRING BULBS such as tulips, daffodils, anemones, hyacinths, and squill when the soil temperature is below 60°F/16°C. If you're planting bulbs in masses, an auger greatly speeds the process of digging holes. Digging beds is even easier. Make sure you dig the holes and/or beds to the proper depth for each plant.

Add bonemeal or bulb fertilizer when planting. Mark the locations of your bulbs so you don't mistakenly dig them up, and so you'll know if any are missing come spring.

CLEAN AND OIL GARDEN TOOLS. Slide shovels and forks up and down in a large bucket of sand to clean them.

AT NIGHT BRING IN TENDER CONTAINER PLANTS such as geraniums, tuberous begonias, and fuchsias, as nighttime temperatures may drop precipitously at this time of year.

GRADUALLY ACCLIMATE POTTED PLANTS you wish to bring indoors as houseplants. Add an hour or two to their indoor time each day.

HOW TO PLANT A TREE OR SHRUB SOLD IN A CONTAINER

1 Remove the plant from its container by placing the container on its side and rolling it on the ground while tapping it to loosen the roots from the insides. Upend the container and slide the plant out. Spray the soil with a strong jet of water to loosen any roots that may be matted or coiled, then untangle them with your fingers. You may have to cut badly coiled roots.

2 Dig a planting hole twice as wide as but no deeper than the root ball. The plant should sit an inch or so above the surrounding soil. Spread the roots wide so they are pointing outward as much as possible. Backfill the hole with the original

garden soil. (Amending the soil will only encourage the roots to circle around the plant instead of probing outward for nutrients, and slow down the process of adapting to the new site.)

3 Mound soil to create a ridge around the plant to direct water to the roots. The trunk should not be directly exposed to water or it may rot.

TRANSPLANT DECIDUOUS TREES AND SHRUBS after they've gone dormant but before the ground freezes hard. Dormant plants are less likely to suffer from transplant shock. Dig out as much of the root balls as possible. Stake large trees and shrubs.

DIG UP dahlias and tuberous begonias. After the first frost withers and blackens their leaves, cut the plants to the ground and dig up the tuberous roots or tubers with a pitchfork, shaking off the excess dirt from dahlia roots (leave it on begonia tubers). Let dahlia roots dry in the

ABOVE AND BELOW: *The warm colors of fall take the chill off winter's onset.*

sun for several hours, then divide multiple roots with a sharp knife (cutting through the stem base). Allow begonia tubers to dry for several weeks before dividing them. Each tuber should have an eye, where new growth will sprout in spring. For best results, dust tubers or roots with an anti-fungal powder. Store in plastic bags filled with peat moss in a cool place (40° to 50°F/4° to 10°C) until spring, checking periodically to make sure they don't dry out.

CLEAN UP PLANT DEBRIS. Put biodegradable, healthy material in the compost heap. (Try to keep weeds out of it.) Compost any fallen leaves that aren't used to mulch beds. Leaves can also be shredded with a lawn mower and left to decompose on the grass. Rake up and dispose of all diseased and decayed plant material, along with any weeds. Eliminate plants that may harbor insects, such as rotting tree stumps.

KEEP WATERING YOUR GARDEN regularly as long as it's warm enough to keep a garden hose outside. When temperatures dip to freezing, it's time for the hose to come indoors.

PROTECT EVERGREENS from drying out in winter due to a combination of sun, wind, and too little snow cover. If fall weather has been dry, you may want to spray them with an antidessicant, which helps leaves and needles hold in moisture.

DO ONE FINAL WEEDING to minimize weed seeds sprouting in spring.

ORDER YOUR SEED catalogs now!

PLANT TREES AND SHRUBS. Fall planting encourages root development and lets plants get established before spring. At this time of year most trees and shrubs will be sold in containers, and they are often root-bound. Look for large roots girdling the plants above their root balls or poking out through the drainage holes. Root-bound plants will not adapt easily to a new site unless their girdled roots are cut or forced to grow outward. Keep new plantings well watered until winter.

Winter

PROTECT TENDER ROSES. If you live in the far north you may want to protect some of your more tender roses by burying them (for a description of the "Minnesota tip" method, see page 224). Make sure your hardy climbing roses and other vines are securely tied to their supports so winter winds don't take them down.

PLANT TULIP BULBS as late as November.

PERIODICALLY CHECK on your winter mulch, adding more as necessary.

PRUNE EVERGREENS and deciduous background shrubs to shape in early winter before the branches have become brittle from very cold weather (or they may break in the wrong places).

SIPHON GASOLINE out of your mower before storing it for the winter. Old gas destroys carburetors.

CHECK UP ON STORED TUBERS AND TUBEROUS ROOTS to make sure they are not drying out. Sprinkle water over them to keep them moist (but not wet).

PROTECT SHRUBS from unseasonable cold snaps. If one is forecast, plunge three or four stakes into the ground around marginally hardy shrubs and drape burlap or old sheets or blankets over them. The material must not touch the plants or they'll freeze. Remove the material when the weather improves.

PLAN NEXT SEASON'S garden projects. Draw a diagram and write up a plant list. Winter is a good time for reflection on successes and failures as well as future projects. Use a garden journal to record your ideas and thoughts for next spring.

PRUNE FRUIT TREES before buds begin swelling in early spring.

PLACE ORDERS FOR SEEDS and plants. When the seeds arrive, mark packets with optimum sowing dates for your area. You can figure these by using the number of days from germination to maturity—usually printed on the packets—and factoring in the average spring and fall frost dates in your area. Prepare for indoor seed-starting by collecting peat pots and all the other necessary equipment.

Freezing weather may cause young branches of deciduous shrubs, such as viburnums (LEFT) and evergreens (OPPOSITE PAGE), to dry out and break. Cut back plants before winter settles in.

Perennials

Perennials are plants that live for more than two years, as opposed to annuals, which live only one season, or biennials, which live no longer than two. In our cold climate most herbaceous (nonwoody) perennials die back to the ground when winter comes, their fibrous roots remaining dormant until longer, warmer days nudge them awake.

Perennials reproduce by shedding fertile seeds from faded flowers. Some perennials are vigorous self-sowers, and their progeny will rise up every spring for years after the original plants have died.

To keep the plants under control, some gardeners remove ("deadhead") the spent blooms, which prevents the flowers from going to seed and producing new plants. This stimulates the plants to try again by making more flowers. Perennials generally require more aggressive pruning as well. Why? Each plant has its peak bloom time, lasting from a few days to several weeks, and after putting its energy into flower production the plant can be pretty ratty-looking. Cutting plants back neatens their appearance and rejuvenates growth.

ORCHESTRATING A SHOW

The trick to designing a beautiful perennial border is timing the different bloom periods so that you have harmonious color in spring, summer, and fall. A garden of just annuals is colorful but static, while a well-planned perennial garden is constantly changing, even in winter. Growing a perennial garden is a bit like conducting an orchestra; it can take a while to get all the plants in tune, but how gratifying it is when the colors and textures create a pleasing composition.

CHOOSING PLANTS

Before going plant shopping, review the perennials in this chapter and select a blend of early, mid-, and late bloomers that will thrive in your garden's soil and sun or shade conditions. Also choose plenty of annuals (addressed in the next chapter) to fill in gaps during skimpy flowering periods.

To figure out where plants will look best and how many of each kind you need, it's helpful to diagram a planting scheme on paper first. Think about the overall shape of your perennials. Are they tall and skinny? Round? Clumpy? Do they creep, soar, or sprawl? These traits may be more important than flower color, as the plants themselves will be around long after their blooms have faded. Combine plants with contrasting shapes. Do the same with leaf texture and color. Foliage may be coarse or velvety, feathery or spiky, monochrome or multicolored.

Resist the temptation to grow one of everything. Instead, plant in groups of three or more. Repeat these groupings if you have room. Rep-

ABOVE: *A prairie-style birdhouse adds a whimsical touch to a mid-summer display of purple coneflowers and black-eyed Susans, a classic midwestern combination.* OPPOSITE PAGE: *Daylilies massed on a hillside are a beautiful and practical design solution.*

etition lends a sense of order and calm, whereas too many individual plants vying for attention has the opposite effect. While it's generally wise to arrange plants with the shortest in front and the tallest in back, don't hesitate to move them around if the scheme seems boring or out of balance. The plants won't mind as long as you work fast on a cool, cloudy day and remember to water them thoroughly before and after transplanting. Grouping perennials with conifers, grasses, trees, and flowering shrubs in a "mixed border" is a great way to make your garden design varied and interesting.

DIGGING IN

Most garden centers have expanded their inventories in recent years, but if they don't have what you want, you can order from a catalog or an on-line mail-order perennials specialist. Perennials grown from seed may not flower until their second year, a good reason to begin with plants.

Make sure you know how large each plant will grow. Space plants as the labels recommend, planting closer only if you want your garden to look filled in right away or if you're using plants for weed control. Be aware that if you plant closer than recommended, you may eventually have to move some plants to avoid overcrowding, and you should be on the lookout for signs of disease and pest infestations, as these problems spread more quickly when plants are crowded.

Perennials generally have long roots and need a bed at least 1½ feet deep. Amend the soil with organic matter such as compost, leaf mulch, manure, or peat moss before planting

ABOVE: *A stand of Siberian iris shows off one of nature's most penetrating blues.*
RIGHT: *Three hostas in subtly different shades of green contribute to the serenity of this shade garden; gray stones and weathered wood furniture complement the monochromatic scheme.*

36

and layer on more in spring and fall. Roots, earthworms, and micro-organisms will do more soil conditioning for you.

SHEARING AND DIVIDING

While deadheading requires snipping off a spent flower with light scissors or even your thumb and forefinger, shearing is a more radical procedure used when perennials are past their peak. I use hedge shears. The idea is to cut each plant back by a third or a half or, in some cases, all the way to the ground. Amazing as it may sound, this doesn't discourage the plant at all. You'll be rewarded with fresh foliage and possibly more flowers.

Over time a plant may lose vigor, flower less, or develop a hole in its center. In that case, it's time to dig up the plant and split the root mass into two or more chunks before replanting. Dividing plants is a good way to expand your garden—or make new friends. Who wouldn't be charmed by the offer of a free plant?

Pay attention to these simple tasks and water as needed, and your perennials will be trouble free—at least, my Top 10 perennials will. These plants can make even a novice look like a pro!

ABOVE: *Masses of pink and white peonies make a superb formal border for a lawn.*
BELOW: *Sun-loving cranesbill geraniums scramble over a stone wall.*

Black-eyed Susan
Rudbeckia

The award-winning Rudbeckia fulgida sullivantii 'Goldsturm', descended from wild rudbeckias once common on the western prairie, has inherited its ancestors' vigorous and cheerful demeanor.

Rudbeckia is one of the best-loved perennials in the midwestern landscape. Never heard of it? Think again. It's daisylike, with yellow petals surrounding a dark brown eye, on stems that grow to about 2 feet tall. It's often called black-eyed Susan. I especially like it planted in masses or with other prairie plants and grasses in a big, open landscape, where its dazzling color can be fully appreciated. Bees, butterflies, and American goldfinches all flock to it, so if you like to think of your garden as a habitat for wildlife, you'll love rudbeckia. Its sturdy stems and long-lasting petals make this mid- to late-summer bloomer a good cut flower as well. A late-summer shearing not only removes fading leaves and flowers but also encourages fresh growth and even some reblooming. In a small city garden a little goes a long way, so keep rudbeckia in check.

Rudbeckia fulgida sullivantii 'Goldsturm', named Perennial Plant of the Year in 1999, is descended from the native wild species *R. hirta*. Both are easy to grow even in clay and will spread—though not rampantly—and self-sow. The offspring of many varieties can vary considerably from their parents.

PEAK SEASON

Midsummer to fall; seed heads are attractive in winter.

MY FAVORITES

Rudbeckia fulgida is longer blooming and takes the heat even better than R. f. 'Goldsturm'. Its flowers are slightly smaller and the plant is generally more delicate-looking.

R. nitida is sometimes called yellow coneflower; 'Herbstonne' grows to 6 feet tall.

GARDEN COMPANIONS

All the rudbeckias work well in mixed prairie or meadow gardens. Try combining them with

- New England aster • garden phlox
- ornamental grasses such as fountain grass, feather reed grass, or switch grass

When Plant nursery-grown plants in spring, summer, or fall. Spring is best. If planting in summer, wait for a cool, cloudy day and water well. Seeds can be started indoors about 8 weeks before the last spring frost date.

Where Choose a site in full sun with well-drained, average to rich soil. Borders and meadow gardens are ideal.

How Amend the soil with organic matter before planting. Plant in groups of three, five, or more, spacing plants 1½ to 2 feet apart, depending on the variety. Crowding encourages leaf spots and powdery mildew. Water thoroughly and keep the soil moist until plants are established.

TLC Although sometimes listed as drought tolerant, rudbeckias do best with consistent moisture. Once the soil has warmed, apply a 1- to 2-inch layer of organic mulch to retain moisture, improve the soil, and reduce weeds. Remove spent blossoms to keep plants looking neat. Staking may be necessary for taller varieties. A 6-inch layer of winter mulch applied after the ground freezes is a good idea for new plants and in areas without snow cover. Divide overgrown plants every 4 or 5 years in spring, splitting them through the crown and replanting the sections with generous spacing between them.

ABOVE, LEFT TO RIGHT: Rudbeckia hirta 'Prairie Sun', R. h. 'Indian Summer'. LEFT: R. h. 'Rustic Colors'.

39

Daylily
Hemerocallis

As a child I loved the look of orange daylilies: clusters of flowers on leafless stems rising 3 to 5 feet above clumps of strappy leaves. My mother had a different opinion. Certainly those old-fashioned wildflowers *(Hemerocallis fulva)* had little in common with the elegant Oriental lilies she loved. They were available only in orange, yellow, or red; they grew from rhizomes, not bulbs; and they were "uncultured"—like the roadsides, yards, and ditches where they sprung up. Daylilies have come a long way since then, thanks to the efforts of hybridizers obsessed with creating ever-frillier petals, more color and fragrance, smaller varieties, and repeat blooming. But as yet no one's figured out how to make a daylily flower last longer than a day.

Mixed daylilies stake their claim on a sunny corner of this large Nebraska garden. Daylilies steadily multiply when they like their location.

If you're a neatness freak you may find yourself wading into the border three or four times a week with scissors. Always take care to snip off the whole flower so the ugly spent bloom won't be replaced by an even uglier seed head. You might also want to snip off yellowing leaves. Give daylilies proper care and they'll flower from June to October.

PEAK SEASON

Early summer to frost

MY FAVORITES

Some of the more dramatic (and pricier) hybrids have flowers in unique blends of burgundy, purple, coral, peach, and even pale green, often with a second color on the edges or throat.

The newer dwarf daylilies, which grow 1 to 2 feet tall, are everblooming and tidy. 'Stella de Oro' and 'Happy Returns' have yellow flowers. Other dwarf rebloomers include 'Prairie Blue Eyes', whose flowers are lavender with blue eyes and green throats; and 'Little Grapette', with tiny purple flowers and yellow throats. 'Daring Deception' has heavily ruffled lavender flowers with deep purple eyes and edges and yellow throats.

GARDEN COMPANIONS

Daylilies look best in a sunny flower bed all to themselves. But they look good in informal flower gardens, too, where they hide the dying foliage of spring bulbs and add a welcome dash of bright color in lightly shaded areas.

The new everblooming varieties are more compact. Most have bright yellow or gold flowers that complement blue-flowered plants such as

- *Veronica* 'Sunny Border Blue'
- *Salvia nemorosa* 'May Night'
- *Campanula* 'Blue Chips'
- *Geranium* 'Johnson's Blue'

When Plant nursery-grown plants in spring, summer, or fall. Spring is best. If planting in summer, wait for a cool, cloudy day and water well. Plant bare-root plants in spring.

Where Choose a site in full sun or light shade. Modern hybrids need at least 8 hours of sun for best bloom. The soil should be well drained and average to rich. Daylilies are great for mass planting, and once established they are a beautiful way to stabilize a slope.

How Amend the soil with organic matter before planting. Space daylilies 1½ to 3 feet apart, depending on the variety. The plants spread, so give them plenty of room. Water thoroughly and keep the soil moist until plants are established.

TLC Young plants need regular watering. Once the soil has warmed, apply a 1- to 2-inch layer of organic mulch to retain moisture, improve the soil, and reduce weeds. Remove faded blooms regularly to keep plants attractive, and remove the bloom stalks after the last flower fades. Protect young plants with a 6-inch layer of organic mulch after the ground has frozen. Every year in early spring, dig in a controlled-release or complete fertilizer or an organic equivalent, such as fish emulsion or compost. Apply it again 4 to 6 weeks later. Divide plants when clumps become crowded or begin to bloom less, every 4 to 6 years, in spring or right after they finish flowering.

TOP, LEFT TO RIGHT: Hemerocallis *'Little Grapette' (with* Achillea millefolium *'Cerise Queen'),* 'Siloam Pee Wee', 'Indian Love Call'. BOTTOM, LEFT TO RIGHT: *'Mary Todd', 'Iona Rosetta Gold', 'Pink Damask'.*

Hardy Geranium
Geranium

Many years ago I visited a renowned perennial gardener and was surprised when she offered to show me her geraniums. I thought she was referring to pelargoniums, the popular container plants commonly called geraniums. Though I didn't know why she would be showing me annuals, I followed her, expecting to see upright, thick-stemmed plants with scalloped leaves and big, showy flowers. Instead, spilling over a wall at the front of the border, small flowers shone like colorful coins in a lacy bed of finely cut, bright green foliage. "Are they some sort of dwarf?" I asked. My host laughed and said, "These are true geraniums. They are nothing like pelargoniums."

Hardy geraniums are mounding plants that come in all sizes. Some varieties grow taller than 1½ feet. A few have a sprawling growth habit; others are more compact and form tidy clumps. Many flower colors are available, even blue. The individual blooms are not always as eye-catching as pelargoniums', but if you shear plants back after their first flowering they'll bloom again. The plants make a wonderful foil for showier specimens.

Hardy geraniums are also called cranesbill geraniums, after the pointy, beaklike fruit that forms after flowers fade.

Flowers and foliage complement each other beautifully in this pairing of Geranium *'Johnson's Blue' and* G. pratense *'Album'.*

When Plant nursery-grown plants in spring, summer, or fall. Spring is best. If planting in summer, wait for a cool, cloudy day and water well.

PEAK SEASON

Main flush late spring into summer; some rebloom into fall. Some have bronze or red fall foliage.

MY FAVORITES

Geranium sanguineum (bloody cranesbill) has pink or magenta flowers and a low, mounding habit.

G. endressii 'Wargrave Pink' stands 1½ feet tall and has bluish pink flowers. It likes cool weather.

G. 'Johnson's Blue' grows 1 foot tall and gets leggy if not adequately watered and pruned. Its penetrating blue flowers are worth the extra effort.

G. macrorrhizum (big-root geranium) is invaluable for dry shade. It is a low grower with white ('Album') or pink ('Ingwersen's Variety') flowers.

Where Select a site in full sun or partial shade with rich, well-drained soil. A spot with morning sun and afternoon shade is ideal. Heavy shade results in leggy plants with few flowers. Place in the front of a border or in woodland or rock gardens. Some of the bloody cranesbills make effective ground covers.

How Amend the soil with organic matter before planting. Space geraniums 1 to 2 feet apart, depending on the variety. Spreading types can grow to 2 feet across. Water thoroughly and keep the soil moist until plants are established.

TOP: Geranium endressii *'Wargrave Pink'*.
BOTTOM: G. sanguineum.

GARDEN COMPANIONS

Geraniums' fluffy mounds cover up the not-so-great legs of tall plants, as well as the withering foliage of tulips and daffodils. Plant with

- lupines
- catmint
- artemisia
- sedum
- fountain grass and golden hakone grass

- dianthus
- lamb's ears
- creeping thyme
- lady's-mantle

Plant shade-tolerant varieties with

- hosta
- epimedium
- wild ginger
- sweet woodruff

- lily-of-the-valley
- lamium
- foamflower

TLC Once the soil has warmed, apply a 1- to 2-inch layer of organic mulch to keep the soil cool and moist. Geranium plants tend to open up and become leggy and sparse in the center after flowering. Cut back after blooming to get a fresh mound of leaves and some rebloom. Every year in early spring, fertilize by digging in a controlled-release or complete fertilizer or an organic equivalent, such as fish emulsion or compost. To keep plants vigorous divide them every 3 to 5 years, in early spring, by digging them up, gently pulling or cutting apart the root systems, and replanting them; make sure each division has several growth buds and healthy roots. Few insects or diseases plague geraniums, although Japanese beetles can be a problem in some areas. Pick off adults and place them in a pan of soapy water or vinegar.

Hosta

Hosta

Create an all-hosta garden combining plants with subtly different leaf colors and textures. These four are, clockwise from top left, 'Northern Exposure', 'Zounds', Hosta tokudama aureonebulosa, and 'Patriot'.

Until I took up gardening I called all hosta "funkia," the common name for the plainest types, which grow like weeds. These days hosta is very near the top of my favorite-plant list. And while breeders have made it vastly more varied in form and color over the years, all this improving hasn't changed its basic good nature: Hostas are still the most stoical of garden plants, unfazed by our weather extremes, content to live in the shade and to serve as a backdrop for more spectacular specimens. They can be used as a filler in the border, an edging plant, or a ground cover in semishade. They grow and multiply without becoming invasive, look good all season long, and have but one enemy: the slug.

Hostas have flower spikes that can be unremarkable in appearance or quite regal, depending on the variety, but they're never the main attraction anyway. We grow hostas for their magnificent foliage. Their leaves may be wide or slender; smooth or puckered; solid colored, deeply veined, variegated, or striped. An all-hosta shade garden can be beautiful if you combine plants with different foliage colors and textures—a mass of hostas sure beats a thin, weedy lawn.

PEAK SEASON

Late spring to fall

MY FAVORITES

Hosta 'Francee' has green leaves edged in white. 'Gold Standard' has light green leaves that turn golden with dark green margins. 'Golden Tiara' is green-gold. 'Blue Angel' has huge, bluish leaves shaped like hearts, and white flowers. 'Winfield Blue' has blue leaves and lavender blooms.

H. sieboldiana is the puckered-leaf species. 'Frances Williams' is probably the most famous variety, with its blue-green leaves edged in yellow, and white flowers opening from lavender buds.

H. plantaginea has large flowers and blooms late. Look for 'Grandiflora', 'Aphrodite', and 'Royal Standard', a hybrid of *H. plantaginea* and *H. sieboldiana*.

GARDEN COMPANIONS

Plant en masse with early-spring bulbs, primroses, forget-me-nots, and lily-of-the-valley to add interest until hostas come up. Or plant with ferns, meadow rue, and Solomon's seal.

When Plant nursery-grown plants in spring, summer, or fall. Spring is best. If planting in summer, wait for a cool, cloudy day and water well.

Where Most hostas need partial to full shade and well-drained, rich soil. A spot with morning sun can be beneficial for variegated and golden-leafed cultivars. Too much sun will lead to leaf scorch. Hostas are suitable almost anyplace in the shade garden, including along the edges of ponds, as ground covers, and as specimen plants.

How Amend the soil with organic matter before planting. The recommended spacing of plants varies greatly depending on the variety. Be sure to allow enough room for each plant to expand to its full size, which may take 2 to 4 years. Water thoroughly and keep the soil moist until plants are established.

TLC Once the soil has warmed, apply a 1- to 2-inch layer of organic mulch to retain moisture, improve the soil, and reduce weeds. Although established plants are fairly drought tolerant, hostas will grow best if they have even moisture. Cut off the bloom stalks if you find the flowers unattractive. Winter hardiness varies by species and variety. It is a good idea to provide winter protection in colder zones. Plants emerge rather late in spring; mark locations of plants before winter if necessary. Every year in early spring, dig in a controlled-release or complete fertilizer or an organic equivalent, such as fish emulsion or compost. Some hostas self-sow, but they do not come true from seeds so you may need to dig out seedlings. Hostas can go for years without any division. When they do need it, divide plants in early spring just as new growth emerges. Hostas are notorious for their susceptibility to slug damage; handpick the pests or use pans of beer to trap them. The waxy-leafed hostas are a little more resistant.

LEFT TO RIGHT: Hosta *'Golden Tiara'*, H. sieboldiana *'Elegans'*, H. *'Krossa Regal'*, H. plantaginea

Irises

Iris germanica, I. sibirica

Irises are technically bulbous plants: some irises grow from rhizomes; others have fibrous roots. But like daylilies, which also grow from rhizomes, irises belong in the perennial border so we've grouped them with perennials instead of bulbs (see Chapter 11).

The most elaborate-looking irises are the German, or bearded, varieties. "Bearded" refers to the fuzzy hairs that grow from the lower, petal-like sepals. Although quite spectacular at their peak, bearded iris flowers lose their looks in a hurry and must be deadheaded. The plants are not unattractive without their flowers, but I find the leaves of Siberian irises more appealing in a perennial border.

Siberian irises are extremely hardy, and best for beginners. They have blue, purple, or white flowers; no beard; more slender leaves than their bearded cousins; much better resistance to borers and disease; and some shade tolerance. They don't need deadheading, and their seedpods are lovely in dried arrangements.

Siberian irises come in many shades of blue, from pale blue to the deep blue shown here to bluish purple, as well as white and yellow and combinations of all these colors.

German irises (TOP AND BOTTOM) have a more complicated flower than Siberians (MIDDLE), with lower petal-like "beards."

PEAK SEASON

Spring to early summer. The seedpods of Siberian irises are elegant in fall and winter.

MY FAVORITES

Siberian irises grow 3 to 4 feet tall. *Iris sibirica* 'Butter and Sugar' is an award winner with white upper petals ("standards") above yellow sepals ("falls"). 'Ruffled Velvet' is also an award winner, with deep reddish, velvety standards and violet falls. 'Baby Sister' is a low grower with large blue flowers and a white marking ("signal") at the base of each petal. 'King of Kings' is widely regarded as the best white Siberian iris.

German (bearded) irises grow 2½ to 3 feet tall. *I. germanica* 'Beverly Sills' is a coral pink heavy bloomer. 'Immortality' has white flowers with yellow beards and will rebloom. 'Batik' has purple flowers with white splashes. 'Before the Storm' is purple-black with bronze-tipped beards.

GARDEN COMPANIONS

Siberian irises are exquisite when paired with lady's-mantle, hardy geraniums, and other low, mounding plants whose form contrasts well with the delicate verticality of the iris leaves and flower stalks. Bearded irises look good with classic border perennials, such as delphiniums and peonies, as well as by themselves in mixed colors.

When Siberian irises have fibrous roots and are usually available as potted plants; they can be planted in spring, summer, or fall, although spring is preferred. Bearded iris rhizomes are best planted mid-July to early August.

Where Siberian irises like full sun to light shade and well-drained, slightly acidic soil. Plant bearded irises in full sun and well-drained, average to rich soil. Both types are well suited to perennial beds and borders.

How Amend the soil with organic matter before planting. Space irises 1½ to 2 feet apart, depending on the variety. Plant bearded iris rhizomes with the tops just above the soil surface; rhizomes planted too deep are susceptible to rot. Water all newly planted irises thoroughly and keep the soil moist until plants are established.

TLC Both iris types benefit from an application of a balanced fertilizer or an organic equivalent in early spring just as growth begins. Siberian irises require lots of water throughout the growing season; apply an organic mulch to keep moisture in the soil. Cutting off spent blooms makes the plants neater-looking but eliminates the production of attractive seedpods. Siberian irises take a season or two to become established and resent being disturbed; divide them when the clump is shaped like a doughnut, indicating a dead center. Bearded irises go into semidormancy in midsummer and require less water than Siberian irises. Tall bearded varieties may need staking. To keep plants healthy and vigorous, divide bearded irises every 3 to 5 years, 4 to 6 weeks after flowering, in July or early August. Bearded irises are susceptible to iris borers, a serious pest problem. Cut back and dispose of old foliage and rake up debris to help control the pests.

Lady's-mantle
Alchemilla

Take a look at lady's-mantle after a light rain. Its velvety, lily pad–like leaves hold the raindrops like translucent pearls. But that's not why it makes my Top 10. Lady's-mantle is easy to grow and puts up plumes of feathery chartreuse flowers that can make even a petunia suddenly seem glamorous if it's lucky enough to grow beside it. In fact, lady's-mantle makes everything else in the garden ten times prettier. Like hosta, it is a natural companion, self-effacing but never dull. Its subtle colors and soft, mounding habit lend a sense of cohesion, softening strident attention-seekers while coaxing shy beauties out into the limelight.

Quiet and unassuming, lady's-mantle grows in sun or shade and is the perfect companion for shrubs like these old-fashioned hydrangeas.

Lady's-mantle responds well to shearing and doesn't mind some shade (its leaves may burn if it's planted in a dry, hot, sunny location). The flowers are long lasting, may rebloom if deadheaded, and look good even after they've lost their vibrant lime green color.

When Plant nursery-grown plants in spring, summer, or fall. Spring is best. If planting in summer, wait for a cool, cloudy day and water well. Start fresh seeds indoors about 12 weeks before the last expected frost date or outdoors in summer.

Where Choose a site in partial shade with well-drained, rich soil. A spot with morning sun and afternoon shade is ideal. Lady's-mantle can be grown in full sun if you can provide a constantly moist soil. Place in the front of a border, along paths, or in woodland gardens. Mass plantings make an effective ground cover.

How Amend the soil with organic matter before planting. Plant in groups of three to five, spacing plants 1 to 2 feet apart, depending on the variety. Mature plants spread up to 2 feet. Water thoroughly and keep the soil moist until plants are established.

TLC Once the soil has warmed, apply a 1- to 2-inch layer of organic mulch to retain moisture, improve the soil, and reduce weeds. Although established plants are fairly drought tolerant, lady's-mantle will require watering during extended periods of dry weather. Plants self-sow, and the seedlings are easily transplanted. Remove spent flower heads if you don't like their appearance or to discourage self-sowing. Protect young plants with a 6-inch layer of organic mulch after the ground has frozen. In early spring, dig in a controlled-release or complete fertilizer or an organic equivalent, such as fish emulsion or compost.

PEAK SEASON

Late spring to early summer; foliage is attractive spring through fall.

MY FAVORITES

Alchemilla mollis 'Auslese' has the classic greenish yellow sprays of flowers and exquisite cupped foliage. It grows to 1½ feet tall.

A. erythropoda is a dwarf (growing to just 8 inches tall) with blue-green leaves and yellow blooms.

GARDEN COMPANIONS

Plant with

- masses of hardy geraniums and dianthus
- penstemon and Siberian irises
- astilbes in light shade
- late-spring bulbs

ABOVE AND LEFT: *Lady's-mantle knits together an otherwise discordant scheme; its broad, flat leaves and lacy, lime green flowers have a calming effect on plants with brighter flower color or a more angular shape, for example.*

49

Peony

Paeonia

Reliably robust health is required of all my Top 10 perennials, except this one. Its beauty and longevity more than make up for the peony's single weakness: it is vulnerable to certain illnesses, notably a fungal horror called botrytis, which causes flower buds and leaves to blacken and die. Infected parts must be removed immediately. For some reason, red-flowered varieties are more susceptible. Moreover, while peony flowers are spectacular at their peak, you'll want to deadhead fading blooms promptly.

Come August, you may be tempted to do away with the leaves as well. Don't even think about it. They'll need all the time they can get to store energy for next year's flowers, which will be simply gorgeous—also romantic, fragrant, and, well, perfect. They look stunning in a vase.

Herbaceous (nonwoody) peonies are long-lived plants with attractive, shiny green leaves that form rounded shrubs 2 to 4 feet tall and wide. So-called tree peonies are actually deciduous shrubs that can grow to 6 feet

OPPOSITE PAGE, TOP AND BOTTOM: The common peony (Paeonia lactiflora) is the queen of the perennial garden when in bloom in mid-June. Its glossy, dark green leaves are handsome all summer.

tall and produce blooms the size of dinner plates. Tree peonies may also be damaged by late-spring frosts, need significant support for their heavy flowers, and are quite expensive, partly because they're difficult to propagate. Stick to herbaceous peonies until you're more experienced. You won't be sorry.

PEAK SEASON
Late spring into early summer

MY FAVORITES
'Nice Gal' is magenta with big yellow centers and doesn't need staking.

'Festiva Maxima' has double white flowers and good fragrance. 'Sarah Bernhardt' is similar in light pink.

GARDEN COMPANIONS
Plant with

- foxgloves
- hardy geraniums
- Siberian irises
- roses
- clematis
- delphiniums

When Plant nursery-grown plants in spring. Plant tuberous roots late August through September.

Where Select a planting site carefully, as established peonies don't like to be moved. They require at least 6 to 8 hours of sun each day and well-drained, rich soil. Avoid heavy, poorly drained soils and sites with excessive wind. Plants flower less in light shade. Plant in borders or by themselves.

How Prepare the planting hole well, as these plants are often in the ground for decades. Dig a hole 1 1/2 feet deep and 2 feet wide. Fill it with loose, humus-rich soil enriched with superphosphate or bonemeal. Space plants 3 to 4 feet from other plants. This may seem like a lot of room at first, but the plants will fill in, and they need good air circulation to avoid foliar diseases. Plant so that the buds (the points from which stem and leaf growth develop) are no more than 1 1/2 to 2 inches below the soil surface; peonies won't flower if planted too deep. When in doubt, plant a little shallower. Water well after planting.

TLC Peonies require patience. Do not expect much bloom until at least the third season after planting. Water during dry spells, as low moisture can affect flower development. Most types will need some type of support, either in the form of staking or hoops. The first season, mulch the plants after the ground has frozen. Fertilize plants each spring after planting with a topdressing of well-rotted manure, compost, or a balanced fertilizer. Remove spent blossoms to prevent the formation of seeds and to put more energy into the root system. To help prevent botrytis, cut back and dispose of the stems each fall.

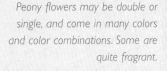
Peony flowers may be double or single, and come in many colors and color combinations. Some are quite fragrant.

Purple Coneflower
Echinacea purpurea

Like magnolias in the Deep South, cactus in Arizona, and ivy in New England, purple coneflowers exude pride of place. They're rugged midwestern prairie plants whose erect stems and durable flowers also make them ideal for a cutting garden.

As their name suggests, coneflowers have unusual shaped blooms. The petals slant downward from the center in a way that gives each bloom a shuttlecock appearance. (Some newer varieties have daisylike flowers, less suitable for a game of badminton.) When the petals fade and fall off, the golden brown center (or "cone") remains, bristling

with seeds. The plant's sturdy stem holds it aloft until it is reduced to a small black nugget, its seeds mostly dispersed. Butterflies and bees are forever flitting among the flowers, and American goldfinches consider the seed heads a real delicacy.

Some gardeners prefer a tidy winter look and cut back coneflowers in the fall. This means fewer seedlings next year. Left unpruned, the seed heads can add interest to the garden in winter. While coneflower clumps do expand, they are not invasive.

The flower shape of this purple coneflower has been "improved" through breeding so it resembles a daisy; petals on the classic coneflower (SHOWN OPPOSITE, AT TOP) slope downward from the center.

When Plant nursery-grown plants in spring, summer, or fall. Spring is best. If planting in summer, wait for a cool, cloudy day and water well.

Where Give purple coneflowers a site in full sun with light to average, well-drained soil. Soggy soils can lead to rot. Plants will bloom in light shade, but they will produce fewer flowers and may get leggy. Borders and meadow gardens are ideal.

How Amend the soil with organic matter before planting. Plant in groups of at least three, spacing the plants 2 feet apart. Crowding encourages leaf spots and powdery mildew. Water thoroughly and keep the soil moist until plants are established.

TLC Pinching back the growing tips of stems in spring results in bushier plants with smaller but more numerous blooms. Remove spent flowers to encourage more bloom, but allow later blooms to form attractive seed heads for winter interest. Plants will self-sow; leave the seedlings undisturbed or move them while they're still young (deep taproots do not transplant well). Winter protection may be necessary in areas without snow cover. Mature plants will tolerate drought and heat. Divide plants only if necessary in spring or early fall by splitting the crowns and replanting. Purple coneflowers are susceptible to aster yellows, a viruslike disease for which there is no cure. Infected plants must be dug up and discarded. Reduce chances of infection by keeping your garden free of weeds. Japanese beetles can also be a problem. Pick off adults and place them in a pan of soapy water or vinegar.

PEAK SEASON

Midsummer into fall

MY FAVORITES

'Bright Star' is a classic purple coneflower that grows to 2 feet tall.

'White Swan' has white flowers and grows 2 to 2½ feet tall; its sibling 'Cygnet White' is more compact, growing to just 1½ feet.

'Magnus' produces petals that grow horizontally from the center, giving flowers a daisylike appearance; it grows well from seeds. 'Ruby Star' is an improved version of 'Magnus'.

The yellow-flowered native species *Echinacea paradoxa* (also known as Bush's coneflower) can be ordered from catalogs that specialize in prairie plants.

GARDEN COMPANIONS

Plant with

- yarrows
- coreopsis
- daylilies
- liatris
- salvia
- upright sedums
- tall, golden grasses, such as feather reed grass

The flowers also are nicely set off by lime green plants like lady's-mantle, and plants with silver foliage such as artemisia and lamb's ears.

ABOVE: *Classic purple-flowered* Echinacea purpurea. BELOW: *E. p.* 'White Swan'.

Salvia

Salvia nemorosa

With some 700 species, salvia is an enormous—and enormously useful—family of plants, ranging from the ubiquitous flaming red annual to low, flowering ground covers to the culinary herb sage and its many close relatives. Russian sage *(Perovskia atriplicifolia)* is no relation but probably got its common name from the silvery leaves and blue flower spikes that resemble those of some salvias.

I depend on perennial *Salvia nemorosa* 'May Night' to keep my very public boulevard garden looking respectable. This narrow strip of earth is subjected to car fumes, pet wastes, road salts, occasional trampling by passersby, and blazing sun. While many plants have a brief moment of glory and then fizzle out, *S. nemorosa* doesn't need much care to retain its good looks well into fall. It is extremely hardy and disease resistant. It doesn't mind long dry spells and isn't finicky about soil. The whole plant can be sheared back to the new growth at the plant's base if dry weather or high winds damage the older leaves. The flowers attract butterflies and hummingbirds.

The deep blue flower spikes of Salvia nemorosa 'May Night' make a stunning combination with S. n. 'Snow Hill' and Geranium sanguineum 'Album'.

PEAK SEASON

Summer to fall

MY FAVORITES

'May Night', named Perennial Plant of the Year in 1997, has deep blue flower spikes 1 1/2 to 2 feet tall that fan out from clumps of gray-green leaves and bloom throughout the summer if deadheaded. After the flowers fall off, they leave behind attractive reddish purple bracts.

'Royal Crimson Distinction' has reddish pink flowers on 1 1/2-foot spikes.

'Ostfriesland' ('East Friesland') also grows to 1 1/2 feet and has deep purple flowers.

GARDEN COMPANIONS

Salvia nemorosa's vertical flower spikes are the ideal complement to full, mounding plants. Try combining it with

- hardy geraniums
- *Dianthus gratianopolitanus*
- *Artemisia* 'Powis Castle' and *Artemisia schmidtiana* 'Silver Mound'
- lady's-mantle

Its blue or indigo color looks good with the lemon yellow dwarf daylily 'Stella de Oro' and the creamier yellow 'Moonshine' yarrow, which has broad, flat flowers and silvery foliage.

When Plant nursery-grown plants in spring, summer, or fall. Spring is best. If planting in summer, wait for a cool, cloudy day and water well.

Salvia nemorosa 'Ostfriesland' ('East Friesland') shows off its tall, purple flower spikes in early summer. Deadheading will extend the blooming period.

Where Salvias require a site in full sun with average to rich soil. Good soil drainage is important, especially in winter. Keep taller varieties out of windy sites. Use salvias in mixed borders or mass plantings.

How Amend the soil with organic matter before planting. Plant in groups of three, five, or more, spacing plants 1 1/2 to 2 feet apart, depending on the variety. Water thoroughly and keep the soil moist until plants are established.

TLC Once the soil has warmed, apply a 1- to 2-inch layer of organic mulch to retain moisture, improve the soil, and reduce weeds. If you want bushier plants, pinch off the growing tips when plants are 6 inches tall. Deadheading will extend the bloom season. Apply a 6-inch layer of winter mulch after the ground freezes. Every year in early spring, dig in a controlled-release or complete fertilizer or an organic equivalent, such as fish emulsion or compost. Divide older plants in early spring when they begin to die out in the center. Mature plants are drought tolerant, but they do best with a consistent moisture supply. Good air circulation helps prevent mildew, which can be a problem.

Upright Sedum

Sedum

Reaching for each other across a narrow path are green-gold fountain grass (Penisetum alopecuroides) and Sedum 'Autumn Joy'.

If I had to choose one plant to give a beginning gardener, it would be *Sedum* 'Autumn Joy', a hybrid of *S. spectabile* and *S. telephium*. It teaches two important lessons: that foliage and shape are just as important as flowers, and that a handful of reliable performers planted in groups of three or more makes a garden, whereas one of everything makes a mess.

With its resilient beauty, an upright sedum anchors a garden as well as any clipped shrub, bringing out the best in showier plants and keeping the peace among them. 'Autumn Joy' looks good in spring, when its fleshy leaves poke up through the dirt; in mid-summer, when its pale green broccoli-like heads slowly age to the color of a fine claret; and even in winter, when its still-intact but now russet-colored seed heads look charming under caps of pure white snow. It is bothered occasionally by aphids but is otherwise disease free. Like all sedums, including the creeping ground covers, the upright sedums are succulents. They can get along with little water, less care.

PEAK SEASON
Midsummer to late fall

MY FAVORITES

Sedum 'Autumn Fire' is an improved 'Autumn Joy' with thicker blooms.

S. 'Vera Jameson' is upright but low-growing (to 9 inches). The color of its magnificent foliage defies description; imagine blue tinged with plum and a hint of green. The foliage sets off rose pink flowers that open in early August.

S. spectabile 'Stardust' and 'Iceberg' have white flowers.

S. telephium 'Matrona' has shiny, wine red stems; deep gray leaves; and pale pink flowers.

S. kamtschaticum 'Variegatum' grows to just 6 inches tall, bearing white-edged leaves and early-blooming yellow flowers.

GARDEN COMPANIONS
Plant with
- black-eyed Susan
- salvia
- dwarf fountain grass
- euphorbia
- feather reed grass
- red-berried creeping cotoneaster for winter interest

When Plant nursery-grown plants in spring, summer, or fall. Spring is best. If you are planting in summer, wait for a cool, cloudy day and water well.

Where Choose a planting site in full sun with average to rich soil. Good soil drainage is important, especially in winter. Sedums will tolerate poor, dry soils better than wet soils, which can lead to root or crown rot. Use sedums in mass plantings, meadow gardens, rock gardens, or mixed borders.

How Amend the soil with organic matter before planting. Plant in groups of three, five, or more, spacing plants 1½ to 2 feet apart, depending on the variety. Water thoroughly and keep the soil moist until plants are established.

TLC Once the soil has warmed, apply a 1- to 2-inch layer of organic mulch to retain moisture, improve the soil, and reduce weeds. Sedums do not require large amounts of fertilizer. In fact, they may become lanky with too much nitrogen. Most come through midwestern winters just fine without protection. Cut plants back to the ground in late winter or early spring, after you have enjoyed their attractive seed heads all winter. Apply a balanced fertilizer or organic matter every spring after planting. Divide plants in early spring only if they become floppy.

ABOVE: Sedum *'Vera Jameson'* with Euphorbia rigida. LEFT TO RIGHT: S. *'Frosty Morn'* and S. *'Autumn Joy'*.

TOP 10 Annuals

What is an annual? My horticultural dictionary offers two definitions: any plant that germinates, flowers, and dies in a single growing season and any plant grown for one season and then tossed out, including plants that would come back year after year (perennials) in a warmer climate but that we can grow here for only one season.

If you live in the Midwest and want lots of flowers all summer long, you're going to grow tender perennials as annuals. Everyone does. In fact, the majority of the annuals on my list are tender perennials.

The chief attribute of annuals is that they bloom incessantly, as long as you snip off their fading flowers. This is called deadheading. Deadheading thwarts the plant in its effort to develop seeds; the plant will usually bear more flowers in continued attempts to produce them. When you do let annuals go to seed, they can be prolific self-sowers, which is either a delight or a nuisance, depending on how you feel about a particular plant popping up everywhere.

STARTING GARDEN PLANTS

You can buy annuals in nursery pots (look for dense, fresh foliage and pinch off flowers of leggier plants to promote new leafy growth), or you can start them from seed. Before sowing seeds in the garden, check the seed packet to make sure they'll have time to flower before the first snowfall. Start them indoors if they need a little more time. For best results, grow them in a sterile, soil-less potting mix under artificial lights. When the ground has warmed up in the spring, dig beds 8 to 12 inches deep and amend the soil with organic material such as compost, peat moss, or leaf mulch. Then transfer your seedlings to the beds.

58

A word about weather: If an annual can't take the heat, it doesn't belong in your garden. Having said that, I should explain that pansies can't take the heat but outperform most other plants in cool weather, making them invaluable in early spring and late fall and earning them a spot on my list. The best annuals are like that: they step up when your garden needs help, filling gaps during those lulls when mainstay plants aren't looking their best.

There are hundreds of wonderful annuals that grow well in the Midwest. My aim is to get you started with a diverse selection: on the next few pages you'll find annuals for sun and shade; annuals in different colors, shapes, and sizes; annuals that can offer tropical splendor or give your garden an old-fashioned English cottage garden look. Use this list to experiment with annuals and discover your own personal style.

PLANTING IN CONTAINERS

Use a professional potting soil for your planters, window boxes, and hanging baskets. Fertilize and water regularly; water once a day in dry periods. When designing a container arrangement, choose at least one plant just for its foliage. Unusual leaf form and color can greatly enhance the beauty of flowering plants by offering subtle or striking contrast. Two of the annuals on my Top 10 list, coleus and sweet potato vine, are foliage-only plants; their flowers are insignificant. Licorice plant and dusty miller are two others, but anything from a dwarf conifer to a willowy ornamental grass can be used to complement flowering annuals. Be creative!

Coleus

Solenostemon scutellarioides (formerly *Coleus* × *hybridus*)

I hated coleus before I took up gardening. It made me think of dank Victorian parlors with oriental carpets, frilly doilies, and terrariums. Coleus *was* a popular houseplant in the 1890s, easy to grow and propagate, and content to live in the shade of curtained rooms. But it came out of the parlor and into the garden in a big way several years ago when experienced gardeners fell in love with its showy foliage, and breeders responded with ever more dazzling varieties. Less experienced but highly opinionated gardeners like me began to eat our words.

The cool gray leaves of dusty miller (Senecio cineraria) contrast with the diverse colors of Wizard Mix coleus. This combination works well in containers and flower beds.

Coleus can be positively psychedelic. Brilliantly colored, variegated foliage includes different combinations of red, orange, purple, white, yellow, pink, maroon, and green. The texture of the leaves ranges from velvety to puckered, and the edges may be smooth or serrated. Coleus looks especially good in containers, alone or paired with quiet companions that don't mind being upstaged. I like to grow it with white begonias or impatiens. I always snip off my coleus's flower spikes so the plant can concentrate on putting out more of those swirly-patterned, multicolored leaves.

When Coleus is a tender perennial, so wait until temperatures are safely above freezing to put plants outside. Plant on a cloudy day, if possible, to reduce transplant shock. Sow seeds indoors 8 to 10 weeks before the last frost date. Seeds need light to germinate, so press them just into the surface of the planting medium. Germination takes 2 to 3 weeks.

Where Plant in partial shade for best leaf color. Too much light will cause wilting and sunburn on leaves; too little light diminishes leaf color. Newer types, especially those with red or purple foliage, are more sun tolerant. The soil should be well drained and rich in humus. Use these neat, well-mannered plants individually as focal points or to add color to mixed plantings or containers. They are a great way to brighten up a shady corner of the garden.

How Loosen the soil to a depth of 10 to 12 inches and work in 2 to 3 inches of compost or other organic matter. (Incorporate a controlled-release fertilizer into containers before planting.) Space plants 8 to 12 inches apart in the ground, closer in containers. Lightly fertilize after planting.

TLC Water as needed to keep the soil evenly moist but not wet. Container plants may need watering daily. Mulch beds with chopped leaves or other fine-textured organic matter to retain moisture, control weeds, and improve the soil. If you didn't use a controlled-release fertilizer at planting time, fertilize every 2 weeks with a half-strength balanced fertilizer. Pinch back leaf tips at least once to encourage bushiness, and remove the insignificant flower spikes as they appear.

PEAK SEASON

Late spring to first frost

MY FAVORITES

'Golden Bedder' has chartreuse foliage.

Rainbow Mix, Wizard Mix, and Fashion Parade (ordered from short to shortest) are colorful blends.

'Dragon Sunset' has deeply carved leaves.

The Fairway series is extra short and densely branched for mass planting.

'Superfine Salmon Lace' has wide salmon leaves with burgundy centers and green margins.

GARDEN COMPANIONS

Most coleuses are too intense for use with other bright-colored annuals, but they do combine well with white flowers (shade-loving annuals such as impatiens, vinca, and begonias) and single-color foliage plants such as sweet potato vine.

ABOVE: Solenostemon scutellarioides *'Solar Sunrise'*. BELOW, LEFT TO RIGHT: *'Mr. Wonderful', a serrated-leaf chartreuse hybrid, a Wizard coleus.*

Flowering Tobacco
Nicotiana alata, N. sylvestris

Yes, flowering tobacco is related to smoking tobacco, their kinship revealed in the large lower leaves that make spacing these plants a challenge (they often become overcrowded down below). Fortunately, nicotiana doesn't smell like cigarette smoke. Its perfume is delightful and carries quite a distance. Generally, the taller the plant the headier the aroma.

Flowers are tubular to trumpet shaped atop bare stems. There are lots of colors to choose from, including red, purple, pink, salmon, and even chartreuse. White-flowering varieties are quite effective in the night garden (deeper colors tend to disappear). The smaller nicotianas are excellent in containers. I always plant them in a window box so that when I open the window their scent drifts into the house. Nicotiana is also an excellent filler plant during lulls in perennial blooming.

Although nicotiana is a tender perennial, you may discover that come spring you won't need to replant it, as it readily self-sows. Hummingbirds and moths are attracted to the flowers.

This dazzling combination of red Nicotiana alata 'Domino Crimson' and blue lobelia dresses up a deck.

PEAK SEASON

Early summer to first frost

MY FAVORITES

Nicotiana alata Sensation Mix includes fragrant white, pink, and red flowers on 3-foot-tall stems. Nicki Mix (1½ feet) has lime green, dusty pink, rose, white, and bright pink flowers.

The Havana series (1½ feet) features large flowers and exceptional colors, including apple blossom, carmine rose, and true lime.

The shorter Domino series (1 foot) is good for containers. It blooms earlier than Nicki nicotianas.

N. sylvestris is the aristocrat of the family, growing to 5 feet tall with long, tubular white flowers and great fragrance.

GARDEN COMPANIONS

Nicotiana's airy form blends especially well with more compact plants like hardy geraniums, dianthus, and lady's-mantle. Tall nicotiana may appreciate the support of sturdier plants in the back of the border.

When Plant nicotiana outside after all danger of frost has passed, on a cloudy day if possible to reduce transplant shock. Sow seeds indoors 6 to 8 weeks before the last frost date. The seeds need light to germinate, so press them just into the surface of the planting medium. Germination takes 2 to 3 weeks.

Where Plant in full sun to light shade in well-drained soil. Nicotiana is a good annual for bringing height to a garden area or container. Plant white varieties in night gardens. Compact varieties make good container plants. Site plants near sitting areas to enjoy the slight fragrance.

ABOVE: *Sweetly fragrant* Nicotiana sylvestris. BELOW: *Lime green* N. alata *'Domino Lime'.*

How Loosen the soil to a depth of 10 to 12 inches and work in 2 to 3 inches of compost or other organic matter. (Incorporate a controlled-release fertilizer into containers before planting.) Space plants 8 to 10 inches apart in the ground (12 to 18 inches for *N. sylvestris*), closer in containers. Lightly fertilize after planting.

TLC Water as needed to keep the soil evenly moist but not wet. Mulch planting beds with chopped leaves or other fine-textured organic matter to retain moisture, control weeds, and improve the soil. If you didn't use a controlled-release fertilizer at planting time, fertilize every 2 weeks with a balanced fertilizer. Plants may self-sow.

Geranium
Pelargonium × hortorum

Geraniums, another tender perennial, are easy to love. They're fast growing and tough, and their profuse pink, salmon, purple, white, crimson, or bicolored blooms are dazzling from a distance (less so close up unless the gardener is scrupulous about pinching off fading blooms and leaves). Geraniums tolerate partial shade (though bloom less) and can really perk up a somber corner. They're often grown in containers, a simple solution to a drab front stoop or rear deck. A single plant quickly fills a big pot, especially with trailing ivy, asparagus fern, or a spiky grass for company. Red-flowering varieties are attractive to hummingbirds.

Geranium leaves are as beautiful as their flowers, as soft as a puppy's ears, with scalloped edges and, in some varieties, interesting patterns. The leaves turn toward the sun, another reason to grow them in pots, which can be rotated frequently to keep an even shape.

Geraniums can be grown from seeds or cuttings, but unless you're a true aficionado seeking unusual leaf and flower color or habit, you should find plenty of smashing geraniums to choose from at a local garden center. By the way, the geranium's botanical name comes from the Greek word *pelargos,* meaning stork—and its seed does look like one.

Happy Thoughts geraniums are vigorous plants with a slightly trailing nature, easily filling beds or containers with their bold flower color and variegated foliage.

PEAK SEASON

Late spring to first frost

MY FAVORITES

'Appleblossom' has rosebud-type, blush pink flowers and dark leaves and doesn't mind the heat.

'Black Magic Rose' is an award winner with nearly black, green-margined leaves, and bright rose florets with a white eye.

The Happy Thoughts series offers unusual leaf patterns and red or pink flower colors.

Vining or ivy-leafed geraniums have glossy leaves.

Many species of scented geraniums are grown for their frilly foliage and citrusy fragrance.

Pelargonium × *domesticum* hybrids have azalea-like flowers and prefer cool nights; these plants are often in plant shows. 'Martha Washington' is a popular "show" variety.

GARDEN COMPANIONS

In the garden, brightly colored geraniums combine well with other flowering annuals, such as

- petunias
- marigolds
- verbena
- marguerite daisy

In pots they look best with another foliage plant for contrast, such as

- trailing ivy
- asparagus fern
- an annual grass

When Plant geraniums outside after all danger of frost has passed, on a cloudy day if possible to reduce transplant shock. Sow seeds indoors 14 to 16 weeks before the last frost date. Seeds need light to germinate, so press them just into the surface of the planting medium. Germination takes 1 to 3 weeks.

ABOVE, CLOCKWISE FROM LEFT: *'Martha Washington'; 'Mabel Grey', a lemon-scented geranium; 'Appleblossom'*

Where Plant in full sun to light shade in average, well-drained garden soil. Geraniums appreciate some shade during the hottest part of the day. Use these long-blooming plants in mixed borders, for massing in beds, or in almost any kind of container.

How Loosen the soil to a depth of 10 to 12 inches and work in 2 to 3 inches of compost or other organic matter. (Incorporate a controlled-release fertilizer into containers before planting.) Space plants 9 to 15 inches apart in the garden, closer in containers. Lightly fertilize after planting.

TLC Water as needed to keep the soil evenly moist but not wet. Geraniums will tolerate dry soil for short periods. Mulch beds with chopped leaves or other fine-textured organic matter to retain moisture, control weeds, and improve the soil. If you didn't use a controlled-release fertilizer at planting time, fertilize every 2 weeks with a balanced fertilizer. Prune dead flowers and encourage branching by pinching back fresh growth to the next set of leaves on the stems.

Impatiens
Impatiens walleriana

Soothing flower color against glossy dark leaves makes 'Super Elfin Lavender' an exceptionally attractive impatiens. Whether planted in pots or directly in the garden, this variety adds depth and beauty to a shady corner.

If a more no-nonsense plant exists, I would love to know about it. This compact species thrives in even dense shade, produces masses of flowers in every color but blue, blooms constantly without deadheading, will double in size if fertilized, and never seems to get sick. It grows equally well in pots and in the garden and fills spaces between plants beautifully, keeping down weeds as it spreads its cushion of flowers. Because the plants are so tidy and simple, they work best in a more formal design. They make a delightful edging for a shade garden.

Before hybridizers came up with cold-tolerant varieties, impatiens was confined to the greenhouse or solarium—this central African native likes hot weather—but it now thrives outdoors as a tender annual or a perennial grown as an annual and is consistently among the top-selling plants in North America. Innovation has kept pace with its popularity: the New Guinea hybrids, often billed as sun lovers but sometimes happier with some light shade during the day, have slightly larger flowers, and glossier and larger leaves that may be variegated or bronze-tinged with red veins.

PEAK SEASON

Late spring to first frost

MY FAVORITES

The best of the strains is Super Elfin, a garden-center staple with large flowers and a very tidy habit. Flower colors include white, pink, salmon, lavender, and red.

The New Guinea hybrids are available in a slightly wider range of colors, including yellow, and generally are best displayed in containers.

GARDEN COMPANIONS

In the garden impatiens looks best massed in groups of a half-dozen or more. It's fun to combine more than one color, as the flowers for some reason never clash.

In pots impatiens combines well with shade-tolerant foliage plants, such as coleus and trailing ivies.

When Plant impatiens outside after all danger of frost has passed, on a cloudy day if possible to reduce transplant shock. Plants are readily available in nursery pots in spring, but they can be started from seeds sown indoors 10 to 12 weeks before the last frost date. Seeds need light to germinate, so press them just into the surface of the planting medium. Germination takes 2 to 3 weeks.

Where Plant in partial to full shade in fertile, well-drained soil. Impatiens is great for edging a pathway or planting in masses under large shade trees. It is the number-one choice for containers in the shade. New Guinea impatiens grow best in full sun to very light shade.

How Loosen the soil to a depth of 10 to 12 inches and work in 2 to 3 inches of compost or other organic matter. (Incorporate a controlled-release fertilizer into containers before planting.) Space plants 6 to 12 inches apart in the ground, closer in containers. Lightly fertilize after planting.

TLC Impatiens is truly low maintenance. The plants require no deadheading or pinching. They do need plenty of water, especially during the heat of summer.

ABOVE: *Unusually showy leaves set New Guinea impatiens apart.* LEFT: *Impatiens walleriana 'Accent Orange'.*

Pansy

Viola × wittrockiana, V. cornuta

Why do pansies captivate small children? Maybe it's the subtle coloration that suggests eyes, nose, and mouth. Artists have been drawing "pansy people" for centuries. The fetching flower has inspired its share of poetry, too.

Pansies are a hybrid of several viola species, with slightly larger flowers and more complex, richer colors. Their flowers come in solid hues from white to almost black (including purples, reds, yellows, oranges, blues, and pinks), as well as bi- or tri-colored patterns. They have a light, pleasing fragrance and are delightful plants for small bouquets.

Like violas, pansies are short-lived perennials that love cool weather. Excellent in containers, they're often set out in pots in early spring, replaced in the heat of summer by petunias or other heat-loving plants, and reinstalled when the colder weather returns. In warmer parts of the Midwest they will bloom on and off all winter.

Newer hybrids are less leggy, forming dense clumps, and so happy in cold weather they bloom almost right up till Christmas. What could be more delightful than finding a pansy face peeking up at you through the snow?

Pansies serve two purposes in this spring planting: they complement the tulips in form and color, and they will cover up the tulips' foliage as it fades.

PEAK SEASON

Late spring to winter

MY FAVORITES

Viola × wittrockiana varieties that tolerate some heat include 'Imperial', 'Flame Princess', and 'Maxim.'

The Joker series, including 'Jolly Joker' and 'Joker Poker Face', has fun colors and patterns.

'Purple Rain' is a trailing variety.

'Accord Black Beauty' is a new hybrid with stunning black flowers and good weather tolerance.

Chalon Mix has ruffled edges.

V. cornuta 'Babyface Ruby & Gold' pansies are deep burgundy with yellow-blotched centers and a compact habit. 'Penny Orchid Frost' has a soft orchid pink center with white frosted edges.

The early-blooming Sorbet series features charming color combinations and interesting whiskerlike patterns.

GARDEN COMPANIONS

Pansies are great with spring bulbs. They also combine well with sweet alyssum and forget-me-nots.

When Pansies can usually be planted outside as soon as they are available at local garden centers, about a month before the last expected spring frost date. They tolerate cool temperatures, but if temperatures threaten to dip below freezing, they'll need some protection. Sow seeds indoors 8 to 10 weeks before moving them outdoors: barely cover the tiny seeds with soil, place the seed flats in the refrigerator for a week to satisfy pansies' cold requirement, then move them to a warm indoor spot; seeds sprout in about 2 weeks. Plant a second crop in mid-August for color after other annuals have been killed by frost.

Where Plant in full sun to partial shade in well-drained soil that is rich in humus. Summer plants will need shelter from afternoon sun. A pot of pansies is a must for an early-spring doorstep. Include pansies in your edible landscape and harvest the colorful flowers for tasty additions to salads.

How Loosen the soil to a depth of 10 to 12 inches and work in 2 to 3 inches of compost or other organic matter. (Incorporate a controlled-release fertilizer into containers before planting.) Space plants 6 to 8 inches apart in the garden, closer in containers. Lightly fertilize after planting.

TLC Water as needed to keep the soil evenly moist but not wet. If you didn't use a controlled-release fertilizer at planting time, fertilize every 2 weeks with a balanced fertilizer. Summer plants will need an organic mulch to help keep the soil cool. Deadhead regularly to prolong flowering, and cut back plants in late June to promote late-summer and autumn bloom. Pansies are vigorous self-seeders and tend to show up in the least likely places, but they're always welcome.

TOP TO BOTTOM: *Pansies come in just about every color and color blend you can think of, from white to orange to purple to black.*

Petunia
Petunia × hybrida

Primetime petunias come in 24 colors. They are low-growing, prolific bloomers, best massed in containers.

The petunia used to be a blowsy flower that tended to fold and flop over in windy, wet weather and get leggy and fall over if not frequently pinched back. *Used* to. New hybrids of this tender perennial offer smaller and sturdier flowers, a more spreading growth habit, and a more stoical attitude in foul weather. They've retained their willingness to tough it out through heat spells, and to last longer than impatiens in the fall as cold weather comes on. Alas, their leaves are still sticky, which makes them magnets for dirt.

Petunias are enormously popular, in the garden and in pots. Probably their single best feature is their incredible color range, which includes shades of white and yellow and the full spectrum of reds and blues. They may be striped, veined, edged in a different color, spotted, or splashed. The flowers may be single or double. Some have frilly edges; others are gently scalloped.

PEAK SEASON

Late spring to first frost

MY FAVORITES

Madness series petunias are fragrant.

Milliflora petunias have tiny flowers and don't need pruning. 'Fantasy' is a profuse bloomer with flowers an inch across. 'Colorsplash' is a vigorous grower with hot pink flowers that are very eye-catching against its yellow and dark green foliage.

Petunia integrifolia is a trailing petunia with small, plum-colored blooms that don't need deadheading; it's excellent in masses.

GARDEN COMPANIONS

Petunias are easy to grow in pots. Try them in a window box with other flowering annuals like salvia, zinnias, and verbena, and trailing foliage plants like licorice plant *(Helichrysum petiolare)* and sweet potato vine.

When Plant petunias outside after all danger of frost has passed, on a cloudy day if possible to reduce transplant shock. Sow seeds indoors 10 weeks before the last frost date. Seeds need light to germinate, so press them just into the surface of the planting medium. Germination takes 1 to 3 weeks.

Where Plant in full sun to light shade in average, well-drained soil. Petunias will tolerate poor soil, but too little light results in leggy plants. A spot out of the wind will help keep plants looking neat. Petunias are best suited to containers. A hanging basket makes a marvelous home for spreading, trailing types like 'Purple Wave'. The Wave-series petunias can also be used as colorful ground covers.

How Loosen the soil to a depth of 10 to 12 inches and work in 2 to 3 inches of compost or other organic matter. (Incorporate a controlled-release fertilizer into containers before planting.) Space plants 10 to 12 inches apart in the ground, closer in containers. Lightly fertilize after planting.

TLC Water as needed to keep the soil evenly moist but not wet. Pinch back young plants to encourage bushiness and more bloom. Deadhead the flowers regularly, and cut back plants in midsummer to encourage a second flush of bloom. Fertilize container plants every 2 weeks.

ABOVE: *Wave-series petunias' trailing habit is ideal for hanging baskets.* LEFT: *Carpet-series petunias are so compact they can be used as ground covers; their small, early-blooming flowers grow on short stems.*

Poppies

Papaver rhoeas, P. somniferum, Eschscholzia californica

Golden California poppies and red Flanders poppies mingle happily in a mass planting grown from seed.

If the pansy was my childhood crush, it was a poppy that ignited a full-blown, grown-up gardening passion. A field of poppies, actually. In France. Driving south through Provence in early spring many years ago, I was awestruck by the way the poppies painted the landscape the most brilliant red, as if the setting sun were casting a fiery glow across the fields.

Flanders Field or Shirley poppies *(Papaver rhoeas)* and opium poppies *(P. somniferum)* come in just about every color; most have yellow or dark brown centers. Examined up close, they are surprisingly delicate, with paper-thin petals precariously balanced atop slender woolly stems. They are lovely in bud when the stems bend like swans' necks. Both types grow well in containers and make excellent cut flowers.

It was a Flanders poppy that I fell for in France, but in my own garden the California poppy *(Eschscholzia californica)* has won my heart with its perky orange flowers and wispy gray-green foliage. Hybridizers have also produced bronze, yellow, cream, red, pink, and scarlet forms.

PEAK SEASON

Late spring to early autumn with successive sowings

MY FAVORITES

Papaver somniferum 'Black Cloud' is a medium-tall opium poppy with large, double, ruffled, dark purple (almost black) flowers; 'White Cloud' is the same with white flowers.

GARDEN COMPANIONS

Sow seeds among tulips. The poppies' bushy foliage will help hide fading tulip foliage.

For a wildflower garden, blend with

- lupine
- coreopsis
- perennial cornflower
- Indian blanket

In a cottage garden, combine with

- lamb's ears
- larkspur
- Shasta daisy
- veronica
- perennial cornflower

Mix seeds of California poppy half-and-half with sweet alyssum for an orange-and-white ground cover. Orange California poppy also combines well with purple or deep blue flowers, such as Chinese forget-me-nots and verbena.

When Poppies grow best in cool weather. Sow seeds in early spring, about 4 weeks before the last frost date. Cover with a thin layer of soil or peat moss so they don't dry out and to aid in germination. You can sow seeds indoors in individual pots 6 to 8 weeks before the last frost date, but transplant with care—poppies resent root disturbance. Make successive sowings every 6 weeks for season-long bloom.

Where Plant in full sun in well-drained soil. Poppies are ideal in meadow or prairie gardens.

How Mix seeds with fine sand to make it easier to see where you've sown. Keep the seedbed moist until seedlings appear. Thin seedlings to 6 to 8 inches apart.

TLC Deadhead to prolong bloom, but let some seeds form for next year's plants. Plants die out in midsummer if the weather is very hot. Poppies can become weedy in some situations. Don't hesitate to pull spent plants if deadheading and pinching back don't perk them up.

ABOVE: Papaver rhoeas.
LEFT: P. somniferum.

Sweet Potato Vine

Ipomoea batatas

Container gardening has soared in popularity, and sweet potato vine is one reason why. Its attractive leaves come in all sorts of colors and patterns that set off flower color beautifully. It also has a delightful cascading habit.

This tender perennial belongs to the same genus as the morning glory and the edible sweet potato but is no relation to the eating potato *(Solanum tuberosum)* or the potato vine *(S. jasminoides)*. It is one of several foliage-only annuals that have really perked up our pots: the dark gray–leafed 'Blackie' has deeply lobed leaves that offer a striking contrast to other plants, including its sibling 'Margarita', which has heart-shaped, lime green leaves.

The large-leafed, bright green foliage of 'Margarita' sweet potato vine provides a stage for the delicate, purplish blue, fan-shaped flowers of scaevola.

When Plant sweet potato vine outside a week or two after all danger of frost has passed, as it is very frost sensitive. Sow seeds indoors in individual pots 6 to 8 weeks before the last frost date. Germination takes 1 to 3 weeks. To speed germination, nick the seed coats with a file or soak seeds for 24 hours in warm water before sowing. Provide seedlings with stakes to wrap around so they don't become tangled.

Where Plant in full sun in average, well-drained soil. Sweet potato vine is very well suited to container culture, but it can also be used to cover a fence or trellis or trail over a spring-blooming shrub or large perennial.

How Loosen the soil to a depth of 10 to 12 inches and work in 2 to 3 inches of compost or other organic matter. (Incorporate a controlled-release fertilizer into containers before planting.) Space plants 8 to 10 inches apart in the ground, closer in containers. Lightly fertilize after planting.

TLC Water as needed to keep the soil evenly moist but not wet. If you didn't use a controlled-release fertilizer at planting time, fertilize every 2 weeks with a balanced fertilizer. A fertilizer high in nitrogen will promote more vigorous growth. You will need to provide strings or a trellis if you want the vines to climb.

ABOVE: Ipomoea batatas *'Margarita' with white daisies and hot pink petunias.* RIGHT: I. b. *'Blackie'*.

PEAK SEASON

Late spring through first frost

MY FAVORITES

'Ace of Spades' has heart-shaped, deep purple leaves.

'Blackie' is a trailing vine with large, almost black flowers.

'Margarita' (sometimes sold as 'Marguerita', 'Marguerite', or 'Margurite') is lime green.

'Carolina Bronze' is a new hybrid with bronze-colored leaves and great vigor.

'Ladyfingers' has deeply cut, dark green leaves.

GARDEN COMPANIONS

This vigorous, tropical-looking plant is a great addition to mixed container plantings with lots of flower color. Try combining a lime green variety with blue or lavender petunias and salmon verbena, purple heliotrope, or purple-leafed fountain grass.

Verbena

Verbena × hybrida, V. bonariensis

Here is a plant that does it all. This tender perennial or annual comes in an incredible array of flower colors, either solid or two-toned thanks to a bright eye (often yellow) at the center of the flower. It can be used in formal plantings but also lends itself to the wild abandon of the cottage garden. In a window box verbena adds fullness or, in its trailing form, a touch of grace as it tumbles over the edge of the planter.

Verbena has lacy flowers and serrated leaves, giving it a dainty, old-fashioned air. Yet when clothed in one of its zingy tropical colors—a brilliant salmon with a yellow eye, for instance—it becomes an exotic seductress. *Verbena bonariensis* is the lanky supermodel, growing to a height of 4 feet or more. This favorite of garden designers has purple pom-pom–type flowers, about the size of golf balls, on slender stems with small, thin leaves. It is quite regal when surrounded by shorter, more compact plants, either in the perennial border or as the centerpiece of a round flower or vegetable bed.

Tall, lavender Verbena bonariensis *blooms in late summer, just in time to attract monarch butterflies.*

PEAK SEASON

Summer to first frost

MY FAVORITES

Verbena x *hybrida* 'Peaches 'N Cream' is a low, bushy award winner with creamy peach–colored flowers. Dwarf Jewels is a blend of brighter flowers in mixed colors. 'Summer Blaze' has red flowers with white eyes.

Tapien hybrids are trailing verbenas, good as ground covers and delightful additions to hanging baskets. The pale lavender 'Tapien Blue Violet' is particularly attractive.

The new Superbena series has larger flowers and excellent mildew resistance, and comes in colors ranging from burgundy to coral to pink.

The Babylon verbenas are the most compact, good for edging or as front-of-the-border filler plants.

The Aztec series blooms early in white, red, or plum colors and is quite disease resistant.

GARDEN COMPANIONS

Verbena looks great with sun-loving annuals like sweet alyssum, salvia, and petunias and with most perennials.

Place *V. bonariensis* behind lower-growing perennials like

- lady's-mantle
- coral bells
- Shasta daisy
- hardy geraniums

When Plant verbena outside after all danger of frost has passed, *Tapien-series verbenas have bright flowers and elegant lacy foliage.* on a cloudy day if possible to reduce transplant shock. Sow seeds indoors 8 to 10 weeks before the last frost date. Germination, which takes 2 to 4 weeks and requires darkness, can be difficult. Place flats in the refrigerator for 2 weeks. *Verbena bonariensis* can be sown outdoors 2 weeks before the last frost.

Where Plant in full sun in average, well-drained soil. Use verbenas in beds, borders, rock gardens, or containers. Low-growing types can be used as edging plants. *V. bonariensis* is great in a perennial border.

How Loosen the soil to a depth of 10 to 12 inches and work in 2 to 3 inches of compost or other organic matter. (Incorporate a controlled-release fertilizer into containers before planting.) Space plants 10 to 12 inches apart in the garden, closer in containers. Lightly fertilize after planting.

TLC Water as needed to keep the soil evenly moist but not wet. Established plants tolerate dry conditions but prefer regular watering. Verbena may stop blooming during periods of intense heat, but it will bloom again with cooler temperatures. Mulch beds with chopped leaves or other fine-textured organic matter to retain moisture, control weeds, and improve the soil. If you didn't use a controlled-release fertilizer at planting time, fertilize every 2 weeks with a balanced fertilizer. Deadhead regularly to encourage bloom. *V. bonariensis* readily self-sows. Reduce the risk of powdery mildew by providing ample spacing to increase air circulation and avoiding overhead watering.

Zinnia
Zinnia

The zinnia is the classic annual for cutting gardens, with its popsicle stick–straight stems and vivid, long-lasting blooms. Flowers come in red, pink, orange, white, and some bicolors. Their form can be cactuslike (with spiky petals around a bright center), ruffled, or pom-pom shaped.

The taller varieties can perk up a fading flower border in late summer if planted in masses, but zinnias are prone to powdery mildew

during hot, humid seasons and should be planted behind shorter plants that can hide their leaves (flowers are not much affected).

I tend to favor the newer, smaller hybrids because they're more disease resistant. *Zinnia angustifolia* 'Crystal White', which has small white flowers with orange centers, makes a wonderfully airy addition to a hanging basket or window box. The extremely vigorous Profusion zinnias can be used to edge an herb or flower garden and also do well in pots. The unusual pale green flowers of *Z. elegans* 'Envy' add a touch of glamour to pots and flower beds.

When Zinnias are one of the few annuals that can be directly sown in the garden after the last frost in late May to early June and still produce flowers. The seeds sprout in a few days in warm soil, and flowers appear in 6 to 8 weeks. You can also start seeds indoors 4 to 6 weeks before the last frost date, but transplant carefully as the young plants resent being moved. Young plants do not tolerate frost exposure.

Where Plant in full sun in well-drained soil. Even partial shade will reduce flowering and weaken stems. Include taller varieties in your cut-flower garden. Lower-growing *Zinnia elegans* varieties do well in containers.

How Keep the seedbed moist until seedlings appear. Once seedlings are up, thin to 4 to 18 inches apart depending on stem height; space shorter zinnias closer together than taller varieties. Water seedlings regularly with a weak solution of fertilizer.

TLC Water regularly. Powdery mildew can be a problem on zinnias. Reduce the risk of infection by providing ample spacing to increase air circulation and avoiding overhead watering. Deadhead faded flowers. Tall varieties may need staking.

OPPOSITE PAGE, TOP: 'Profusion Orange' zinnias combine beautifully with silver licorice plant (Helichrysum petiolare) *and nasturtiums. OPPOSITE PAGE, BOTTOM: A bouquet of bright* Zinnia elegans *flowers has old-fashioned charm.*

PEAK SEASON
Midsummer to first frost

MY FAVORITES
Zinnia angustifolia Crystal series (also sold as Star series) has a compact growth habit and orange, yellow, or white flowers that bloom constantly.

Z. elegans 'Envy' has pale chartreuse flowers. Blue Point zinnias are taller, with giant, dahlia-type flowers perfect for the vase.

Profusion zinnias, award-winning hybrids between *Z. angustifolia* and *Z. elegans,* have prolific orange, cherry red, or white flowers that don't need deadheading.

GARDEN COMPANIONS
Zinnias blend well with bright, daisylike flowers such as asters and calendulas. For a dazzling container, combine 'Profusion Orange' zinnias with lime green–leafed 'Margarita' sweet potato vine and magenta-flowered *Petunia integrifolia.*

TOP TO BOTTOM: Zinnia elegans 'Envy', Z. angustifolia 'Profusion Orange', Z. a. 'Crystal White'

Deciduous Shrubs

Shrubs get no respect. We refer to them as bushes, prune them into the most unnatural shapes, or simply neglect them and then rip them out when they grow leggy and disheveled. Yet what would we do without forsythias, lilacs, spirea, and hydrangeas?

Unlike annuals and perennials, shrubs don't leave us in the fall. Evergreen shrubs, called conifers, stay with us year-round (they're addressed along with evergreen trees beginning on page 128). Deciduous shrubs lose only their foliage in winter; the woody branches remain intact, along with the buds that will produce next season's leaves and flowers. As winter wanes and the weather turns warm, the buds open. The dazzling yellow flowers of forsythia announce the arrival of spring in the Midwest. Fragrant lilacs mark the transition from spring to summer. Hydrangeas' giant, colorful blooms capture summer's ripe opulence, then mellow to golden tan as autumn nips the air.

EASY CARE

Shrubs are the least demanding of all our plants, with the possible exception of trees: they hold up in dry, hot weather and are resistant to pests and disease. They come in all shapes and sizes. Many of them have handsome foliage and long-blooming flowers. They harmonize well with other plants.

Whether planted as single specimens, in a mixed border, or as a hedge, shrubs give our gardens definition and structure. They create a sense of enclosure. They screen out unfortunate views. They help draw the eye to focal points. They offer shelter from high winds. More than any other design element—including stone cherubs, tiered fountains, and arbored gates—

shrubs dictate a garden's mood and style: geometric shapes and tight pruning signal formality, while a more natural growth habit lends a garden an informal, romantic air.

MUCH TO OFFER

Shrubs may be underappreciated, but I feel a correction coming on. A well-known direct-mail wholesaler in Michigan that sells only flowering shrubs reports that its business is booming. Every year its catalog gets thicker and glossier.

Gardeners have figured out that a mixed border of trees, shrubs, perennials, and conifers is easier to maintain and often more interesting to look at than the classic perennial border. Shrubs provide the same range of bloom times as perennials do, and many have fall and winter interest as well. Viburnums have small flowers in spring, then berries that turn pink to red to black. Cotoneasters bear small, deep green leaves that gradually turn crimson as winter approaches, and their brilliant red berries remain through

ABOVE: *Deep lavender lilacs, a spring bloomer, set off bright yellow tulips.* OPPOSITE PAGE: *The brilliant pinkish purple flowers of* Rhododendron *'PJM', developed in Minnesota to withstand prolonged subzero winter temperatures, have become a harbinger of spring in the far north.*

winter. Some dogwoods have bright red or yellow stems that also hold their color year-round. Hydrangea blooms cling to their branches long after they've faded to the color of wheat, perfect for holiday wreaths and table arrangements.

THINK AHEAD

Choosing the right shrubs for a particular site is critical. I hate to think how many times I've

ABOVE: *Forsythia in early-spring bloom makes a waterfall effect over a stone wall.* LEFT: Hamamelis × intermedia 'Diane' *is a winter-blooming witch hazel with striking red flowers.*

been captivated by a young specimen at a garden center and either failed to read the label or rationalized that I could curb the growth of an oversize plant through pruning. Better to buy the plant whose mature size fits your space. Most of the shrubs listed here come in many sizes and shapes; if you fall in love with cotoneasters' leaf color and berries, you'll need to figure out if it would look best as an upright hedge or a low, spreading ground cover. Lilacs and hydrangeas are available in dwarf or tree forms. Also, if you want a flowering shrub to combine with perennials, make sure you know when it blooms, and don't make the mistake of pruning at the wrong time and removing flower buds.

Careful pruning is the key to transforming a so-so shrub into a showstopper. Unless you wish to create a tight, formal hedge by shearing (removing the tips of all branches), shrubs look best when pruned to their natural shape. The best way to do this is by thinning; that is, cutting off selected branches to the next living branch or all the way to the ground, but removing no more than a third of the plant at one time. Thinning lets light into the center of the plant and stimulates new growth there, resulting in a bushier, healthier look. To make sure all parts of a hedge are exposed to sunlight, shape the plants so they're a bit fatter at the bottom.

OFF TO A GOOD START

Shrubs are sold as either bare-root, balled-and-burlapped, or container plants. Bare-root plants are sold in spring and should be soaked in water for 2 hours before going into the ground. Container and balled-and-burlapped plants can be planted anytime; fall planting is often recommended. Plants that have been growing for a while in pots may become rootbound. This is especially common if plants are purchased late in the season. These plants' roots should be forcibly spread apart so they don't girdle the stem—that is, grow in tight circles around it. Sometimes, slashing the roots with a pruning knife is necessary to stimulate roots to grow outward.

The planting hole should be no deeper than the root ball but wide enough to encourage roots to stretch out. After planting, backfill the hole with unamended garden soil. Roots won't probe farther than the immediate vicinity if

they're given a perfect soil mix at the start.

Shrubs need room to grow and good air circulation to ward off illness; space them according to label instructions. If you are making a hedge or screen, plants may be spaced a bit closer together.

Give your shrubs adequate water and fertilize them now and then—but above all, appreciate them. They do work awfully hard.

ABOVE: *Bridal wreath spirea forms flower clusters all along its arching branches in late spring or early summer.* BELOW: *Hydrangea macrophylla produces deep blue flowers when grown in acid soil, pink flowers in alkaline soil.*

Cotoneaster

Cotoneaster

Ten years ago I went shopping for mulch and came home with twelve creeping *Cotoneaster horizontalis* shrubs. That was one impulse purchase I haven't regretted. My cotoneasters have consistently garnered more compliments—and prompted more queries—than any other plant in my garden. In early summer it's the tiny, blush pink flowers that attract the notice of passersby; then it's the berries, which glow brilliant orange by autumn, setting off the glossy, deep green–turned–crimson foliage. Visible through the berries and tiny leaves are gnarled branches groping outward like arthritic fingers.

Over the years my "river of cotoneaster," as I call the planting that softens the edges of my boring front walk, has taken a fair amount of abuse. I've lost a few plants, but the river repairs itself by spreading out to fill any gaps and flows on. A single shrub can grow to 15 feet across. You can also grow cotoneaster as an upright hedge. Because it stands up to hard pruning, you can keep it pretty much any size you like.

A low border of Cotoneaster horizontalis *is a fluid extension of the evergreen Canada hemlocks behind it.*

PEAK SEASON

Spring through fall

MY FAVORITES

Cotoneaster horizontalis grows 2 to 3 feet tall with arching branches that can spread 15 feet wide. It has glossy leaves and pale pink flowers that are followed by red berries. Its leaves turn red in fall, and its berries may persist all winter, gradually turning deep maroon.

C. apiculatus grows to 3 feet tall. It has a graceful arching habit, pinkish flowers, and red berries. 'Tom Thumb' grows just 3 to 6 inches tall, forming a low cushion that's great for rock gardens, draping over a wall, or lining a path.

C. racemiflorous 'Songaricus', an upright hedge type, grows 6 to 8 feet tall. It has gray-green foliage, masses of white flowers, and pink fruit.

GARDEN COMPANIONS

Cotoneaster looks good with ground covers like variegated ivy (*Hedera helix* 'Glacier') and euonymus (*Euonymus fortunei* 'Variegatus'); low, mounding plants like hardy geraniums, 'Sea Foam' rambling shrub roses, thyme, and catmint; and taller plants like euphorbia and lavender.

When For best results plant cotoneasters in early spring, but they can be planted all season long if they are watered well.

ABOVE, LEFT: *Cotoneasters bear red berries and vibrant foliage in autumn.* TOP RIGHT: Cotoneaster horizontalis. BOTTOM RIGHT: *In spring, the plants are covered with white or pink blossoms.*

Where Cotoneasters grow best in full sun but don't mind light shade. They prefer fertile, well-drained soil. Use cotoneasters in mass plantings, as ground covers, or in rock gardens.

How Plant cotoneasters at the same depth they were growing in the containers, spacing according to the mature size of the plants. Water immediately after planting.

TLC Consistent watering is most important during the first 2 years. Keep the soil evenly moist from spring until the ground freezes, watering when the top 2 inches of the soil is dry. Once plants are established, apply 2 to 4 inches of shredded bark or wood-chip mulch around them as soon as the ground warms in spring and replenish as necessary throughout the growing season. Feed in spring with a 10-10-10 fertilizer or an organic equivalent sprinkled around the base of the plants and watered in well. Plants grown in the northernmost areas should be covered with winter mulch. Cotoneasters require very little pruning, but dead or diseased wood should be removed (you can do this anytime). Plants are difficult to transplant after the first 2 years.

Dogwood
Cornus

This *Cornus kousa bearing white, flower-like bracts complements a green-and-white planting scheme with chartreuse hostas* (LOWER LEFT) *and variegated euonymus* (LOWER RIGHT).

The most popular dog-woods for midwestern gardens are redtwig (or red-osier) dogwoods, members of the *sericea* species, formerly known as *stolonifera* and still called that in many books and catalogs. Redtwig dogwoods have an amazing ability to spread by sending out sucker-like "stolons," which are actual-ly prostrate branches that tun-nel into the soil and root there, creating brand new shrubs if you let them. New shoots also pop up from the underground roots, which spread quickly. Regular spadework and prun-ing of drooping branches keep the shrubs in check.

Redtwig dogwoods are famous for their brilliant crim-son stems, which hold their color right through winter. Mine grows by a tall cedar picket fence and looks quite stunning against a fresh blanket of snow. These easy-to-grow shrubs have a graceful habit and lovely, slender leaves. Some varie-ties have yellow or purple stems.

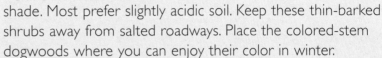

When The best time to plant dogwoods is early spring, but they can be planted all season long if they are watered well.

Where Almost all dogwoods grow best in sun, but some, including pagoda dogwood, prefer partial shade. Most prefer slightly acidic soil. Keep these thin-barked shrubs away from salted roadways. Place the colored-stem dogwoods where you can enjoy their color in winter.

How Plant dogwoods at the same depth they were growing in the containers, spacing according to the mature size of the plants. Be sure to give tree types ample space. Balled-and-burlapped shrubs should be planted so that the root flares are right at the soil surface. Remove as much of the burlap and wire holding the root ball as possible without injuring the roots. Water immediately after planting.

TLC Consistent watering is most important during the first 2 years. Keep the soil evenly moist from spring until the ground freezes, watering when the top 2 inches of the soil has dried out. Once plants are established, apply 2 to 4 inches of shredded bark or wood-chip mulch around them as soon as the ground warms in spring and replenish as necessary throughout the growing season. Shrub types will benefit from a spring application of 10-10-10 fertilizer or an organic equivalent applied around the base of the plant. Prune off dead portions of stems in early spring. Red-twigged types should have about a third of the stems cut out each spring to encourage new growth, which has the best color.

PEAK SEASON

Spring through late summer for foliage. Most also have spring flowers and late-summer fruits, but not all are showy. Some have colorful bark and interesting branching habits, which add winter interest.

MY FAVORITES

Cornus sericea 'Cardinal' has coral stems that turn cherry red in fall. 'Flaviramea' (yellowtwig dogwood) has gold stems.

C. alba 'Argenteomarginata' (formerly *C. a.* 'Elegantissima') is similar to *C. sericea* but has green-and-white variegated leaves.

C. alternifolia (pagoda dogwood) has large, soft white flower clusters and a horizontal branching habit. It is often grown as an ornamental tree.

C. kousa (kousa dogwood) is like *C. alternifolia,* with a horizontal branching habit and profuse, flowerlike bracts. 'China Girl' has white bracts. 'Rosabella' has pink bracts.

GARDEN COMPANIONS

Use shrub-type dogwoods in a shrub border with hemlock, viburnum, and lilacs; as hedges; and in mass plantings.

ABOVE: Cornus sericea *'Flaviramea'*. BELOW, LEFT: C. sericea. RIGHT: C. alba *'Argenteomarginata'*.

Forsythia

Forsythia

Mother Nature knows just what we need after a long, hard winter: a few rays of golden sunshine. Forsythia does a remarkably good imitation. Its dazzling yellow flowers bloom before the shrub leafs out and before most other shrubs flower. Though ubiquitous in regions where the plant is reliably hardy, forsythia still manages to lend a touch of the exotic to the late-winter landscape. Flowers range in color from a soft lemon yellow to bright gold, depending on the variety. Shrubs may be spreading or upright, dwarf or tall, and leaves are often variegated or turn purplish bronze in fall.

Forsythia branches hold their flowers for weeks and are striking alone in a tall glass vase or in a Japanese-style arrangement with other spring bloomers. If you want to jump-start spring, you can force forsythia to bloom early by cutting branches when they're still in bud. The warmth indoors will trick the buds into thinking it's time to open.

PEAK SEASON

Early spring

MY FAVORITES

Forsythia × intermedia 'Lynwood' is an old-time favorite.

'New Hampshire Gold' is extremely cold-hardy.

'Golden Peep' is a dwarf from France with profuse gold flowers.

'Golden Times' has green-and-gold variegated leaves.

Forsythia 'Meadowlark' has early yellow flowers and is very hardy.

GARDEN COMPANIONS

The yellow flowers of forsythia are wonderful with

- early-spring bulbs that have blue flowers, such as scilla, muscari, and hyacinths
- yellow and white daffodils
- tall, white tulips

When The best time to plant forsythias is early spring, but they can be planted all season long if they are watered well.

Where To get the best show of flowers, plant forsythias in full sun. They prefer fertile, well-drained soil. Use them in mixed shrub borders where their foliage can fade into the background after they are done blooming. They can also be used as hedge plants.

How Plant forsythias at the same depth they were growing in the containers, spacing according to the mature size of the plants. Water immediately after planting.

TLC Consistent watering is especially important during the first 2 years; after that, forsythias will tolerate dry spells. Keep the soil evenly moist from spring until the ground freezes, watering when the top 2 inches of the soil has dried out. Once plants are established, apply 2 to 4 inches of shredded bark or wood-chip mulch around them as soon as the ground warms in spring and replenish as necessary throughout the growing season. Feed in spring with a 10-10-10 fertilizer or an organic equivalent sprinkled around the base of the plants and watered in well. The best bloom is on year-old wood. Cut one-third of the oldest stems back to the ground right after blooming to encourage new growth. Severely overgrown, untidy plants should be sheared to the ground in spring and allowed to grow back over the next few years. Plants may produce suckers, which can be dug up in early spring and replanted or discarded. Extreme winter temperatures or late-spring cold snaps can damage flower buds, reducing spring bloom.

ABOVE: Forsythia × intermedia 'Lynwood'. RIGHT: Forsythia's tiny, four-petaled flowers grow along the length of the branches. The shrub will leaf out after the flowers are spent.

Hydrangea
Hydrangea

Hydrangeas have a distinctly old-fashioned look. Their large blooms—some resembling lace caps, others like cotton candy from a distance—are made up of thousands of delicate flowerets. These clusters, or "panicles," may be white, blush pink, or sky blue. The color of *H. macrophylla* flowers depends on the availability of aluminum in the soil, which is determined by soil pH. Acidic soils produce blue flowers, and alkaline soils produce pink ones. The flowers last a long time and still look attractive as they change color and begin to fade, holding up well in dried arrangements.

Hydrangea foliage is attractive and dense, and the shrubs come in various shapes and sizes. The PeeGee makes a wonderful small specimen tree, especially when pruned to a horizontal canopy. The oakleaf hydrangea has beautiful bronze fall foliage and peeling bark, but may not survive a rugged upper Midwest winter.

Hydrangeas complement other plants well and never look messy, though they will wilt in prolonged heat and drought. Place them where they'll get some afternoon shade and they'll be happy.

Hydrangea macrophylla *will produce flowers this blue if grown in acid (low pH) soil. In alkaline soil they'll turn pink. Add aluminum sulfate to lower pH, lime to raise it.*

PEAK SEASON

Mid- to late summer

MY FAVORITES

Hydrangea paniculata 'Grandiflora' is a PeeGee with big white blooms that fade to pink. 'Tardiva' is similar but blooms later.

H. arborescens 'Annabelle' produces snowball-like flowers that change from green to pure white. It tolerates light shade. 'White Dome' has white, lace cap–style blooms that give it a Victorian look.

H. macrophylla 'Nikko Blue' has blue lace-cap flowers and tolerates extreme cold. 'Tokyo Delight' has small, bright pink, lace-cap flower heads.

H. quercifolia 'Alice' is an oakleaf hydrangea with huge white panicles; its foliage turns to pink and then burgundy in fall.

GARDEN COMPANIONS

Plant hydrangeas in a mixed border with other shrubs, trees, and tall, slender perennials like hollyhocks or low, mounding ones like catmint and hardy geraniums. Hydrangeas also make excellent hedges; plant 'Annabelle' behind a tightly pruned low box or cotoneaster hedge or, for a more informal look, 'Little Princess' spirea, whose pale pink flowers set off the hydrangea's blooms as they turn from white to lime green over the course of the summer.

When The best time to plant hydrangeas is early spring, but they can be planted all season long if they are watered well.

ABOVE, LEFT: Hydrangea quercifolia *blossoms.* TOP RIGHT: H. arborescens *'Annabelle'.* BOTTOM RIGHT: *Pink flowers of* H. macrophylla *'Tokyo Delight'.*

Where Hydrangeas vary in their light requirements from full sun to partial shade. They all prefer well-drained soils high in organic matter. Less-hardy and vining types will need a protected location in colder zones. Their shade tolerance makes hydrangeas good candidates for the north side of buildings or under shade trees. Their late-summer color is a great addition to a mixed shrub border.

How Plant hydrangeas at the same depth they were growing in the containers, spacing according to the mature size of the plants. Water immediately after planting.

TLC Consistent watering is especially important during the first 2 years, but even mature plants will wilt at the first signs of drought. Keep the soil evenly moist from spring until the ground freezes, watering when the top 2 inches of the soil has dried out. Once plants are established, keep 2 to 4 inches of shredded bark or wood-chip mulch around them throughout the growing season. Feed in mid-June with a 10-10-10 fertilizer or an organic equivalent sprinkled around the base of the plants and watered in well. Prune anytime to remove dead or diseased wood and crossing branches.

Lilac
Syringa

Lilacs are said to be the most aromatic of all plants when in bloom; their scent is still the only flower fragrance that I can conjure up even in the dead of winter. Maybe that's because I grew up in a house with lilac hedges on all four sides. Their heady perfume wafting into my bedroom window announced that spring had come at last. In the neighborhood where I live now, most of the houses date back to the 19th century, and so do a few of the lilac hedges. Neighbors with heavy-blooming hedges always share the wealth with those less well endowed, and everyone's house is filled with lilacs for 2 or 3 precious weeks in May.

The old-fashioned, common lilac *(Syringa vulgaris)* is a big, blowsy bush that needs plenty of elbowroom. The newer hybrids offer a range of bloom times, so you can extend the flowering period well into summer. The summer-blooming Japanese tree lilac is a dramatic alternative to the traditional lilac hedge.

ABOVE: Syringa vulgaris. BELOW, TOP: S. v. 'Primrose'. BELOW, BOTTOM: S. v. 'Ludwig Spaeth'.

PEAK SEASON

Spring or early summer

MY FAVORITES

Syringa × *hyacinthiflora* 'Evangeline' doesn't sucker (a huge asset) and has early, light purple, double flowers. 'Anabel' is a double-flowering, early pink bloomer.

S. × *prestoniae* 'Donald Wyman' is an early bloomer with big purple flowers.

S. julianae 'George Eastman' has flowers ranging from cerise to wine red.

S. meyeri 'Palibin' is a dwarf Korean lilac with reddish purple flower buds that open to a lavender pink.

S. pubescens patula 'Miss Kim' has small, disease-resistant leaves; soft purple flowers; and reddish bronze fall foliage. It is often grown as an ornamental tree.

S. vulgaris 'Ludwig Spaeth' has reddish purple to dark purple flowers. 'Primrose', one of the newer hybrids, has pale yellow blooms.

GARDEN COMPANIONS

Plant lilacs with 'Sugar Tyme' flowering crabapple trees or spring-flowering shrubs like sweet mock orange (*Philadelphus coronarius*).

OPPOSITE PAGE: *A mass planting of white tulips in front of a lavender-flowered lilac makes a stunning spring composition.*

When The best time to plant lilacs is early spring, but they can be planted anytime during the growing season if they are watered well.

Where Lilacs grow best when they receive full sun at least 6 hours a day. Shrubs planted in partial shade will bloom less and are more susceptible to powdery mildew. Lilacs are lovely as specimen plants, in small groups, and in hedges.

How Plant lilacs at the same depth they were growing in the containers, spacing according to the mature size of the plants. Be sure to give tree types ample space. Balled-and-burlapped shrubs should be planted so that the root flares are right at the soil surface. Remove as much of the burlap and wire holding the root ball as possible without injuring the roots. Water immediately after planting.

TLC Keep the soil evenly moist from spring until the ground freezes, watering when the top 2 inches has dried out. Once plants are established, keep 2 to 4 inches of shredded bark or wood-chip mulch around them throughout the growing season. Feed in spring with a 10-10-10 fertilizer or an organic equivalent. Remove spent blossoms right after blooming to encourage more blooms the next year. Prune dead or diseased branches anytime. To keep common lilacs from becoming overgrown, remove one-third of the older branches annually. Prune to reduce height and maintain form right after flowering.

Potentilla

Potentilla fruticosa

You may have noticed that this indestructible shrub is beloved by fast-food chains. Don't let that cool your own budding

The sprightly yellow flowers of this Potentilla fruticosa *are nicely set off by burgundy-leafed Japanese barberry* (Berberis thunbergii). *All potentillas are easy to grow and tough as nails.*

passion for potentilla. It's a commonplace plant, true enough, but there is a good reason for that: Potentilla is a wonder, blooming incessantly from June through September on long, gracefully arching branches. It is impervious to drought, oblivious of pests, immune to illness. If you must veer off the beaten path, grow one with red, pink, or white flowers instead of yellow ones. The best of the whites by far is 'Abbotswood', a low shrub that has a very neat, rounded shape. I planted three along a low fence. The sprightly white flowers, so small and profuse they look like new-fallen snow, never fail to attract lots of attention—for which they must compete with the opulent pink blooms of a 'William Baffin' climbing rose and the purple flowers of a 'Jackmanii' clematis. Not bad.

PEAK SEASON

Late June to frost

MY FAVORITES

'Abbotswood' grows 3 feet tall and wide and is covered for long periods with profuse white flowers. It has excellent shape and is very hardy.

'Apricot Whisper' has orange flowers, light green leaves, and an oval shape.

'Red Ace' has red flowers with yellow centers. It tends to fade in very hot weather.

'Goldfinger' has yellow flowers, dark green leaves, and an oval shape.

'Pink Beauty' was developed in 1999 at the University of Manitoba. It has bright green foliage and long-lasting pink flowers.

GARDEN COMPANIONS

Potentillas can be tucked into a perennial border for a splash of flower color but are best grouped together as an edging for a flower bed or as a low hedge. White-flowered varieties go well with everything; yellow flowers are best with blue-flowering plants, such as salvia, veronica, delphinium, campanula, and lavender. Plant *Potentilla fruticosa* 'Primrose Beauty' (pale yellow flowers) with purple-leafed bugleweed (*Ajuga reptans* 'Atropurpurea').

When The best time to plant potentillas is early spring, but they can be planted all season long if they are watered well.

Where Potentillas thrive in hot sites in full sun, and they can tolerate wind, salt, and drought. Shade reduces flowering. Red, pink, and orange varieties require cool summers to flower best and do not always do as well in the Midwest. All types tolerate a wide variety of soils as long as they have good drainage. Potentillas make good informal hedges and are well suited to shrub borders and rock gardens. Their tough nature means they can be used in spots many other plants wouldn't survive.

How Plant potentillas at the same depth they were growing in the containers, spacing according to the mature size of the plants. Water immediately after planting.

TLC Consistent watering is most important during the first 2 years. Keep the soil evenly moist from spring until the ground freezes, watering when the top 2 inches of the soil has dried out. Once plants are established, apply 2 to 4 inches of shredded bark or wood-chip mulch around them as soon as the ground warms in spring and replenish as necessary throughout the growing season. Feed in mid-June with a 10-10-10 fertilizer or an organic equivalent sprinkled around the base of the plants and watered in well. New stems produce more flowers than older ones, so cut one-third of the old stems to the ground in late winter to keep plants vigorous and blooming. Spider mites can be a problem on potentillas. Spray plants with a forceful jet of water early in the morning to stop an infestation from becoming severe.

ABOVE: Potentilla fruticosa.
RIGHT: P. f. *'Pink Beauty'*

Rhododendron

Rhododendron

Rhododendrons and azaleas used to be the sort of plants northern gardeners gazed at longingly in southern gardens. The cold-hardy PJM rhododendron series changed all that, with an iridescent purple–flowering rhododendron that took the Midwest by storm. When breeders at the Minnesota Landscape Arboretum introduced the hardy Northern Lights azaleas, scintillating shades of orange, yellow, red, and white were added to the color spectrum.

Azaleas belong to the rhododendron family and have many similiarities to rhododendrons, but there are subtle differences. Rhododendrons are usually evergreens; and their leaves are less pointy, darker green, and thicker—almost rubbery in texture. Many cold-tolerant azaleas are deciduous, losing their leaves in winter, and have smaller leaves and flowers.

Be sure to choose only cold-tolerant varieties and give them an acid soil, partial shade, and consistent moisture. Alas, you still have to live in a temperate climate to grow rhododendrons as big as a house.

Rhododendrons come in a wide range of flower colors and can be combined in massed plantings like this one featuring pinks and yellows.

TOP: *Northern Lights azalea.* MIDDLE: *'Hino-Crimson' azalea.* BOTTOM: Rhododendron ponticum.

PEAK SEASON

Late spring. PJM hybrids have some fall leaf color.

MY FAVORITES

Rhododendron 'PJM' is a cold-tolerant rhododendron that has penetrating, light purple flowers in early spring and glossy green leaves that turn bronze in winter.

R. yakushimanum is a rhododendron with a dense, spreading habit. Leaves open gray, then turn glossy dark green with tan undersides; flowers are bell-like. 'Yaku Princess' tolerates cold well.

R. mucronulatum 'Cornell Pink' is a deciduous rhododendron with very early–blooming pink flowers that open before the leaves.

Northern Lights hybrid azaleas are deciduous, are extremely hardy, and have flaming fall foliage and late-blooming flowers in tight clusters in a wide range of colors. Varieties include 'Apricot Surprise', 'Orchid Lights', 'White Lights', and 'Rosy Lights'.

GARDEN COMPANIONS

Azaleas and rhododendrons look good in masses and with woodland plants like ferns, hostas, pulmonarias, and wild ginger (*Asarum*).

Mix different azalea colors for a colorful display.

When Plant rhododendrons and azaleas in early spring.

Where Choose a site in partial shade, ideally on the north or east side of a building to prevent winter burn, but avoid deep shade. Deciduous azaleas can tolerate full sun with ample water. All types need rich, well-drained soil high in organic matter. Rhododendrons are excellent as single specimens, but they also look great as massed plantings.

How All rhododendrons and azaleas require a pH of 4.5 to 5.5. Test the soil and amend as needed before planting. Plant at the same depth shrubs were growing in the containers, spacing according to the mature size of the plants. Plant balled-and-burlapped shrubs so that the root flares are right at the soil surface. Remove as much of the burlap and wire holding the root ball as possible without injuring the roots. Immediately after planting the shrubs, water with an acidic water-soluble fertilizer solution.

TLC Keep the soil evenly moist from spring until the ground freezes, watering when the top 2 inches of the soil is dry. Once plants are established, keep 2 to 4 inches of an acidic mulch such as pine needles, pine bark, or shredded oak leaves around them throughout the growing season. Feed in spring with an acidic fertilizer and again right after plants bloom. Stop watering in mid-September to encourage plants to begin hardening off for winter, but saturate the soil just before the first freeze to make sure plants go into winter with moisture around their roots. Remove dead or damaged branches anytime. To encourage bushier plants, cut back stems on mature plants by one-third right after flowering.

Spirea
Spiraea

Spiraea pruniflora *is always exquisite in bloom, with its impressive 6-foot height and long, drooping branches creating a fountain effect.*

I live in a tall clapboard house that my great-grandfather built in 1882. I'm not sure if the bridal wreath spirea beside the front porch dates back to his occupancy, but it sure looks it. This is the quintessential old-fashioned shrub, with its fountain of long, arching branches; feathery leaves; and sprays of tiny white flowers in early summer. Always a bit messy, bridal wreath has been "improved" over the years, but it wasn't on my list when I went plant shopping to replace shrubs lost when we had the front porch rebuilt. Instead I went crazy for *Spiraea japonica* 'Little Princess'. I lugged home 12 of them. *S. japonica* combines the wispy charm of bridal wreath with trendier virtues like a tidy, low, mounding growth habit; light green (or bright gold) leaves against pinkish purple flowers; a long bloom time; and low maintenance. Give your 'Little Princess' lots of sun, along with a haircut every 3 years, and it will always look great.

PEAK SEASON

Midspring through summer

MY FAVORITES

Spiraea japonica 'Little Princess' is a low, mounding shrub that grows to 2½ feet tall with small, pale lavender flowers at the stem ends. 'Magic Carpet' grows 1½ to 2 feet tall with brilliant yellow leaves and red leaf tips, and pinkish purple flowers.

S. × vanhouttei is the old-fashioned bridal wreath with white flowers on arching branches. It grows to 6 feet tall and 8 feet wide. 'Renaissance' is resistant to mildew and rust.

GARDEN COMPANIONS

Plant low, mounding types in front of a taller hedge of flowering hydrangeas or 'Mohawk' viburnum. The dwarf 'Magic Carpet' looks great as a ground cover combined with rambling roses such as 'Sea Foam' and hardy geraniums.

When The best time to plant spireas is early spring, but they can be planted all season long if they are watered well.

Where Spireas grow best in full sun but will tolerate partial shade. They prefer fertile, well-drained soil. They will not do well in boggy or constantly wet conditions or in highly alkaline soils. Most low-growing spireas should be planted in groups for best effect, but bridal wreath types are often grown as specimen plants.

How Plant spireas at the same depth they were growing in the containers, spacing according to the mature size of the plants. Mass plantings sometimes look better when spaced closer than is recommended. Water immediately after planting.

TLC Keep the soil evenly moist from spring until the ground freezes, watering when the top 2 inches of the soil has dried out. Once plants are established, apply 2 to 4 inches of shredded bark or wood-chip mulch around them as soon as the ground warms in spring and replenish as necessary throughout the growing season. Feed in spring with a 10-10-10 fertilizer or an organic equivalent sprinkled around the base of the plants and watered in well. Summer-flowering spireas bloom on new wood and should be pruned in late winter to avoid cutting off the current season's flower buds. Overgrown plants can be cut to the ground in early spring to control size or rejuvenate plants. Prune to remove dead or diseased branches anytime. Remove dead flower heads to keep plants tidy and encourage a later flush of modest bloom.

ABOVE, LEFT: Spiraea japonica *'Goldflame'*. ABOVE, RIGHT: S. × vanhouttei. LEFT: S. j. *'Magic Carpet' with switch grass* (Panicum virgatum).

99

Viburnum
Viburnum

Although viburnums are a varied family of shrubs, almost all have year-round interest. Many produce large white or pink flowers in spring, followed by clusters of red or black berries in late summer. Viburnums also have handsome foliage. *Viburnum × burkwoodii* 'Mohawk' has dark green, velvety leaves with a pleasantly sculpted shape, while *V. trilobum* 'Wentworth' has pointier, lighter green leaves. Both are effective as background plants in a woodland garden. They like a bit of shade but otherwise aren't picky about soil or situation. Mine seem to thrive in the dry shade of an enormous white oak.

Leatherleaf viburnum, which tolerates full shade, grows quite tall, making it useful for screening unsightly views or buildings. Korean spice viburnum has a spicy fragrance in early spring when its pink buds open to white, snowball-like flowers. Autumn temperatures turn this delightful shrub's leaves a deep burgundy color.

LEFT: Viburnum trilobum's *graceful, drooping branches are covered with large white flowers in spring.* ABOVE: *Many viburnums produce red berries in summer.*

When The best time to plant viburnums is early spring, but they can be planted all season long if they are watered well.

Where Most viburnums grow best in full sun, but many do well in partial to even full shade. They prefer well-drained, fertile, slightly acid soil, but are tolerant of less-than-ideal conditions. Use shrub-type viburnums in shrub borders, as hedges, or in mass plantings. Some can be pruned as small trees. Place the heavy-fruiting types where you can enjoy their fall and winter interest.

How Plant viburnums at the same depth they were growing in the containers, spacing according to the mature size of the plants. Mass plantings sometimes look better when spaced closer than is recommended. Be sure to give tree types ample space. Water immediately after planting.

TLC Consistent watering is especially important during the first 2 years, but even mature plants will wilt at the first signs of drought. Keep the soil evenly moist from spring until the ground freezes, watering when the top 2 inches of the soil has dried out. Once plants are established, apply 2 to 4 inches of shredded bark or wood-chip mulch around them as soon as the ground warms in spring and replenish as necessary throughout the growing season. Feed in spring with a 10-10-10 fertilizer or an organic equivalent sprinkled around the base of the plants and watered in well. Prune to reduce height or improve form just after flowering. Remove a few older stems every few years to keep plants vigorous.

PEAK SEASON

Spring through fall

MY FAVORITES

Viburnum x burkwoodii 'Mohawk' grows to 7 feet tall and has lustrous green leaves with orange-red fall color.

V. opulus 'Compactum' (European cranberry bush) grows to 6 feet tall; bears showy, doily-like flowers against deep green leaves; and produces red berries in late summer.

V. rhytidophyllum (leatherleaf viburnum) resembles rhododendron but doesn't require acid soil. It bears bright red autumn berries.

V. carlesii (Korean spice viburnum) has a spicy scent and early pink buds that open to white snowball flowers.

V. furcatum has round leaves that turn bronze in late summer.

V. × carlcephalum (fragrant snowball) grows 6 to 10 feet tall and has slender gray leaves that turn reddish purple in fall. Sweet-scented, creamy white flower clusters bloom in spring. It's hardy to Zone 39.

GARDEN COMPANIONS

Plant viburnum with other flowering shrubs like dogwood and lilac, and low, bushy perennials like euphorbia, whose foliage turns from lime green to reddish gold as summer progresses. In warmer regions, plant *V. furcatum* with *Rhododendron cinnabarinum concatenans*.

ABOVE: Viburnum trilobum. BELOW: V. × carlcephalum (fragrant snowball).

Witch Hazel

Hamamelis

Witch hazels are fascinating shrubs, boasting angular or zigzagging branches and some of the more unusual flowers in the plant kingdom. Their bold colors and odd shapes, like small yellow or red spiders, cover bare branches in winter—*after* their leaves have turned yellow and fallen off. Most plants are still sleeping when witch hazels burst into bloom, and this peculiar timing, combined with a surprisingly sweet fragrance, makes their exotic flowers welcome indeed.

Hamamelis virginiana, the common witch hazel, is extremely hardy. Newer hybrids such as 'Arnold Promise' and 'Jelena' combine cold tolerance with prettier flowers and leaves; they grow to 15 feet tall and have an open, spreading shape, sometimes with multi-trunks. Don't fret too much about unseasonable cold snaps; witch hazels' flowers are unfazed even when the mercury falls to the low 20s.

For best flowering give witch hazels sun, and skip over them when you prune your spring-blooming shrubs. Wait to prune until after witch hazels have flowered or you may cut off the buds and miss a season of bloom.

Witch hazels are January bloomers in southern parts of the Midwest, including Indiana, and among the earliest spring bloomers elsewhere in the region. Here Hamamelis × intermedia 'Primavera' in winter.

PEAK SEASON

Late winter into early spring. Some varieties have foliage with good fall color.

MY FAVORITES

Hamamelis × intermedia hybrids are very hardy, are early blooming, and grow to 15 feet tall. 'Arnold Promise' has light yellow flowers and grows to 10 feet wide, with an upright, open habit. 'Diane' has gold fall foliage and coppery red flowers and grows to 10 feet tall by 10 feet wide. 'Jelena' has large leaves, a vigorous spreading habit, yellow flowers tinged with red, and good fall color. 'Moonlight' has strongly fragrant, yellow flowers; gold leaves in fall; and an upright habit. 'Pallida' is low (8 feet) and wide (15 feet), with pale yellow flowers and a sweet scent.

GARDEN COMPANIONS

Witch hazel looks best in a partially shady woodland setting planted with evergreens to set off their intense flower color.

When The best time to plant witch hazels is early spring, but they can be planted all season long if watered well.

Where Flowering is most abundant in full sun, but witch hazels will tolerate partial shade. If you grow them in heavy shade their branches may weaken and break off. Witch hazels prefer well-drained soil high in organic matter. They grow naturally along the edges of woods. Take advantage of their shade tolerance and use them as understory shrubs, being aware that occasionally the branches may break off.

How Plant witch hazels at the same depth they were growing in the containers, spacing according to the mature size of the plants. Balled-and-burlapped shrubs should be planted so that the root flares are right at the soil surface. Remove as much of the burlap and wire holding the root ball as possible without injuring the roots. Water immediately after planting.

TLC Keep the soil evenly moist from spring until the ground freezes, watering when the top 2 inches of the soil is dry. Once plants are established, apply 2 to 4 inches of shredded bark or wood-chip mulch around them as soon as the ground warms in spring and replenish as necessary throughout the growing season. Feed in spring with a 10-10-10 fertilizer or an organic equivalent sprinkled around the base of the plants and watered in well. Prune only to remove dead or crossing branches or suckers or to improve the shape. Larger types can be pruned as small trees.

ABOVE, LEFT: Hamamelis × intermedia *'Diane'*. ABOVE, RIGHT: H. × intermedia. BELOW: H. × i. *'Allgold'*.

*Trial zone

Trees

Try to imagine your neighborhood stripped of its trees. You would feel exposed. The natural landscape would seem out of kilter. Trees settle our homes and gardens into the larger landscape. They give us a sense of our world as a three-dimensional space. They put ceilings on our gardens. They turn our streets into green cathedrals.

Trees have their practical virtues, too. They clean the air, and their roots prevent erosion by holding soil in place. They serve as windbreaks. Their nuts and berries are dietary staples for countless species of birds and other small creatures.

In this chapter I'll cover deciduous trees. You'll learn about evergreen trees and shrubs in the next chapter. Deciduous trees retain their branches and stems year-round but lose all their foliage in autumn; in spring new leaves unfurl from leaf buds that formed the previous summer. Trees of this type often form flower buds as well, which bloom in spring, summer, or fall, depending on the species.

TYPES OF TREES

Trees come in many shapes and sizes. What distinguishes them from shrubs is their growth habit. While shrubs are bushy, with numerous stems growing up from the base of the plants, trees typically grow a single stem, or trunk, with leaf buds forming on branches higher up the trunk to create a dense canopy, or crown. Their branches may curve gently upward from the trunk to form the shape of a vase; they may grow out from the trunk horizontally; or they may even have a "weeping" habit, meaning that their branches actually grow downward. Some trees' branches grow out and then up, like the candles on a menorah.

SMALL IS BIG

Small trees can be just as dramatic as large ones. Instead of finding your nose pressed against the giant trunk of a 50-foot-tall oak, you can admire the whole tree, top to bottom. Small trees make excellent focal points. Garden designers often place a single, exquisite tree—a river birch, for example—in a corner and arrange the rest of the plantings so as to draw the eye there.

Small trees are also attractive in pairs or groups. The French claim credit for inventing the allée. These are trees planted in two straight rows, evenly spaced, to give a sense of formality, order, and perspective. In a small garden, ornamental dwarf trees can produce a similar

ABOVE: *A double row (allée) of linden trees forms either a tunnel or a hedge on stilts, depending on your perspective, screening unsightly views beyond the garden wall. The branches were pleached, or woven together, to form a single canopy.* OPPOSITE PAGE: *The brilliant fall foliage of a sugar maple (Acer saccharum).*

effect, lining a walk or driveway, for example. Less formal but just as soothing to the eye is a single row of evenly spaced trees. On a sunny slope running the full length of my house, where pounding sun and poor soil spelled doom for all but the toughest weeds, a row of six 'Sugar Tyme' flowering crabapple trees came to the rescue. They hold the soil in place and filter the strong morning sun.

I prune these trees to keep them tidy and to curb their growth. Alas, pruning stimulates new growth, and that's not always a good thing. To be honest, I wish I'd bought a dwarf variety instead. I am constantly cutting off suckers that shoot up in all the wrong places, including from the roots, and my trees have developed tiny bristling twigs that keep sun from penetrating deep into the canopy. Unless you're after a formal effect (a tightly clipped hedge or a topiary, for instance), most trees look best and stay healthiest when they are allowed to assume their natural shape and are pruned only to remove diseased or damaged limbs or to thin the canopy so more sunlight can reach the interior branches. That means choosing the right tree in the first place.

DECIDING ON A TREE

Landscapers often remark that the most common mistake do-it-yourselfers make when they buy trees is underestimating their mature size. It's amazing how quickly a single one can turn a sunny space into a shade garden. You won't feel nearly so fond of your tree when it begins killing off your sun-loving peonies. It's also important to know a tree's soil and water requirements. Trees are heavy feeders and very thirsty. In a dry spell it's the perennials that are the first to wilt, while the nearby shade tree never shows the least discomfort.

ABOVE: *The stunning pink flower of Magnolia* × loebneri *'Leonard Messel'.* RIGHT: *'Crimson Queen' Japanese maple, with its feathery, bronze foliage and horizontal branching habit, is an excellent foil for plants with contrasting shape, color, and texture, such as rhododendrons and spiky grasses.*

with unamended garden soil. Roots won't probe farther than the immediate vicinity if the soil mix is too perfect. Bare-root trees may need to be staked.

If you suspect rodents are nibbling at a trunk, you can deter them by applying a tree wrap or plastic tree guard. A circle of mulch will keep down weeds at the base of the tree and, more important, protect the trunk from your lawn mower. Though young trees benefit from some fertilizing and a cover of mulch to hold in moisture, the trees I'm recommending here shouldn't need much of your time to maintain excellent health.

Oaks, in particular, are notorious water hogs. If you're set on having one, you may be limited to growing dry-shade plants underneath it.

Trees are sold as bare-root, balled-and-burlapped, or container plants. Bare-root plants must be planted immediately (soak them for 2 hours first). Burlap should be removed before planting or else it will wick water away from the roots. Container plants are often root-bound; you'll need to force roots that are growing in circles to change course, even if this means slashing a few with a pruning knife.

The planting hole should be three or four times wider than the root ball and backfilled

Eastern Redbud
Cercis canadensis

Though the tree is called redbud, the buds of the native *Cercis canadensis* are closer to purple than red. They open in early spring on bare branches, just as most other trees and shrubs are beginning to leaf out. The exquisite flowers are followed by large, heart-shaped leaves and interesting beanlike pods that may cling to the tree well into winter.

Eastern redbud sets a woodland landscape ablaze with blooms. The tree will unfurl its leaves after flowering.

Eastern redbud has a rounded head and grows quickly to 30 feet in height. It is rapidly gaining popularity all over the Midwest, as much for its stately, upright posture and spreading branches as for its flowers. It is happiest in a woodland setting. In warmer states like Indiana, redbud is a beloved harbinger of spring. In the north, the flowers are always at risk of being nipped by a late frost. Gardeners in Zones 1B and 43 should purchase only Northland strain eastern redbud and plant it in a protected site.

When Plant redbud as soon as you can work the ground in spring.

Where Redbud prefers partial shade but will tolerate full sun or shade. It grows best in well-drained soil high in organic matter. Soil should not be heavy or consistently moist. Plant a single redbud as a focal point where it will have plenty of room to grow into its lovely mature form.

How Remove the tree from its container carefully, keeping the root ball intact. Plant at the same depth as it was in the container, in a hole deep and wide enough to accommodate the roots without crowding. Plant a balled-and-burlapped tree so that the root flare is right at the soil surface, cutting and removing as much of the burlap and wire as possible without injuring roots. Gently firm soil around the roots and water thoroughly, making sure there are no air pockets. A half-cup of starter fertilizer solution (diluted according to the product's instructions) can be watered in around the base.

TLC Keep the soil evenly moist from spring until the ground freezes in fall, especially during the first 2 years. Water deeply to encourage deep root growth. Apply 2 to 4 inches of organic mulch such as shredded bark or wood chips and replenish as needed throughout the growing season. Trees will benefit from an application of 10-10-10 fertilizer or an organic equivalent every other spring. Annual shaping should be done in late winter. You may prune off dead, damaged, or diseased branches anytime.

PEAK SEASON

Long-lasting purplish pink or white flowers bloom in spring before leaves appear. Leaves often turn yellow in fall. Pods may cling to branches into winter.

MY FAVORITES

'Flame' has double pink flowers and grows vigorously.

'Royal White' and 'Alba' are both good varieties with white flowers.

GARDEN COMPANIONS

To emphasize its flowers, plant redbud in front of tall evergreens.

ABOVE: *Cercis canadensis.* RIGHT: *Redbud's bright flowers and elegant, spreading shape look striking against a dark background of evergreen white pines.*

Flowering Crabapple
Malus

Malus is a huge family of trees. Certain crabapples are grown for eating and cooking, but the varieties featured here are chiefly ornamental—and there's one for just about every garden situation. Some crabapples have a horizontal branching habit that is well suited to the tranquil mood and flowing lines of a Japanese garden; others stand tall and erect and look wonderful in rows along a street, driveway, or fence. The flowers come in white, pink, or various shades of red, followed by attractive fruits that vary in size and color depending on the species and variety. Branch color ranges from tan to gray to purplish red.

In the introduction to this chapter I told you about the 'Sugar Tyme' crabapple trees I planted along the side of my house. When I read the label all I saw was "upright, oval." Turns out I didn't give the trees nearly enough elbowroom. Don't get me wrong. I love my trees, and they don't seem to mind that I prune them hard. They keep right on flowering heavily in spring, and their abundant red fruits hang around all winter. But next time I'll go with the dwarf *Malus sargentii* 'Tina', which has white flowers and red fruits like 'Sugar Tyme' but is less than half the size.

Dwarf flowering crabapples are good choices for semiformal groupings of two or more. Prune them to their natural shape.

PEAK SEASON

Abundant, fragrant, white, pink, or red flowers bloom in spring. Some have persistent fruits that add winter interest.

MY FAVORITES

M. 'Prairifire' has a rounded canopy, pink flowers, and exceptional disease tolerance.

M. 'Sugar Tyme' has an upright, oval shape; white flowers; and long-lasting red fruit.

M. 'Donald Wyman' has a broad canopy, white flowers, long-lasting fruit, and glossy leaves.

M. sargentii has a dense branching habit and profuse white flowers that are lovely against its sturdy, dark limbs. 'Tina' is a charming dwarf version.

GARDEN COMPANIONS

In the filtered shade beneath your crabapple trees, plant spring bloomers such as

- primroses
- early-spring bulbs
- shade-loving annuals like impatiens and begonias

TOP TO BOTTOM: Malus 'Prairifire', the charming flower clusters of M. 'Gorgeous', M. 'Snowdrift'

When Plant crabapples as soon as you can work the ground in spring.

Where Crabapples flower best in full sun. A site with good air circulation decreases the chances of leaf spot diseases. Give trees well-drained soil with a slightly acidic to nearly neutral pH.

How Remove the tree from its container carefully, keeping the root ball intact. Plant at the same depth as it was in the container, in a hole deep and wide enough to accommodate the roots without crowding. Plant a balled-and-burlapped tree so that the root flare is right at the soil surface, cutting and removing as much of the burlap and wire as possible without injuring roots. Gently firm soil around the roots and water thoroughly, making sure there are no air pockets. A half-cup of starter fertilizer solution (diluted according to the product's instructions) can be watered in around the base.

TLC Keep the soil evenly moist from spring until the ground freezes in fall, especially during the first 2 years. Water deeply to encourage deep root growth. Apply 2 to 4 inches of organic mulch such as shredded bark or wood chips and replenish as needed throughout the growing season. Crabapples will benefit from an annual application of 10-10-10 fertilizer or an organic equivalent in spring. Protect the thin bark of young trees with plastic cylinders or hardware cloth and tree wrap. Prune annually in late winter to increase air circulation and ward off leaf spot diseases. Rake up and dispose of any infected leaves in fall.

Some varieties, including 'Donald Wyman' and 'Snowdrift', can live in Zone 45.

Hawthorn
Crataegus

Hawthorns belong to the rose family, and like roses they are admired for their flowers and fruits, and respected (but not loved) for their sharp thorns. Birds are attracted to the showy fruits, which resemble tiny red apples, and sometimes nest in the protection of the thorny canopy.

The best of the hawthorns is the native *Crataegus viridis* 'Winter King', a vase-shaped tree that grows to 30 feet tall and has white flowers in handsome clusters. Its silvery stems nicely set off the red berries, which last as long as the birds don't find them, sometimes

all through winter. The fruits are often used in holiday decorating.

Crataegus ambigua (Russian hawthorn) is the hardiest of the hawthorns and resembles 'Winter King', but with smaller fruits and more twisted branches.

The name "hawthorn," by the way, combines the tree's two most distinctive features, the berries, technically known as "haws," and the thorns.

Red berry clusters decorate the branches of this thornless hawthorn (Crataegus crus-galli inermis) in late summer.

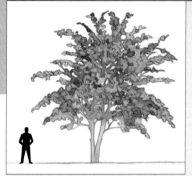

When Plant hawthorns as soon as you can work the ground in spring.

Where Hawthorns prefer limestone regions and sandy loam but will grow in ordinary garden soil in full sun. They are tolerant of city conditions and drought, and their thorns make them suitable as barrier plantings. Be careful about planting thorned varieties where small children can be injured.

How Remove the tree from its container carefully, keeping the root ball intact. Plant at the same depth as it was in the container, in a hole deep and wide enough to accommodate the roots without crowding. Plant a balled-and-burlapped tree so that the root flare is right at the soil surface, cutting and removing as much of the burlap and wire as possible without injuring roots. Gently firm soil around the roots and water thoroughly, making sure there are no air pockets. A half-cup of starter fertilizer solution (diluted according to the product's instructions) can be watered in around the base.

TLC Keep the soil evenly moist from spring until the ground freezes in fall, especially during the first 2 years. Water deeply to encourage deep root growth. Apply 2 to 4 inches of organic mulch such as shredded bark or wood chips and replenish as needed throughout the growing season. Trees will benefit from an application of 10-10-10 fertilizer or an organic equivalent every other spring. Annual shaping to thin out excess twiggy growth should be done in late winter. Prune off dead, damaged, or diseased branches anytime. Fireblight and cedar-apple rust can be problems. The varieties recommended here are less susceptible to hawthorn rust, another potential problem.

PEAK SEASON

Hawthorn bears showy white flowers in spring and attractive, bright red, applelike fruits in fall.

MY FAVORITES

Crataegus viridis 'Winter King' has glossy leaves in spring followed by creamy white flower clusters, then red "haws." It tolerates diverse growing conditions.

C. phaenopyrum (*C. cordata*) 'Fastigiata' is similar to 'Winter King' with a narrower, columnar shape and smaller fruits. 'Princeton Sentry' is shaped like a pyramid and has few thorns.

C. crus-galli inermis is thornless. Don't confuse it with *C. crus-galli,* which has thorns up to 3 inches long.

GARDEN COMPANIONS

Keep it all in the family (and burglars at bay) by planting your hawthorns in a mixed border with some really thorny shrub roses.

ABOVE: Crataegus. RIGHT: *Hawthorns' creamy white flowers grow in clusters that may cover the entire canopy. They emerge in April, following the glossy green leaves.*

Hornbeam
Carpinus

Hornbeam is compact and tidy, with a dense, leafy canopy and pretty, nutlike fruits that hang in drooping clusters. The leaves last well into fall; and the trunk's smooth, gray-blue bark lends an air of sophistication to the garden. It is excellent both as a boulevard plant and for making allées (for example, along a driveway). European gardeners use *Carpinus betulus* to make "hedges on stilts" by planting them close together in straight rows and training the canopies to grow together through frequent shearing.

The European species has a tighter, more pyramidal shape than the native American hornbeam *(C. caroliniana).* American hornbeam

European hornbeam Carpinus betulus 'Fastigiata' has an upright, pyramidal form when young and becomes more oval or teardrop shaped as it ages.

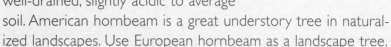

When Hornbeams can be difficult to transplant and should be planted in early spring for best results.

Where Hornbeams prefer sun to partial shade, but American hornbeam will grow in heavy shade. They all like well-drained, slightly acidic to average soil. American hornbeam is a great understory tree in naturalized landscapes. Use European hornbeam as a landscape tree.

How Remove the tree from its container carefully, keeping the root ball intact. Plant at the same depth as it was in the container, in a hole big enough to accommodate the roots without crowding. Plant a balled-and-burlapped tree so that the root flare is right at the soil surface, cutting and removing as much of the burlap and wire as possible without injuring roots. Gently firm soil around the roots and water thoroughly, making sure there are no air pockets. A half-cup of diluted starter fertilizer can be watered in around the base.

TLC Keep the soil evenly moist from spring until the ground freezes in fall, especially during the first 2 years. Water deeply to encourage deep root growth. Apply 2 to 4 inches of organic mulch such as shredded bark or wood chips around the base of European hornbeam. Avoid mulching under American hornbeam, to discourage sucker growth. Regular mowing should keep suckers down on lawn trees. Fertilization is not required. Annual shaping should be done in late winter. Prune off dead, damaged, or diseased branches anytime. European hornbeam tolerates clipping, and young branches can be interwoven to form an effective barrier.

tolerates both sun and heavy shade, doesn't mind being waterlogged, and is often found along rivers as an understory plant. Its leaves fall off earlier than the European hornbeam's do; otherwise the two species are quite similar. Both have very hard wood and grow fairly slowly.

PEAK SEASON

Hornbeam's smooth, slate gray bark has undulations that look like muscles rippling under its surface. The dark green leaves turn yellow, orange, or red in fall.

MY FAVORITES

Carpinus betulus 'Fastigiata', the most common European hornbeam, has a striking flamelike shape.

C. caroliniana is native and very hardy. It has a round head.

GARDEN COMPANIONS

European hornbeams are right at home in a formal setting with clipped conifers, boxwood hedges, and perfect lawns. Plant American hornbeams in a more natural setting with moisture-loving shrubs like flowering dogwood and trees like willows.

ABOVE: Carpinus caroliniana. BELOW: C. betulus 'Pendula', a weeping form of European hornbeam.

Linden

Tilia

Lindens are lovely formal trees. Here Tilia americana 'Redmond' shows off its perfect pyramidal shape.

Lindens are the picture-perfect city tree, good choices for parks and boulevards. They are tall and narrow, usually forming a slender pyramid. This cone-shaped canopy is densely covered with glossy green, heart-shaped leaves. In early summer unusually fragrant, pale green flowers hang in clusters. The flowers are followed by small, nutlike berries attached to bracts.

The native American linden *(Tilia americana)* grows to a height of 80 feet. While it is an attractive tree, its European cousin, the little-leaf linden *(T. cordata),* has surpassed it in popularity in recent years, thanks to its slightly shorter stature and perfectly symmetrical crown. It also isn't bothered by poor soil or car fumes, which makes it a great street tree.

In the garden, a single linden makes a handsome focal point, but it casts a dense shadow. Plant it where you'd like to have a cool spot for lounging with a book. Expect bees to join you when the tree is in flower.

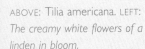

When Plant lindens as soon as you can work the ground in spring.

Where Lindens are very adaptable, but they prefer full sun and soil that is slightly acidic to slightly alkaline. The large size of American linden restricts its use to estate gardens and parks, but the little-leaf linden, which is smaller in stature, is well suited to most residential landscapes.

How Remove the tree from its container carefully, keeping the root ball intact. Plant at the same depth as it was in the container, in a hole deep and wide enough to accommodate the roots without crowding. Plant a balled-and-burlapped tree so that the root flare is right at the soil surface, cutting and removing as much of the burlap and wire as possible without injuring roots. Gently firm soil around the roots and water thoroughly, making sure there are no air pockets. A half-cup of starter fertilizer solution (diluted according to the product's instructions) can be watered in around the base.

TLC Keep the soil evenly moist from spring until the ground freezes in fall, especially during the first 2 years. Water deeply to encourage deep root growth. Apply 2 to 4 inches of organic mulch such as shredded bark or wood chips and replenish as needed throughout the growing season. Prune off sprouts at the base of the trunk and dead, damaged, or diseased branches anytime. The thin bark of young trees is susceptible to damage from winter sun and string trimmers. Protect trees with plastic cylinders or wrapping materials.

PEAK SEASON

Fragrant, creamy white flowers appear in early summer, and attractive green foliage turns yellow in fall.

MY FAVORITES

Tilia cordata 'Greenspire' is an excellent little-leaf linden that can be sheared into hedges if formal structure is needed in a garden.

T. americana 'Redmond' has glossier leaves than the species and a more pyramidal shape.

GARDEN COMPANIONS

Lindens' erect, formal bearing makes them good choices for planting along a boulevard or fence, with begonias or other shade-loving annuals clustered below.

ABOVE: Tilia americana. LEFT: *The creamy white flowers of a linden in bloom.*

117

Magnolia
Magnolia

Surely there is no lovelier tree than the classic southern magnolia, *Magnolia grandiflora.* While that particular species is off-limits to midwestern gardeners, breeders have come up with wonderful magnolias that do just fine in the cold and snow. Most notable of these are the star magnolias *(M. stellata),* whose flowers are shaped like stars and come in white, pink, yellow, or lavender. The flowers bloom early, before the leaves unfurl. This makes for some anxious moments when late frosts are forecast, for once the flowers are nipped by frost they're done for. Fortunately, flowers aren't star magnolias' only virtue. Glossy, dark green leaves and gray bark make these slow-growing trees handsome specimens, small and stately and sure to elicit compliments.

The native *M. virginiana* (sweet bay magnolia) is hardy in warmer parts of the Midwest. Some of the saucer magnolias *(M. × soulangeana)* can take the cold but tend to fare badly in hot, dry, windy places.

Giant, cup-shaped blossoms of Magnolia × soulangeana (saucer magnolia) cover wide-spreading, smooth, gray branches in spring before the tree leafs out.

When Plant magnolias as soon as you can work the ground in spring.

Where Magnolias grow and flower best in full sun. A site out of winter winds will help protect flower buds. In Zone 43, avoid planting in low-lying areas that can trap cold air in late spring. Magnolias grow best in rich soil high in organic matter with a slightly acidic to nearly neutral pH. Single plants make superb focal points. Give them plenty of room so they can mature naturally into their full size.

PEAK SEASON

Showy flowers appear in early spring, usually before the leaves.

MY FAVORITES

Magnolia stellata has star-shaped, early-spring flowers in many colors.

M. 'Ann' and *M.* 'Jane', both crosses between *M. stellata* 'Rosea' and *M. liliiflora* 'Nigra', open later in spring so are less likely to be nipped by frost. 'Ann' has purplish red blooms; 'Jane' has pink flowers.

M. virginiana has creamy white flowers that bloom sporadically all summer and have a sweet fragrance. 'Henry Hicks' remains evergreen at cold temperatures.

GARDEN COMPANIONS

Plant star magnolias in mixed borders where their flowers can enjoy the company of early-spring bulbs like scilla, daffodils, and early tulips; later on, their glossy green leaves and handsome gray bark will look good with flowering shrubs and perennials. Magnolias are also well suited to Japanese-style gardens.

How Remove the tree from its container carefully, keeping the root ball intact. Plant at the same depth as it was in the container, in a hole deep and wide enough to accommodate the roots without crowding. Plant a balled-and-burlapped tree so that the root flare is right at the soil surface, cutting and removing as much of the burlap and wire as possible without injuring roots. Gently firm soil around the roots and water thoroughly, making sure there are no air pockets. A half-cup of starter fertilizer solution (diluted according to the product's instructions) can be watered in around the base.

TLC Keep the soil evenly moist from spring until the ground freezes in fall, especially during the first 2 years. Water deeply to encourage deep root growth. Maintain 2 to 4 inches of organic mulch such as shredded bark or wood chips throughout the growing season. Magnolias will benefit from an annual application of 10-10-10 fertilizer or an organic equivalent in spring. Prune right after flowering only for form or maintenance.

ABOVE: Magnolia × soulangeana. RIGHT, FROM TOP TO BOTTOM: M. 'Ann', M. stellata (star magnolia), M. 'Lois'.

Maple

Acer

While not as grand as an oak or as elegant as a river birch, the sugar maple does just about everything a tree is supposed to do. Its full, round canopy sits atop a straight trunk. Its large, pointy leaves, recognizable at once to anyone who loves maple syrup, supply dense shade in summer. Then fall comes and turns the canopy into a ball of flame. Although I love the autumn brilliance of sugar and red maples, their shallow roots and heavy shade make it tough to grow anything below them. My garden is better suited

to the daintier types, like the flowering amur maple; paperbark maple *(Acer griseum)*, with its cinnamon-colored bark that is constantly peeling; and the airy Japanese maples. The latter are not reliably hardy where I live, but I grow them anyway. Last year I planted them in containers and overwintered them in the garage. Somehow they survived.

LEFT: *'Mondy' amur maple displays glorious fall foliage. Growing to 25 feet tall and wide, amurs are among the smaller maples.* ABOVE: *Flower clusters dot a sugar maple* (Acer saccharum) *in spring. The tree grows about 40 feet wide and 60 feet tall.*

When Plant maples as soon as you can work the ground in spring.

Where Most maples prefer full sun but will grow in partial shade. Young trees like well-drained, slightly acidic soil. Their brilliant fall color makes them good as specimen plants in mixed borders. Amur maples create a good screen or hedge when spaced 2 feet apart.

How Remove the tree from its container carefully, keeping the root ball intact. Plant at the same depth as it was in the container, in a hole deep and wide enough to accommodate the roots without crowding. Plant a balled-and-burlapped tree so that the root flare is right at the soil surface, cutting and removing as much of the burlap and wire as possible without injuring roots. Gently firm soil around the roots and water thoroughly, making sure there are no air pockets. A half-cup of starter fertilizer solution (diluted according to the product's instructions) can be watered in around the base.

TLC Keep the soil evenly moist from spring until the ground freezes in fall, especially during the first 2 years. Water deeply to encourage deep root growth. Apply 2 to 4 inches of organic mulch such as shredded bark or wood chips and replenish as needed throughout the growing season. Not all maples require fertilization. Those that do will benefit from a spring application of 10-10-10 fertilizer or an organic equivalent sprinkled around the base of each tree and watered in well. To avoid heavy sap flow, do annual shaping in winter or after leaves are fully open. Prune off dead, damaged, or diseased branches anytime. The thin bark of maples is susceptible to damage from winter sun and string trimmers. Young trees should be protected with plastic cylinders or wrapping materials.

PEAK SEASON

Maples' most outstanding feature is their fall color, which may be yellow, orange, or red. They also have inconspicuous spring flowers, clean summer foliage, and winged fruits in mid- to late summer that are tinged with pink or red.

MY FAVORITES

Acer tataricum ginnala (amur maple) grows to 25 feet and has yellow flowers and red leaves in fall. 'Flame' is shorter.

A. japonicum (fullmoon maple) grows 20 to 30 feet tall with feathery leaves and a graceful habit. A single tree makes a lovely focal point.

A. palmatum (Japanese maple) includes some of the smallest and most delicate of the maples, with deeply cut leaves and multiple stems. 'Bloodgood' grows to 15 feet tall with bronze-red leaves in spring and summer that turn scarlet in fall.

GARDEN COMPANIONS

The smaller maples are excellent specimen plants in a mixed border or in the dappled light of a woodland garden with hostas, epimediums, and ferns. Plant Japanese maples with witch hazel; with the velvety, deep green foliage of Hinoki false cypress (*Chamaecyparis obtusa*) behind it; or with paperbark maples.

ABOVE: Acer saccharum. BELOW: A. palmatum *'Ever Red' is a diminutive Japanese maple, forming a 7-foot mound of weeping branches.*

Oak
Quercus

A mature bur oak (Quercus macrocarpa) is the embodiment of splendor and permanance, with its impressive branches and deeply furrowed bark.

One of the toughest decisions I ever made was to take down a 150-year-old bur oak. My contractor assured me that either the tree or the house had to go; they were at war, and the tree was winning. I still dream about that tree. It had a perfect vase shape, which meant that its long, arching limbs made excellent entrance ramps for the squirrels living in the attic. The tree completely encircled the house, embraced it like a babe in arms. Oaks will do that if you plant them too close.

Like my tree, many oaks growing in lawns and gardens were never actually planted but sprouted from acorns in the wild. Bur, white, red, shingle, and pin oaks are common varieties. All oaks produce acorns and have deeply furrowed gray-brown bark, which gives them their look of rugged invincibility. Red oak is probably the best for planting in residential landscapes, as its unusually deep roots don't bother nearby plants and its high branching habit creates the open shade that many plants thrive in.

PEAK SEASON

Oaks have something to offer the landscape all year, including clean summer foliage, fall color, and interesting winter silhouettes.

MY FAVORITES

Quercus macrocarpa (bur oak) grows slowly to 80 feet tall, with deeply furrowed bark and large acorns. It is extremely tough and hardy.

Q. rubra (red oak) grows quickly to 75 feet. Its high branching habit (creating open shade), deep roots, and need for good soil make it an excellent choice for gardens.

Q. imbricaria (called shingle oak because early pioneers used it to make shingles for their cabins) grows slowly to 60 feet, preferably in moist, rich soil. It has smooth, glossy, unlobed leaves and can be pruned heavily.

Q. palustris (pin oak) grows to 80 feet tall with a slender, vaselike shape, drooping lower branches, and pointy leaves.

GARDEN COMPANIONS

Oaks look good in a large, open lawn. They are also excellent garden plants. Epimedium, wild ginger *(Asarum),* and other plants that tolerate dry shade do well beneath oaks.

When Plant oaks as soon as you can work the ground in spring. Many types are difficult to transplant and should be planted while they are still young.

Where Oaks grow best in full sun but will tolerate partial shade. They require a rich, slightly acidic soil. Give trees plenty of room to grow and avoid planting them under power lines.

How Remove the tree from its container carefully, keeping the root ball intact. Plant at the same depth as it was in the container, in a hole deep and wide enough to accommodate the roots without crowding. Plant a balled-and-burlapped tree so that the root flare is right at the soil surface, cutting and removing as much of the burlap and wire as possible without injuring roots. (Acidify the soil before planting pin oak, which is susceptible to iron chlorosis when soil is too alkaline.) Gently firm soil around the roots and water thoroughly, making sure there are no air pockets. A half-cup of starter fertilizer solution (diluted according to the product's instructions) can be watered in around the base.

TLC Keep the soil evenly moist from spring until the ground freezes in fall, especially during the first 2 years. Water deeply to encourage deep root growth. Apply 2 to 4 inches of organic mulch such as shredded bark or wood chips and replenish as needed throughout the growing season. (For pin oaks, add soil amendments as needed to maintain a slightly acidic pH.) Avoid disturbing the root zone; trenching or compacting soil there can damage or kill an oak. To prevent oak wilt, don't prune trees from April 15 to July 1, when insects that can spread it are most active. Restrict pruning to removal of dead, diseased, or crossing branches.

ABOVE: Quercus palustris. BELOW: *Red oak (Q. rubra) leaves in fall.*

River Birch
Betula nigra

It's not often that I recommend just one variety of a Top 10 plant. After all, part of the fun is opening your eyes to how diverse most plant families are: If you don't like the tall version, try the dwarf. If blue isn't your color, grow the kind with the white flowers. Like the look of a plant but don't want it to creep? Chances are there's an upright version.

Betula nigra 'Heritage' does have relatives, but none can compare to this most famous member of the river birch clan. Most trees have a single trunk; 'Heritage' likes to fork at ground level, forming a V. Since its peeling, golden bark is one of its chief attractions, most people think two trunks are better than one.

The best river birch, Betula nigra 'Heritage', typically has a forked trunk, delicate limbs, peeling bark, and diamond-shaped leaves that turn yellow in fall.

River birch is native and grows quickly in its youth. The trunk and branches are initially beige; as the outer layer peels away a creamy-colored inner bark is revealed that ages to apricot. On older trees, the bark curls off in sheets.

'Heritage' loves a hot, humid climate and is able to tolerate poor drainage. It also looks great in winter, when its bark is more noticeable.

PEAK SEASON

River birch's ragged bark is attractive all year and complemented in summer by clean, green foliage.

GARDEN COMPANIONS

River birch looks good in an informal setting with dogwood, as well as with evergreens like hemlock and with large-leafed hostas.

When Plant river birch as soon as you can work the ground in spring.

CLOCKWISE FROM LEFT: *River birch's peeling bark adds interest in winter; Betula nigra; a close-up look at the unusual apricot-colored bark of 'Heritage' river birch*

Where River birch prefers sun but will grow in partial shade. It likes well-drained, slightly acidic to average soil. It tolerates moist or even wet sites but not drought. Plant it where you can enjoy the interesting bark.

How Remove the tree from its container carefully, keeping the root ball intact. Plant at the same depth as it was in the container, in a hole deep and wide enough to accommodate the roots without crowding. Plant a balled-and-burlapped tree so that the root flare is right at the soil surface, cutting and removing as much of the burlap and wire as possible without injuring roots. Gently firm soil around the roots and water thoroughly, making sure there are no air pockets. A half-cup of starter fertilizer (diluted according to the product's instructions) can be watered in around the base.

TLC Keep the soil evenly moist from spring until the ground freezes in fall, especially during the first 2 years. Water deeply to encourage deep root growth. Maintain 2 to 4 inches of organic mulch such as shredded bark or wood chips throughout the growing season. Do annual shaping in summer to avoid heavy sap flow.

125

Serviceberry

Amelanchier

Serviceberries often have multiple trunks that grow to about 25 feet tall. The crimson fall foliage of this young Amelanchier canadensis sets off the soft gray bark beautifully.

Although serviceberries are most common in their shrub form, the trees deserve more attention and seem finally to be getting it. They have pretty gray trunks and airy canopies that are covered in tiny white flowers in early spring. Birds love the purple berries that follow, but if you act fast when they first appear you might gather enough to make serviceberry preserves, also known as juneberry or shadblow preserves, as *Amelanchier* is known by all three common names. The trees' smooth, green leaves turn red-orange as temperatures drop. Serviceberries are also lovely against the snow, especially if the birds haven't made off with all the berries.

I planted a row of 'Autumn Brilliance' serviceberries to divide my garden in two. When I look out over the garden from my back porch, the trees lead my eye to a shady hosta garden and a birdhouse—and away from an ugly utility pole directly overhead. Their dainty appearance belies a tough temperament. No need to baby these hardy, disease-resistant trees.

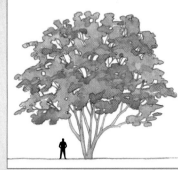

PEAK SEASON

Attractive but short-lived white flowers bloom in spring, followed in late summer by purplish berries that attract wildlife. Serviceberries have excellent fall color in shades of red, orange, or yellow.

MY FAVORITES

Amelanchier x *grandiflora* 'Autumn Brilliance' and 'Princess Diana' have white flowers in early spring, dark blue fruits, and red fall foliage.

A. laevis 'Cumulus' makes an excellent border screen.

GARDEN COMPANIONS

Serviceberries bloom early, so give them some company. They look great with early-spring daffodils, crocuses, and wild tulips.

When Plant serviceberries as soon as you can work the ground in spring.

Where Serviceberries prefer partial shade but tolerate full sun. Young trees like well-drained, slightly acidic soil. Single serviceberries make excellent focal points, especially when pruned as small trees. The trees are also ideal for naturalized settings.

How Remove the tree from its container carefully, keeping the root ball intact. Plant at the same depth as it was in the container, in a hole deep and wide enough to accommodate the roots without crowding. Plant a balled-and-burlapped tree so that the root flare is right at the soil surface, cutting and removing as much of the burlap and wire as possible without injuring roots. Gently firm soil around the roots and water thoroughly, making sure there are no air pockets. A half-cup of starter fertilizer (diluted according to the product's instructions) can be watered in around the base.

TLC Keep the soil evenly moist from spring until the ground freezes in fall, especially during the first 2 years. Water deeply to encourage deep root growth. Apply 2 to 4 inches of organic mulch such as shredded bark or wood chips and replenish as needed throughout the growing season. Once mature, trees will tolerate fairly dry conditions. Serviceberries do not require fertilization. Annual shaping to keep an open crown should be done in late winter. Prune off dead, damaged, or diseased branches anytime. Remove suckers from the base of the trees as they appear.

ABOVE, TOP TO BOTTOM: Amelanchier; *a cluster of serviceberry fruits; delicate white spring flowers.* LEFT: *A single serviceberry in high summer, covered in small berries.*

127

Evergreen Conifers

Conifers are cone-bearing plants. Most are evergreen, with leaves that are shaped like needles or fronds. While most conifers carry their seeds in woody cones, some bear them in structures that are more like berries or fruit. Junipers, for example, bear clusters of dense, pale blue berries; yews produce fleshy red berries.

Conifers' leaves are usually tougher textured than the broad, flat leaves of most deciduous shrubs, and they drop off gradually instead of all at once in autumn. This eases the annual chore of raking and bagging leaves, and enriches the soil as the needles decompose, maintaining the low pH most conifers prefer. The needles make an attractive mulch that keeps down weeds and holds moisture in the soil.

Conifers also tend to grow slowly, so they don't develop extensive root systems. While a woody tree or shrub may seriously compromise nearby plants, conifers are much less intrusive. In short, conifers are good citizens wherever they live—but to gardeners in cold climates conifers are a godsend, offering many of the same qualities as broad-leafed evergreens but with a much better ability to cope with our winters' dehydrating triple whammy of cold, wind, and sun.

COLOR AND FORM

With 650 species to choose from, you can be picky. The six we recommend for midwestern gardens are extremely hardy, maintenance free, and versatile. Colors range from green to gold to gray-blue. While most prefer full sun (junipers insist on it), yews and hemlocks like partial shade. The taller conifers tend to grow upright, like spires or pyramids, and take on interesting silhouettes as they mature, though a few

(notably spruce) never lose their Christmas-tree shape. The smaller conifers tend to mimic the shapes of the taller ones while adding a few flourishes of their own: some form low mounds; others carpet the ground. Yews and arborvitaes can be sheared for a more formal look, either as individual specimens or as a hedge, but most conifers will grow into pleasing shapes without your guidance.

PLANTING

Early spring planting is ideal, although fall is also a good time—and you'll find the best selection and lowest prices in fall. As with deciduous trees and shrubs, don't go shopping until you know where sun and shade fall in your garden, how much space you have for each plant, and what size and shape it will be when fully grown.

Conifers are usually sold as container plants. Before planting, pull apart any tangled roots and spread them out, cutting those that are determined to grow in concentric circles, using a pruning knife. Plant as you would a decidu-

ABOVE: *A pot of annuals resting on a chair finds shelter among the soft-needled branches of a white pine.* OPPOSITE PAGE: *A metallic gazing ball pulls a piece of sky into the sculpted greenery of an Illinois conifer garden.*

ous tree or shrub, digging the hole no deeper than the root ball but three or four times wider and backfilling with unamended garden soil to encourage roots to grow outward. Space conifers as the plant labels advise unless you're planting a hedge, in which case you may want them closer together.

129

American Arborvitae

Thuja occidentalis

Arborvitaes have feathery, flat sprays of foliage and tiny cones. Like yews they are staid and structural. But unlike yews they can't take much shade, and their leaves are softer to the touch, smoother and more pliable, and a lighter green. Arborvitaes also come in more interesting shapes than yews do. These include spheres, cones, slender columns, and plump pyramids, all in various sizes. That means no clipping is necessary to shape your shrub into a ball; 'Globosa' already *is* a ball.

Individual arborvitaes take pruning well, however, and an annual haircut is a good idea because shearing allows maximum leaf exposure to the sun and stimulates the shrub to grow fresh, new foliage. To make sure all parts of an arborvitae hedge are exposed to sunlight, always clip the plants so they're wider toward the bottom or the lower branches will grow sparse.

'Europe Gold' arborvitae, named for its yellow foliage, forms a neat pyramid about 8 feet tall. It can also be pruned as a hedge.

PEAK SEASON

Year-round. Scalelike, flattened foliage comes in various shades of green.

MY FAVORITES

Although the species, *Thuja occidentalis,* grows upright to 30 to 60 feet tall, many varieties are smaller.

'Techny' is a pyramidal shrub that grows to 10 feet tall and has dark green foliage. It can be sheared to check growth.

'Emerald' is columnar, growing to 12 feet tall, with lighter green leaves.

'Hetz Midget' is a dwarf that grows to 2 feet tall, with dense foliage and a rounded shape.

'Globosa' is slightly larger than 'Hetz Midget' and also globe shaped. It can be sheared as a low, rounded hedge.

GARDEN COMPANIONS

Columnar arborvitaes anchor beds of mounding and creeping plants like hardy geraniums, rambling shrub roses, catmint, and low false cypress *(Chamaecyparis).* Grown as a tall hedge, arborvitaes make an excellent backdrop for tall perennials like delphinums, phlox, and lilies. The cone-shaped types look good framing masses of lavender.

When Plant arborvitaes as early as you can work the ground in spring. They also can be successfully planted in early fall if given ample water.

Where Arborvitaes like full sun or light shade and fertile, well-drained soils. They are popular plants for hedges, foundation plantings, screens, and windbreaks (except in hot, dry locations—the needles will turn brown).

How Carefully remove each plant from its container, keeping the root ball intact. Plant at the same depth as it was in the container, in a hole deep and wide enough to accommodate the roots without crowding. Plant balled-and-burlapped shrubs so that the root flares are right at the soil surface, cutting and removing as much of the burlap and wire as possible without injuring roots. Gently firm the soil around the roots and water thoroughly, making sure there are no air pockets. A half-cup of a starter fertilizer solution (diluted according to the product's instructions) can be watered in around the base. Give each shrub space to grow to its full height and width, with the exception of hedge plants, which are usually planted closer.

ABOVE: Arborvitae *'Techny'*. BELOW: *Globe-shaped* Thuja occidentalis *'Woodwardii' will grow to 3 feet in diameter. Its foliage turns brownish green in winter.*

TLC Keep the soil evenly moist from spring until the ground freezes in fall, especially during the first 2 years. Water deeply to encourage deep root growth. Apply 2 to 4 inches of organic mulch such as shredded bark or wood chips and replenish as needed throughout the growing season. Cut off winter burn in early spring. Prune arborvitaes just after new growth has emerged. Formal hedges can be pruned again later in the season, but not after mid-August.

Canada Hemlock

Tsuga canadensis

I vaguely associated hemlock with poison until I happened to be visiting a friend's garden 7 or 8 years ago and noticed an unusually graceful tree with long, languorously drooping branches growing against a tall cedar fence. It looked terribly fragile, which, my friend told me, is all a pose. Hemlocks are native and very tough, as long as you give them some wind protection, keep them out of polluted air, and plant them in well-drained, acidic soil. I fell in love with my friend's hemlock and decided I had to have one, too. What I didn't know was that Canada hemlock grows 40 to 60 feet tall! The good news is that it takes shearing well and is often used as a formal clipped hedge.

The wide, weeping form of Tsuga canadensis 'Pendula' hides the bare trunks of taller background trees.

Mine is now a tidy 12 feet and holding. By the way, the poison hemlock taken by the Greek philosopher Socrates belongs to the carrot family.

PEAK SEASON

Year-round. Fanlike sprays of foliage on horizontal branches, abundant pendulous cones, and cinnamon red bark are all assets.

MY FAVORITES

The species, *Tsuga canadensis,* has gracefully drooping, long branches and an airy structure; it tolerates some shade. It's an excellent landscape plant but can also be clipped as a tight hedge.

'Aurea' has golden foliage when young, aging to green. It grows to 15 feet or more.

'Pendula' (Sargent weeping hemlock) grows to 20 feet tall and twice as wide, but with pruning it can be kept to a gently cascading 3- to 5-foot mound.

GARDEN COMPANIONS

Hemlocks look best surrounded by ferns, wild ginger (*Asarum*), hostas, and spreading Japanese yews. They also make an excellent clipped hedge for a perennial border. The weeping type ('Pendula') looks good with rock-garden plants.

When Plant hemlocks as early as you can work the ground in spring. They also can be successfully planted in early fall if given ample water.

Where Choose a site with partial shade, good drainage, and cool, acidic soil. Avoid hot sites with alkaline soil. Hemlocks are susceptible to air pollution and salt damage from roadways, so they do not make good street trees. They are useful as screens or clipped hedges. The weeping form, 'Pendula', makes an interesting focal point; it will need shelter from wind and possible winter protection in Zones 1B and 43.

How Plant hemlock at the same depth as it was in the container, in a hole deep and wide enough to accommodate the roots without crowding. Plant a balled-and-burlapped tree so that the root flare is right at the soil surface, cutting and removing as much of the burlap and wire as possible without injuring roots. Gently firm soil around the roots and water thoroughly, making sure there are no air pockets. A half-cup of an acidic starter fertilizer solution (diluted according to the product's instructions) can be watered in around the base. Give single trees plenty of space to grow to their full height and width; hedge plants are usually spaced closer.

TLC Keep the soil evenly moist from spring until the ground freezes in fall, especially during the first 2 years. Water deeply to encourage deep root growth. Apply 2 to 4 inches of organic mulch such as shredded bark or wood chips and replenish as needed throughout the growing season. Hemlocks benefit from a spring application of an acidic fertilizer. Remove any winter-damaged branches in early spring, and prune lightly in early summer to shape.

ABOVE: Tsuga canadensis. RIGHT: *The small cones of Canada hemlock are less than 1 inch long.*

Juniper
Juniperus

Junipers are among the toughest plants around. Unfortunately, they are rarely displayed to best advantage. The low-growing, spreading types are all too often used as a substitute for grass, usually at commercial establishments too busy to mow. Junipers look much better with lots of interesting company. They are wonderful in rock gardens with stone and gravel and small plants bursting with color. A richly textured mat of creeping juniper has a way of knitting disparate elements together, soothing the eye with its fluid grace.

I grow *Juniperus horizontalis* as a ground cover among shrub roses on a troublesome slope that is dry, rocky, and pounded by the sun all day. Junipers thrive in such rugged terrain, and the blue-gray leaves and berries look great with the rose blossoms' pink and blush tones.

My Italian-born neighbor uses junipers for vertical interest: he planted 12 columnar 'Welchii' junipers along a high, wrought-iron fence. The 8-foot-tall spires enliven an otherwise flat landscape, and add a touch of Italy.

A river of low juniper winds among smooth boulders and fountain grass (Pennisetum).

PEAK SEASON

Year-round. Juniper foliage may be dark green, blue, silver-blue, or golden yellow, depending on the variety. Honey-colored cones gradually darken to bluish black in late summer.

MY FAVORITES

Juniperus communis 'Compressa' has green foliage and grows slowly to 2 to 3 feet tall, making it excellent in rock gardens.

J. scopulorum 'Welchii' is very slender with silvery green foliage and grows to 8 feet tall.

J. horizontalis 'Wiltonii' (blue rug juniper) is a vigorous, creeping ground cover with silvery blue foliage that grows 4 inches tall and 8 to 10 feet wide. Many other varieties grow 8 to 12 inches tall and 6 to 8 feet wide, including 'Blue Chip' (silver-blue), 'Blue Mat' (gray-green), 'Emerald Spreader' (bright green), and 'Prince of Wales' (dark green).

GARDEN COMPANIONS

Plant low-growing, creeping junipers with upright dwarf conifers like Alberta spruce and feathery, mounding shrubs like gold false cypress (*Chamaecyparis*). All junipers are great with shrub roses; in herb gardens with lamb's ears, sage, and lavender; and in rock gardens.

When Plant junipers as early as you can work the ground in spring. They also can be successfully planted in early fall if given ample water.

LEFT: Juniperus communis 'Compressa'. RIGHT: J. horizontalis 'Blue Chip' is a creeping juniper that spreads up to 8 feet along the ground.

Where Junipers prefer sunny locations and light, sandy soil but will grow in almost any situation. About the only thing they can't tolerate is constantly wet soil. Use this diverse group of evergreens to hide a foundation or as a hedge or windbreak. Shrub types can be used as ground covers or in rock gardens or flower borders.

How Plant juniper at the same depth as it was in the container, in a hole deep and wide enough to accommodate the roots without crowding. Plant a balled-and-burlapped tree or shrub so that the root flare is right at the soil surface, cutting and removing as much of the burlap and wire as possible without injuring roots. Gently firm soil around the roots and water thoroughly, making sure there are no air pockets. A half-cup of a starter fertilizer solution (diluted according to the product's instructions) can be watered in around the base. Give each tree or shrub plenty of space to grow to its full height and width.

TLC Water well until plants are established. After that, keep the soil on the dry side. Apply 2 to 4 inches of organic mulch such as shredded bark or wood chips in spring and replenish as needed throughout the growing season. To help reduce chances of winter drying and browning, make sure plants go into winter well watered. Remove any winter damage in spring. Junipers benefit from a spring application of an acidic fertilizer. Prune new growth of spreading junipers annually in early summer to maintain their size and shape and to prevent them from dying out in the middle. Upright junipers benefit from a gentle pruning each year. Try to retain the natural shape of the plants.

135

Pine

Pinus

Pines are among those conifers that begin life boringly, as rather scruffy, pyramid-shaped plants, and grow more interesting as their upper branches open up or develop a more rounded habit. There are so many types of pines that it's hard to generalize about them, their only common characteristic being their bundles of long needles and pendulous cones. The needles grow in clusters of two, three, five, or sometimes more.

White pines are the most majestic of trees, but in my opinion they belong in a wilderness setting or a very large landscape garden or park. Dwarf, weeping, and trailing varieties, however, are quite lovely in smaller gardens. Dwarf varieties of *Pinus mugo* are also excellent, especially in rock gardens; their deep green, tuftlike needle clusters and twisting branches add a touch of the exotic.

I've always loved Scotch pines, too, with their golden branches and bluish green foliage, but recently they've been plagued by fatal nematodes and can't be recommended.

Pinus mugo looks most at home in a Japanese-style garden like this one. Perennial lamb's ears are in the foreground.

PEAK SEASON

Year-round

MY FAVORITES

Pinus thunbergii (Japanese black pine) is a handsome tree that reaches 20–100 feet. 'Majestic Beauty' doesn't mind polluted air or salt.

P. cembra (Swiss stone pine) is hardy and slow growing to 70 feet or more, with dense even foliage. It's great in small gardens.

P. strobus 'Nana' is a dwarf white pine, growing 4 feet tall by 7 feet wide, with a graceful, airy branching habit. It's excellent in containers and rock gardens. 'Horsford' grows 1 to 2 feet tall, has a globular shape, and bears light green needles.

P. nigra (Austrian black pine) is a resilient, densely branched, pyramid-shaped tree. It will grow to 40 feet and makes an excellent screen or windbreak.

P. mugo grows slowly to 10 feet tall with long, feathery, dark green needles; the growth habit can be prostrate, pyramidal, or low and shrubby. 'Gnom' and 'Mops' are dwarf versions, excellent in rock gardens.

GARDEN COMPANIONS

Use Japanese black pine to anchor a formal landscape composed of clipped evergreens in various shapes and sizes. Dwarf pines look good with rock-garden plants and in small woodland gardens with ferns and hostas.

TOP: *Pinus thunbergii* (Japanese black pine), MIDDLE: *P. strobus* 'Horsford', BOTTOM: *P. nigra* (Austrian black pine)

When Plant pines as soon as you can work the ground in spring. They can be planted in early fall if given ample water.

Where Pines grow best in full sun in acidic soil. They are very sensitive to salt damage from roadways. Landscape uses include hedges, windbreaks, and background plantings; smaller specimens make good accents.

How Carefully remove the pine from its container, keeping the root ball intact. Plant at the same depth as it was in the container, in a hole deep and wide enough to accommodate the roots without crowding. Plant a balled-and-burlapped tree or shrub so that the root flare is right at the soil surface, cutting and removing as much of the burlap and wire as possible without injuring roots. Firm soil around the roots and water thoroughly, making sure there are no air pockets. A half-cup of an acidic starter fertilizer solution (diluted according to the product's instructions) can be watered in around the base.

TLC Keep the soil evenly moist from spring until the ground freezes in fall, especially during the first 2 years. Water deeply to encourage deep root growth. Apply 2 to 4 inches of organic mulch such as shredded bark or wood chips and replenish as needed throughout the growing season. Remove winter-burned branches in early spring. Pines benefit from a spring application of an acidic fertilizer. Prune annually in early summer by cutting back the upward-growing new growth ("candles") by half. This encourages bushier growth and better-shaped plants.

137

Spruce
Picea

Ask a child to draw a picture of an evergreen and you will get a Christmas tree every time, one that looks exactly like a spruce. Even though other types make better Christmas trees because they hold their needles longer, spruce is still the prototype, thanks to its perfectly symmetrical pyramid shape and the way its cones hang like, well, Christmas ornaments from its short-needled branches.

The spruce is far more useful in the outdoor landscape than in the living room. The Colorado blue spruce is a favorite lawn specimen in the lower Midwest. The Serbian spruce is an exceptionally handsome tree, probably the loveliest of the spruces, with its dark green needles and willowy form. Its branches don't thin out at the bottom, and it loves hot, humid weather. The dwarf Alberta spruce is delightful in rock gardens. It is a member of the extremely hardy white spruce family.

Black Hills spruce (Picea glauca densata) is a handsome, slow-growing specimen plant, good for large, sweeping lawns. It will eventually attain a height of 20 feet.

PEAK SEASON

Year-round

MY FAVORITES

Picea abies 'Gregoryana' is a dwarf Norway spruce with a dense, irregular, mounding habit and dark green needles.

P. omorika (Serbian spruce) is the most handsome spruce, growing to 60 feet tall with a graceful conical habit and dark green needles. 'Nana' is the dwarf, growing 4 to 10 feet tall.

P. orientalis is a dense, cone-shaped tree that grows to 60 feet tall with short needles. 'Skylands' has golden foliage and grows to 20 feet tall.

P. glauca albertiana 'Conica' is a dwarf Alberta spruce with soft leaves that emerge as pale green, then deepen in color. Its cone shape and small size (6 to 8 feet tall) make it an excellent accent plant.

P. pungens 'Glauca globosa' is a dwarf Colorado spruce with a compact habit that grows to 3 feet tall and wide and has vivid blue-gray needles. It's another great accent plant.

GARDEN COMPANIONS

Plant dwarf and weeping spruce varieties as accent plants in mixed borders. Plant blue-needled types to contrast with dark green trees and shrubs or as lawn trees. *P. pungens* 'Koster', a small, upright blue spruce, looks great with the blue, grassy spikes of *Festuca glauca* 'Elijah Blue' in front of it.

When Plant spruces as early as you can work the ground in spring.

Where Spruces grow best in full sun; even partial shade will result in thinner foliage. They prefer soil slightly on the acidic side with some organic matter mixed in. Good drainage is essential. Avoid sites with drying winds. Landscape uses include hedges, windbreaks, and background plantings; smaller specimens are good accent plants. Avoid planting spruce trees in small yards or too close to buildings; they will quickly outgrow those sites.

How Carefully remove the plant from its container, keeping the root ball intact. Plant at the same depth as it was in the container, in a hole deep and wide enough to accommodate the roots without crowding. Plant a balled-and-burlapped tree or shrub so that the root flare is right at the soil surface, cutting and removing as much of the burlap and wire as possible without injuring roots. Gently firm soil around the roots and water thoroughly, making sure there are no air pockets. A half-cup of an acidic starter fertilizer solution (diluted according to the product's instructions) can be watered in around the base.

TLC Keep the soil evenly moist from spring until the ground freezes in fall, especially during the first 2 years. Water deeply to encourage deep root growth. Apply 2 to 4 inches of organic mulch such as shredded bark or wood chips and replenish as needed throughout the growing season. Spruces benefit from a spring application of an acidic fertilizer. Most require very little pruning and are best left to grow into their natural shape. Any pruning to shape trees should be done in late spring; snip off no more than one-third of the new growth.

ABOVE: Picea omorika *(Serbian spruce).* BELOW: *Many varieties of Colorado spruce* (P. pungens) *have blue needles.*

Yew

Taxus

An avid gardener I know, born and raised in Minnesota, moved to England recently because he wanted to grow "a great, undulating yew hedge." To him an artfully sheared yew hedge as tall as a house epitomized the rewards of gardening. In England, which has a more temperate climate than ours, yews grow quickly and are frequently used as hedges or screens to give gardens their basic form and structure. They do wonders for midwestern gardens, too, albeit on a smaller scale.

When left alone yews are anything but eccentric. Their cones don't drip (they don't *have* cones, but cuplike red berries); their branches don't weep or twist themselves into sinister shapes. But they are fun to shear into fanciful topiaries. Yews are to our gardens what the little black dress is to women's wardrobes—exceptionally adaptable. They are also absolutely essential for shade gardens. For an effect that is decidely *not* like that of an English garden, plant spreading yews as a ground cover in an informal woodland setting.

When Plant yews as early as you can work the ground in spring. They also can be successfully planted in early fall if given ample water.

Where Yews will grow in sun or shade, but keep them out of drying winds. They like soils that have excellent drainage and are high in organic matter. Use them in shrub borders, as large ground covers or hedges, or right up against the house as foundation plantings.

How Carefully remove the plant from its container, keeping the root ball intact. Plant at the same depth as it was in the container, in a hole deep and wide enough to accommodate the roots without crowding. Plant a balled-and-burlapped tree or shrub so that the root flare is right at the soil surface, cutting and removing as much of the burlap and wire as possible without injuring roots. Gently firm soil around the roots and water thoroughly, making sure there are no air pockets. A half-cup of starter fertilizer solution (diluted according to the product's instructions) can be watered in around the base. Give each tree or shrub plenty of space to grow to its full height and width.

TLC Keep the soil evenly moist from spring until the ground freezes in fall, especially during the first 2 years. Water deeply to encourage deep root growth. Apply 2 to 4 inches of organic mulch such as shredded bark or wood chips and replenish as needed throughout the growing season. Yews benefit from a spring application of fertilizer. Spreading types should be allowed to grow naturally with very little pruning. Shear upright forms in spring and again in midsummer if necessary. Yews are a favorite food of deer; shrubs may require protection.

OPPOSITE PAGE: *The densely packed needles of* Taxus × media *'Hicksii' make it a good candidate for use as a tall screen or hedge.*

PEAK SEASON

Year-round. The scented, spreading branches have attractive leaves that are dark green above and lighter green below.

MY FAVORITES

Taxus cuspidata (Japanese yew) is a spreading shrub with dark green needles and arching branches. 'Capitata' will grow to 25 feet tall unless new growth is pinched back; it has a pyramidal form and profuse red berries. 'Nana' is a low grower (to 3 feet) with a more rounded habit.

T. × media 'Hicksii' is a narrow, upright grower, to 12 feet tall and 4 feet wide; it makes an excellent screen. 'Densiformis' grows 3 to 4 feet tall and 5 feet wide.

T. baccata 'Semperaurea' has golden foliage. It grows slowly to 6 feet tall.

GARDEN COMPANIONS

Use the upright types as screens or hedges or as a backdrop for perennials. Grow the spreading types among ferns, hostas, and lily-of-the-valley. Put *T. baccata* 'Semperaurea' with *Hosta sieboldiana* 'Elegans', which has deeply veined blue leaves.

ABOVE: Taxus cuspidata. BELOW: T. cuspidata *shows off its bright red berries.*

If planted in protected areas.

Vines

Climbing vines have a special charm that goes beyond adding vertical interest to a garden. I think it has to do with the way they reach out to others to form endearing partnerships: if you let me cling to you, I'll make you look beautiful. You see it in the way they embrace arbors, trellises, fences, houses, even the trunks of trees.

Vines may seem hopelessly dependent, but I see them as resourceful and tough. After a little help getting started—maybe a bit of twine to hold them in place—you'll be reaching for the pruners more often than the scissors and twine ball. Their instinct is to grow toward the sun.

TYPES OF VINES

Vines such as ivy, whose leaves form a thick, carpet-like mass of green, cling to even the slickest surfaces with their sticky aerial rootlets. Climbing hydrangeas and trumpet creepers are clingers, too, with twining stems and "sticky feet" that will provide added support if you grow them on a trellis or an arbor. Clematis and grapevines send out slender

tendrils that will curl around a strand of wire, a bamboo pole, a slat in a trellis, or a twig. Honeysuckle and wisteria depend solely on twining stems to hold them in place.

SEEDS VS. PLANTS

Annual vines—such as morning glory, nasturtium, and hyacinth bean—are easy to grow from seed. They flower in mid- to late summer and often self-sow. Some have seedpods as handsome as their flowers. Many annual vines (including the three mentioned above) also happen to have exceptional foliage and are quite attractive even when they're not in bloom.

Perennial vines are typically slow to get established. If you've decided to grow one

LEFT: *Morning glories make a pretty floral "roof" for a rustic arbor.* BELOW: *Climbing hydrangea's snow white flower clusters brighten a fence in dappled shade.* OPPOSITE PAGE: *A purple-flowering clematis embraces a bronze garden statue.*

location and just a little bit of guidance, they'll do well in your garden. A few of them are pretty aggressive, and you may need to rein them in now and then. Wisteria, for example, made the list in spite of its sometimes rather brutish nature, since this spectacular vine is well worth the effort it takes to keep its growth in check. Clematis needs occasional pruning, too, though not to curb an invasive streak. Well-timed pruning improves its flowering and vigor. In the TLC sections I'll tell you how to prune each vine that needs it. Gardening, after all, isn't entirely labor free.

of the perennial vines on my Top 10 list, start with a potted plant, not seeds—unless you don't mind waiting 3 or more years for the vine to flower. If the vine is already growing up a trellis or stake in the container, the support can be transplanted into the garden with the plant, but you'll need to help the vine make the transition to its permanent support.

PRUNING

All the vines featured here were chosen for their beauty and their reputations as reliable performers in the Midwest. Given the right

Clematis
Clematis

When I'm out plant shopping, I can always spot beginning gardeners in the first flush of an infatuation with clematis. They gaze longingly at the elegant petals and the charming way the perennial vine scales its miniature plastic trellis. Then, after a few deep sighs, they move on. I know just what they're thinking: Some day I'll be skilled enough to take one of these beauties home. Some day I'll have clematis cascading over the mailbox, or threading through a tall shrub rose, or scrambling up the trunk of a flowering crabapple tree—just as it does in the garden books. But clematis is for experts, not for know-nothing gardeners like me.

But the fact is, clematis gets a bad rap. If you choose the right variety for your climate, soil, and site, and if you prune it properly and make sure its roots are shaded, you'll find that clematis is among the easiest and most rewarding of all flowering plants. Yes, even if you're a novice. *Especially* if you're a novice, as experienced gardeners won't feel a tenth as proud as you will when friends come over to admire your clematis at its floriferous peak.

Large-flowered, sky blue to lavender Clematis 'Will Goodwin' and magenta C. 'Ernest Markham' both begin blooming in early summer.

PEAK SEASON

Flowers bloom in early spring, summer, or fall, depending on variety, followed by wispy seedpods.

MY FAVORITES

Clematis montana (anemone clematis) flowers in early spring. It is easy to grow but not hardy in the far north.

C. × Jackmanii, a large-flowered summer bloomer, is a sure thing for beginners whose biggest worry is the weather. It is extremely hardy, and its deep purple blooms will thickly cover a trellis from midsummer to fall.

C. 'Will Goodwin' bears large lavender-blue flowers in early summer and on and off for the rest of the summer. Other early-summer bloomers include 'Nelly Moser', whose pale pink petals have a darker pink stripe down the center, and 'Niobe', which bears masses of deep crimson flowers.

Sweet autumn clematis, variously sold as *C. terniflora* and *C. paniculata,* is a reliable late bloomer with small white flowers from August to October. It is hardy only in Zones 42 and 43.

GARDEN COMPANIONS

Clematis can do wonders for an ordinary mailbox or light post, especially when combined with a climbing rose or morning glory. It also goes well with delphiniums, lilies, peonies, and 'Annabelle' hydrangeas.

TOP TO BOTTOM: Clematis 'Nelly Moser', a long-blooming favorite; the late-season charmer C. terniflora (sweet autumn clematis); sultry C. 'Niobe'

When The best time to plant nursery-grown clematis is early spring.

Where Plant in rich, loose, fast-draining soil in full sun or light shade. Roots like to be cool, but the top of the plant requires 6 to 8 hours of sunlight. An eastern exposure is best. South- and west-facing plantings must be mulched to keep roots cool. Plant vines next to a trellis, a tree trunk, or an open framework to provide support.

How Loosen soil to a depth of 10 to 12 inches and work in generous amounts of compost or other organic material. Incorporate a controlled-release fertilizer into the soil before planting. Plant vines at the same depth they were growing in the container. Water well with a half-strength solution of fertilizer.

TLC Keep the soil evenly moist from spring until the ground freezes, watering when the top 2 inches of soil has dried out. Apply 2 to 4 inches of shredded leaves, bark, or wood-chip mulch around plants as soon as the ground warms in spring, and replenish as necessary throughout the growing season. Give plants a complete liquid fertilizer monthly during the growing season. Stems are easily broken so use care when attaching to supports. The twisting leafstalks may need help climbing. Pruning varies with the type of clematis. Spring bloomers flower on old wood; prune them a month after flowering to restrict sprawl. Summer and fall bloomers flower on new stems; prune them in spring before leaf and flower buds swell.

Climbing Hydrangea
Hydrangea anomala petiolaris

Most gardeners first learn about climbing hydrangea when they're looking to add a vertical dimension to a shady garden. Few flowering vines do well in shade, but climbing hydrangea actually thrives in it. Another virtue is its versatility as a climber. Its aerial rootlets cling tenaciously to brick or stone. A climbing hydrangea can also be trained to a trellis or other support.

I grow climbing hydrangea in partial shade on a simple metal arch that marks the entrance to an open, sunny garden. In early summer, clusters of what appear to be tiny, pale green berries appear. They are panicles, the buds of flowers that eventually form broad clumps in the lace-cap style. The blossoms are pure white and last for weeks before fading to a pleasant brownish gold color. The vine's heart-shaped leaves are glossy green all summer; in fall they turn reddish bronze.

The weathered timbers of a pergola are barely visible under the dense leaves and lacy flower clusters of climbing hydrangea, a shade-tolerant vine that's indestructible once established.

Climbing hydrangea is slow to get established and may not flower for the first several years, but once adapted to its site, the vine is a showstopper.

PEAK SEASON

White flower clusters bloom in mid-summer. Dark green foliage is attractive all season. Older plants have peeling, cinnamon-colored bark.

MY FAVORITES

Hydrangea anomala is slightly less hardy and has smaller flowers and longer, pointier leaves than *H. a. petiolaris*. It is lovely in June and July.

Decumaria barbara (wood vamp) is a native cousin that's hardy as far north as Chicago and is a tenacious climber with handsome, dark green leaves. Its creamy white flowers are fragrant but otherwise insignificant.

GARDEN COMPANIONS

Climbing hydrangea looks wonderful against brick or stone, especially when in bloom or when the leaves turn crimson in fall. Combine it with other shade-tolerant plants. The white flowers go well with white- or pink-flowered Japanese anemones, astilbe, and the tall white spires of cimicifuga. Or plant it with a glossy-leafed, shade-tolerant ground cover such as European wild ginger (*Asarum europaeum*), pachysandra, ajuga, or myrtle at its feet.

When The best time to plant climbing hydrangea is early spring. Nursery-grown plants can be planted throughout the growing season if they are watered well.

Climbing hydrangea's tiny flowers form lace-cap clusters several inches wide.

Where Climbing hydrangea likes rich soil and full sun or light shade. Avoid very dry sites. Aerial roots cling readily to wood, brick, and stone.

How Loosen soil to a depth of 10 to 12 inches and work in generous amounts of compost or other organic material. Incorporate a controlled-release fertilizer into the soil before planting. Plant at the same depth the plant was growing in the container. Water immediately after planting.

TLC Keep the soil evenly moist from spring until the ground freezes, watering when the top 2 inches of soil has dried out. Consistent watering is especially important during the first 2 years, but even mature plants will wilt at the first sign of drought. Apply 2 to 4 inches of shredded bark or wood-chip mulch around plants as soon as the ground warms in spring and replenish as necessary throughout the growing season. Fertilize in spring with a 10-10-10 fertilizer or an organic equivalent sprinkled around the base of plants and watered in well. Plants bloom on old wood, so prune after flowering only as needed. It may take up to 2 years before a vine clings well to a flat surface.

*Plants may survive in protected locations in southern parts of Zone 43.

Dutchman's Pipe

Aristolochia durior (A. macrophylla)

This is a big, leafy perennial vine that's great for covering a wall or growing on a trellis to screen a porch. Although its name comes from the curious shape of its flowers, the foliage is its most remarkable feature: twining stems 10 to 20 feet long bear kidney-shaped leaves in dense layers, like shingles on a house.

Dutchman's pipe is a woodland native. It belongs to the same family as wild ginger *(Asarum);* both plants have large, broad leaves that obscure the flowers, which are held close to the stem. Finding the flowers is great fun, especially for children. (Beware that parts of Dutchman's pipe are toxic when ingested.) I grow both plants together. A patch of wild ginger sits at the foot

Dutchman's pipe makes a solid green screen when grown up a fence. The vine's big, heart-shaped leaves are the perfect foil for the patterned foliage of a coleus planted in a formal urn.

ABOVE: *The leaves of Dutchman's pipe can grow more than a foot long. The 3-inch-long flowers are shaped like curved smoking pipes.* BELOW: *Dutchman's pipe combines well with ferns in dappled shade.*

of a trellis leaning against an oak tree. The vine scrambled up the trellis in a single season and now drips from the tree's lower branches.

Dutchman's pipe is easy to grow from seed, very hardy, and disease resistant. It appreciates a fertile, moist site and full sun but can tolerate dense shade. If it gets too aggressive, it can be cut back in late winter or early spring. The vine doesn't do well in windy areas, so give it some shelter.

PEAK SEASON

Inconspicuous but interesting flowers bloom late spring to early summer; leaves are glossy deep green all season.

GARDEN COMPANIONS

Dutchman's pipe looks good with woodland plants like trillium, pulmonaria, epimedium, Solomon's seal, and Japanese painted ferns (*Athyrium nipponicum*), and it makes an excellent backdrop for a shady flower border.

When The best time to plant Dutchman's pipe is early spring. Nursery-grown plants can be planted all season if they are watered well. Seeds can also be sown directly in the ground in fall.

Where Plant in average to rich, well-drained soil. Dutchman's pipe grows best in full sun but tolerates shade, and even heavy shade in southern areas. It does not tolerate dry soils or windy areas. Grow it where you want a dense privacy screen or deep shade.

How Loosen soil to a depth of 10 to 12 inches and work in 2 to 3 inches of compost or other organic matter. Incorporate a controlled-release fertilizer into the soil before planting. Plant at the same depth plants were growing in the containers, spacing them 15 to 20 feet apart. Provide a sturdy support. Water immediately after planting.

TLC Keep the soil evenly moist from spring until the ground freezes, watering when the top 2 inches of soil has dried out. Apply 2 to 4 inches of shredded bark or wood-chip mulch around plants as soon as the ground warms in spring and replenish as necessary throughout the growing season. Plants will respond well to an annual spring application of 10-10-10 fertilizer or an organic equivalent sprinkled around the base of plants and watered in well. Cut back vines in late winter if they get too heavy.

Honeysuckle

Lonicera

Honeysuckle is a delightful perennial vine, well behaved and graceful, with clusters of brilliant yellow, orange, or red flowers that bloom sporadically all summer. Its thick, almost serpentine stems wind around their support as they grow upward. Occasionally a branch will drift away from the support and wave about in the air; tie it in place with twine while it's still young and pliant. Honeysuckle vines become gnarled and rigid over time, which adds to the vine's appeal. Their leaves are large, leathery, and round, a fine backdrop for the warm flower color.

I have three trumpet honeysuckle vines, and by far the happiest—that is, the most vigorous, floriferous, and healthy-looking—is the one that grows in full sun over a metal arch. Honeysuckle tolerates some shade, but too much shade or poor air circulation will invite fungal problems. The vine also will get ratty-looking if it is chronically deprived of adequate moisture or crowded. Give it a trellis of its own, an arbored gate, or even a mailbox, and it will more than rise to the occasion.

A 'Dropmore Scarlet' honeysuckle vine at peak bloom spills over a garden bench.

PEAK SEASON

Tubular orange, red, or yellow flowers bloom from early spring to late summer. Red or purple berries in late summer attract birds.

MY FAVORITES

Lonicera sempervirens (trumpet honeysuckle) gets its name from the shape of its large red or orange flowers, which grow in clusters, or whorls, of six. 'Sulphurea' (also sold as 'Flava') has yellow, unscented flowers in April.

L. × brownii 'Dropmore Scarlet' is a hybrid of *L. sempervirens* and *L. hirsuta* and probably the best honeysuckle vine for all regions. It is extremely hardy and has red flowers that attract hummingbirds, though the flowers aren't fragrant.

L. × heckrottii (goldflame honeysuckle) has fragrant carmine flowers that open to show some yellow.

GARDEN COMPANIONS

Honeysuckle looks good on a fence behind small to midsize perennials with blue or lavender flowers, such as veronica, salvia, lavender, or catmint, or sharing the fence with a blue-flowering clematis like 'Will Goodwin'. It's also attractive behind low shrub roses and other plants with bright flowers. Just make sure they don't obscure the vine or cut off its air supply.

When The best time to plant honeysuckle is early spring. Nursery-grown plants can be planted all season if they are watered well.

Where Plant in fertile soil in full sun except where noted.

How Loosen soil to a depth of 10 to 12 inches and work in generous amounts of compost or other organic material. Incorporate a controlled-release fertilizer into the soil before planting. Plant honeysuckle at the same depth it was growing in the container. Provide a support for the vines' twining stems. Water immediately after planting.

TLC Keep the soil evenly moist from spring until the ground freezes, watering when the top 2 inches of the soil has dried out. Consistent watering is especially important during the first 2 years, but even mature plants will wilt at the first sign of drought. Apply 2 to 4 inches of shredded bark or wood-chip mulch around plants as soon as the ground warms in spring and replenish as necessary throughout the growing season. Fertilize in spring with a 10-10-10 fertilizer or an organic equivalent sprinkled around the base of plants and watered in well. Prune after flowering to maintain shape. Next year's flowers will bloom on new wood. Regular washing with the garden hose will help keep aphids from becoming a serious problem.

ABOVE: *Lonicera x tellmaniana grows best in filtered shade.* RIGHT: *Trumpet-shaped honeysuckle blooms are carried in whorls.*

Hyacinth Bean Vine
Dolichos lablab (Lablab purpureus)

Hyacinth bean vine is a colorful, rough-and-tumble twining annual that will quickly cover a fence, lamppost, or bean tepee, as long as the support is wrapped in wire mesh.

I still remember my first encounter with hyacinth bean vine. I was driving in an old part of town and passed a Victorian streetlight covered in vines—masses of purplish green leaves, from which sprung clusters of lavender-pink flowers that looked like sweet peas. Closer inspection revealed that a collar of wire mesh had been attached to the post to support the vine. Clearly this wasn't the work of a city employee. I rang the doorbell of the nearest house, and the owners confessed that they had planted the seeds on city property and had been doing this for years.

If you don't have a streetlight handy, you can make a delightful centerpiece for a kitchen garden by growing hyacinth bean vine up a bean tepee. Lash three 10-foot bamboo poles together at the top with twine, set the poles in the ground, wrap wire mesh around them, then plant seeds at the base of the poles. Or sow some at the base of a trellis, arbor, or fence. If you plant seeds in early spring, the vines will be covered in flowers by late August. The flowers are followed by edible purple pods, 2½ inches long and very showy.

PEAK SEASON

Hyacinth bean vine bears rose-purple stems and leaves all season, and purple flowers and glossy purple fruits in late summer.

MY FAVORITES

Dolichos lablab 'Darkness' has purple flowers. It grows 15 to 30 feet tall.

GARDEN COMPANIONS

Hyacinth bean vine looks great in a kitchen garden with other vining plants such as nasturtiums, cucumbers, melons, and squash—or sharing a trellis with the small tubular red flowers and dainty foliage of cardinal climber, which blooms at the same time.

When Plant nursery-grown plants or seeds outside after all danger of frost has passed. For earlier bloom, sow seeds indoors in individual pots 6 to 8 weeks before the last frost date. Soak seeds in warm water overnight before sowing and barely cover them with soil. Germination takes 2 weeks. Hyacinth bean vine resents transplanting, so handle seedlings carefully.

Where Plant in full sun in average to rich, well-drained soil. Use this showy vine to decorate trellises, walls, arbors, and railings.

How Loosen soil to a depth of 10 to 12 inches and work in 2 to 3 inches of compost or other organic matter. Incorporate a controlled-release fertilizer into the soil before planting. Space plants 9 to 12 inches apart. Provide strings, netting, or a trellis for the vines to climb on. Water with a half-strength solution of fertilizer.

TLC Water as needed to keep the soil evenly moist but not wet. Mulch with chopped leaves or other fine-textured organic matter to retain moisture and control weeds. Harvest edible pods when they have turned from dark purple to brown. Hyacinth bean vine may self-seed; deadhead if you don't want seedlings next year.

ABOVE: *Sweet pea–shaped flowers bloom on hyacinth bean vine in late summer.* LEFT: *Handsome, shiny purple pods follow the flowers.*

Ivy

Hedera helix, Parthenocissus quinquefolia, P. tricuspidata

If you like an old-fashioned, traditional look, you'll love ivy. From a single planting, this perennial vine can take off quickly in all directions. As a ground cover it smothers weeds and seldom needs trimming; as a vine it softens and adds character to a stone facade.

Boston ivy *(Parthenocissus tricuspidata)* scales tall buildings. It's the ivy that covers just about everything architecturally significant in the Northeast. English ivy *(Hedera helix)* has thick leaves with a distinctive arrowhead shape; they create a dense mat of greenery that turns crimson in fall. Virginia creeper *(P. quinquefolia)* is a coarser, more rugged plant whose small but profuse leaves make an excellent cover for eyesores that you want to camouflage from view. Mine grew up a trellis on the back wall of my house, took off across a telephone wire, and within a few weeks had traversed the length of my garden and scrambled up a utility pole to a blinding security light, softening and diffusing it. Aggressiveness can be a good thing.

Boston ivy (Parthenocissus tricuspidata) *clings to the side of a barn, with flowering* Campanula portenschlagiana *at its feet.*

PEAK SEASON

English ivy holds its leaves year-round. All three ivies change color in fall.

MY FAVORITES

Hedera helix 'Baltica' is a small-leafed English ivy with white veins and a purplish hue in winter. It's among the hardiest ivies. 'Atropurpurea' has purple leaves whose color intensifies in cold weather. 'Hahn's Self Branching' is a miniature ivy that's fun to grow up a small trellis stuck into a container. Though hardy only in the southern parts of the Midwest, it can be overwintered as a houseplant.

Parthenocissus tricuspidata (Boston ivy) has light green, glossy leaves that turn orange to burgundy in fall. It is extremely hardy.

P. quinquefolia 'Engelmannii' (Engelmann ivy) is a form of Virginia creeper; like Boston ivy it will cover just about any surface in a hurry, but with a smaller, coarser, darker green leaf and a looser growth habit.

GARDEN COMPANIONS

Climbing ivies tend to run over other climbers, so use them as a backdrop for garden plantings. Roses and spring bulbs look good against an ivy screen.

When The best time to plant all of these vines is early spring, but nursery-grown plants can be planted throughout the growing season if they are watered well.

CLOCKWISE FROM LEFT: *English ivy* (Hedera helix) *growing on a stone wall; fast-growing Engelmann ivy, a form of Virginia creeper; Boston ivy with autumn color.*

Where All three vines are tolerant of a wide range of soil conditions but prefer rich, moisture-retentive soil. English ivy must have shade in hot climates. Boston ivy prefers full sun, and Engelmann ivy tolerates sun to full shade. English ivy is most often planted as a ground cover but can also scale low stone walls. It's also good for hanging baskets and topiaries. Boston ivy is used to cover brick and stone walls and building facades. Virginia creeper covers walls, facades, and fences.

How Loosen soil to a depth of 10 to 12 inches and work in generous amounts of compost or other organic material. Incorporate a controlled-release fertilizer before planting. Plant ivies at the same depth they were growing in their containers. Water well with a half-strength solution of fertilizer.

TLC Keep the soil evenly moist from spring until the ground freezes, watering when the top 2 inches of the soil has dried out. Apply 2 to 4 inches of shredded leaves, bark, or wood-chip mulch around the plants as soon as the ground warms in spring and replenish as necessary throughout the growing season. These plants generally do not need additional fertilizer or winter cover.

Morning Glory

Ipomoea

Morning glory's popularity is easy to understand: here's an annual vine that's flashy and simple to grow. Children seem to find it irresistible. Small fingers

Morning glories can easily be trained to scramble over a picket fence. Their flowers open when the sun comes up, then close in the afternoon.

can get a good grip on the big, nutlike seeds, which hardly ever fail to germinate. The vine will reseed readily, too, unless the flowers are deadheaded just as they've begun fading and any seedlings that do appear are pulled up promptly.

As the name suggests, this vine's glory lies in its morning-blooming flowers. Colors include white, pink, red, purple, and blue. Unless you start the seeds early indoors, your morning glory won't bloom until July or August. But since that happens to be when most garden plants are in the doldrums, you'll appreciate the floral fireworks even more.

Morning glory's pretty, heart-shaped leaves form a dense green mass that makes the vine ideal for hiding an ugly chain link fence. The vine attaches itself by putting out curly tendrils. Just wrap a big piece of wire mesh around whatever you want the vine to grow on, sit back, and watch your morning glory take off.

PEAK SEASON

Showy, trumpet-shaped flowers bloom from summer to first fall frost.

MY FAVORITES

Ipomoea tricolor 'Heavenly Blue' is the most familiar morning glory, with penetrating sky blue flowers. Award-winning 'Pearly Gates' has white flowers. 'Flying Saucers' has blue-and-white-striped flowers.

I. nil 'Scarlet O'Hara' has red flowers.

I. purpurea 'Grandpa Ott's' was brought to the U. S. in the last century from Bavaria. It has small purple flowers and is a prolific self-seeder.

I. alba (moonflower) has fragrant white flowers that open after sundown or on dark days.

I. quamoclit (cardinal climber) has tiny, tubular red flowers and delicate foliage resembling palm leaves.

For *I. batatas* (sweet potato vine), a foliage-only plant popularly used in containers, see page 74.

GARDEN COMPANIONS

Plant morning glory at the base of climbing roses to provide color after roses have bloomed. Plant 'Heavenly Blue' with pale yellow 'Moonbeam' coreopsis or ever-blooming 'Stella de Oro' daylilies at its feet, perhaps along a fence. Cardinal climber is so delicate it can grow over other vines, and its red flowers harmonize well.

When Plant nursery-grown plants outside after all danger of frost has passed, on a cloudy day if possible to reduce transplant shock. Seeds can be sown directly in the ground about a week before the last frost date. Or sow indoors in individual pots 6 to 8 weeks before the last frost date. Soak seeds in warm water overnight or nick hard seed coats before planting to help germination, which can take 1 to 3 weeks. Morning glory resents transplanting, so handle seedlings carefully.

Where Plant in full sun in average, well-drained soil. Morning glories provide background color in borders and work well as container plants with support.

How Loosen soil to a depth of 10 to 12 inches and work in 2 to 3 inches of compost or other organic matter. Incorporate a controlled-release fertilizer into the soil before planting. Space plants 8 to 10 inches apart. Provide some sort of support—strings, a trellis, or a woody vine—at planting time to prevent small plants from becoming tangled. Water with a half-strength solution of fertilizer.

TLC Water as needed to keep the soil evenly moist but not wet. Mulch with chopped leaves or other fine-textured organic matter to retain moisture and control weeds. If you didn't use a controlled-release fertilizer at planting time, fertilize every 2 weeks with a balanced fertilizer.

ABOVE: *A blend of three morning glory varieties—I. tricolor 'Flying Saucers', 'Heavenly Blue', and 'Crimson Rambler'.* BELOW: *Feathery-leafed cardinal climber (I. quamoclit).*

Nasturtium
Tropaeolum

Nasturtium is prized by dirt gardeners and garden snobs alike. It has the sort of architectural features that appeal to designers—flat, lily pad–like leaves and tropical-looking flowers. It also happens to be a delightful plant for beginners, with large seeds and simple needs. Nasturtium likes poor soil and won't bloom if conditions get too comfy. It doesn't mind dry weather either. Its leaves may get a bit tatty, but you can just snip them off. All the better to see those delicate flowers, which the leaves are otherwise likely to hide.

I start my nasturtiums indoors, then transplant the seedlings to my kitchen garden. The vining types grow anywhere from 15 inches to 10 feet long on curling leaf stems. I grow the short vines and bush types; the former share a bean tepee (three bamboo poles tied together at the top with twine) with cardinal climber and hyacinth bean vine.

Nasturtium is a good cut flower. Its blooms come in lots of colors, usually creams, peaches, oranges, reds, or a combination of those. The leaves can be gray-blue to bluish purple or variegated. Young leaves, flowers, and unripe seed pods have a peppery flavor and may be used in salads.

Their curling leaf stems will attach to any support, including a neighboring plant, but nasturtium vines are just as happy trailing from a planter atop a porch or deck railing.

When Plant nursery-grown nasturtiums outside after all danger of frost has passed. Seeds can be sown directly in the ground 1 to 2 weeks before the last frost date. For earlier bloom, sow seeds indoors in individual pots 4 to 5 weeks before the last frost date. Nasturtiums resent transplanting, so handle seedlings carefully.

Where Plant in full sun to light shade in poor to average, well-drained soil. Rich soils produce plants with lots of foliage but few flowers. Use bush nasturtiums in containers or for edging gardens; use climbers to decorate trellises.

PEAK SEASON

Showy red, orange, or yellow flowers bloom from late spring to first frost; the foliage is attractive all season.

MY FAVORITES

Tropaeolum tuberosum is a tuberous perennial nasturtium with grayish green leaves and tubelike orange flowers. It climbs 6 to 10 feet. 'Ken Aslet' has red-streaked yellow flowers and blue-green leaves.

T. majus is the old-fashioned annual nasturtium with large, fragrant, single or semidouble flowers that bloom until frost. Seed mixes are available for both climbing and bush types in brilliant mixed colors.

GARDEN COMPANIONS

Grow nasturtiums in a kitchen garden with herbs and vegetables. Combine the bush and vining types around a trellis as a centerpiece.

How Loosen soil to a depth of 10 to 12 inches and work in 2 to 3 inches of compost or other organic matter. Incorporate a controlled-release fertilizer into the soil before planting. Space plants 12 to 18 inches apart. Vines climb by gripping supports with coiling leafstalks, but they may need some help getting started on a trellis or arbor. Water with a half-strength solution of fertilizer.

ABOVE: *The variegated leaves and brilliant flowers of* Tropaeolum majus *'Alaska Mixed'*
BELOW: T. m. *'Jewels of Africa'*

TLC Water as needed to keep soil evenly moist but not wet. Mulch beds with chopped leaves or other fine-textured organic matter to retain moisture and control weeds.

*Plants dislike hot, humid weather and do best where summers are cool.

159

Trumpet Creeper
Campsis radicans

If you want to cover something like a gazebo with big, brilliant orange flowers, and if you love hummingbirds, plant trumpet creeper. But keep in mind the vine's single drawback, a tendency to trample everything in its path. The vine puts out aerial shoots, which is how it manages to scale just about any structure to a height of 30 or 40 feet. The dark green, serrated leaves unfurl in late May. Clusters of trumpet-shaped, 3-inch-long, flame-colored flowers bloom from June through September, followed by attractive woody seedpods that may last all winter.

Trumpet creeper is actually a slow-growing vine, but it is determined. Keep it away from the house, as its stems will clog

Though perfect for covering eyesores or obscuring an ugly view, trumpet creeper Campsis x tagliabuana *'Madame Galen' may become a little too aggressive unless you keep it in check.*

gutters and downspouts, cover up windows, and poke their way through any exposed cracks and crevices. In the far north, subzero temperatures will freeze the vine to the ground, forcing it to retrace its steps the following spring.

PEAK SEASON
Trumpet-shaped, orange-scarlet flowers bloom in summer.

MY FAVORITES
Campsis radicans 'Flava' has yellow flowers and grows 30 to 40 feet. 'Praecox' bears scarlet flowers earlier in the season.

C. × tagliabuana is showier but less hardy than *C. radicans*. 'Mme. Galen' bears orange-red blooms. 'Crimson Trumpet' has deep red flowers.

GARDEN COMPANIONS
Place plants in front of trumpet creeper that will benefit from a solid green background after the vine has finished flowering. Roses, daylilies, lilies, rudbeckias, and other sun-loving perennials are all good choices.

When The best time to plant trumpet creeper is early spring. Nursery-grown plants can be plant-

Trumpet creeper flowers are long blooming and loved by hummingbirds.

ed throughout the growing season if they are watered well. Seeds can be sown directly in the ground in spring or fall.

Where Plant in average, well-drained soil in full sun to partial shade, (Trumpet creeper requires full sun and a protected location in Zone 43.) It tolerates city pollution. Trumpet creeper clings to wood, brick, and stucco surfaces with aerial rootlets. Use it for large-scale screening.

How Loosen soil to a depth of 10 to 12 inches and work in 2 to 3 inches of compost or other organic matter. Incorporate a controlled-release fertilizer into the soil before planting. Plant trumpet creeper at the same depth it was growing in the container. Water immediately after planting.

TLC Keep the soil evenly moist from spring until the ground freezes, watering when the top 2 inches of soil has dried out. Apply 2 to 4 inches of shredded bark or wood-chip mulch around plants as soon as the ground warms in spring and replenish as necessary throughout the growing season. Thin plants regularly. In colder zones, the plant will die back to the ground each winter. Suckering roots may invade nearby gardens.

Wisteria
Wisteria

This perennial vine's remarkable beauty more than offsets its sometimes aggressive nature. Chinese wisteria

Growing wisteria over an arbor or pergola transforms a backyard into an exotic retreat. The Japanese wisteria W. floribunda 'Longissima Alba' shown here bears flower clusters up to 2 feet long that dangle from the vine like elongated bunches of grapes.

(W. sinensis) has the longest bloom time, flowering about a week earlier than Japanese wisteria *(W. floribunda),* but Japanese wisteria has longer racemes (flowers clusters) and is hardier and better suited to the Midwest. In the far north, however, most of us are content to grow the native Kentucky wisteria *(W. macrostachya);* the hardiest variety, developed at the University of Minnesota Landscape Arboretum, is called 'Aunt Dee'.

I grow 'Aunt Dee' over a metal arch I rigged up myself. Initially I had to tie the slender young stems to the arch, but now the stems are as fat as my garden hose and wrapped so thickly around their support that they seem to be holding it up. The smooth, light gray bark contrasts well with the light green foliage, but it's the pendulous flowers that are to

PEAK SEASON

Fragrant, pendulous flower clusters bloom late spring to early summer. The glossy foliage is attractive all season.

MY FAVORITES

Wisteria floribunda (Japanese wisteria) is often sold as *W. multijuga*. Its fanlike leaf clusters are 1 foot long and its racemes are 1½ to 2 feet long. 'Longissima' has violet flowers. 'Rosea' is lavender-pink.

W. macrostachya 'Aunt Dee' is a Kentucky wisteria with 8- to 12-inch racemes of bluish purple flowers.

GARDEN COMPANIONS

Plant wisteria on an arbor or a pergola with clumps of shade-tolerant hardy geraniums or a ground cover like myrtle, ajuga, or pachysandra at its feet.

die for. At first I was frustrated by the vine's slowness to flower—it takes several years—but when it finally did bloom, the thrill was almost comparable to that of watching my children take their first steps. I should note that 'Aunt Dee' has flower clusters slightly shorter than those of its Asian cousins, and they spring out a bit in all directions.

When The best time to plant wisteria is early spring. Nursery-grown plants can be planted all season if they are watered well.

Where Plant in full sun. Wisteria will grow in light shade, but you'll have fewer flowers. Plants tolerate a wide range of soils as long as they are well drained. Hot, dry, compacted soils are the exception. Grow wisteria as a focal point in your garden. Draped over an arbor or pergola, it makes a shady refuge.

How Loosen soil to a depth of 10 to 12 inches and work in generous amounts of compost or other organic material. Incorporate a controlled-release fertilizer into the soil before planting. Plant at the same depth the plant was growing in the container. Provide a sturdy, well-anchored support to handle the weight of mature vines. Water immediately after planting.

TLC Keep the soil evenly moist from spring until the ground freezes, watering when the top 2 inches of soil has dried out. Consistent watering is especially important during the first 2 years, but even mature plants will wilt at the first sign of drought. Apply 2 to 4 inches of shredded bark or wood-chip mulch around plants as soon as the ground warms in spring and replenish as necessary throughout the growing season. Wisterias generally do not need supplemental fertilizer. Prune side branches back after flowering, always leaving at least six leaves per branch. Remove excess branches to improve light penetration and flowering. Wisteria does not have the ability to cling to surfaces. Instead, its stem and side branches twist around supports. Without supports, the vine will crawl along the ground. It may take several years before wisteria has a good bloom.

The flowers of Japanese wisteria (Wisteria floribunda) are the most fragrant of all the wisterias. Its leaves turn an attractive golden color in autumn.

Once upon a time, American vegetable gardens were laid out in straight rows and fenced to keep out livestock or wild animals. Plants were grown from seeds harvested the previous year, and produced bumper crops that were tasty and fragrant but short-lived once harvested, so much was dried or canned.

As the interests of agribusiness took precedence over those of backyard growers, new vegetable hybrids were developed that had tougher skin to survive the rigors of shipping and a longer shelf life in the supermarkets. Seed catalogs featured these new, improved hybrids, but home gardeners found that newer wasn't always better. An "improved" tomato, for example, might have tougher skin (to avoid bruising when shipped) but inferior flavor, fragrance, or color variety. Home gardeners began saving and trading the seeds of plants they called heirlooms—varieties that had not changed in generations and still retained the flavor, juiciness, fragrance, color, or whimsical shape that made "homegrown" mean something special.

AESTHETIC INFLUENCES

As appreciation for distinctive flavors and colors grew, so did interest in food crops as garden plants. The form of the vegetable garden itself began changing, becoming more eclectic, imaginative, and pleasing to the eye. Influenced by flower gardeners, who were combining annuals with perennials, flowering shrubs, ornamental trees and conifers, grasses, and native plants, food gardeners began growing plants like parsley, fennel, leaf lettuce, cabbage, beans, and dill for their looks as well as their taste. Herbs were often grouped together in pots by the back door, handy for cooking and lovely to look at.

A reverse flow of knowledge was occurring as well, as flower gardeners learned from food gardeners about the effects of toxic chemicals and the benefits of organic gardening methods. Composting is now a routine practice among all gardeners, and garden books always recommend amending garden soil with organic matter to encourage micro-organisms and earthworms to do the work chemicals used to do.

THE "KITCHEN GARDEN"

These changes in the content and form of the food garden are embodied in what we call the modern kitchen garden. Besides herbs and vegetables, kitchen gardens often include dwarf fruit trees, clipped shrubs, and flowers, along with design elements such as geometric pat-

ABOVE: *Swiss chard, parsley, basil, onions, and many other edible plants share this mixed garden with flowering annuals.* OPPOSITE PAGE: *'Early Girl' tomatoes are a good choice for climates with a short growing season.*

terns that impose a sense of order on abundant plant growth, and artfully designed functional structures (fences, trellises, benches) that add to the beauty of the garden.

In choosing the best herbs and vegetables for midwestern gardens, I looked for plants that possess all the traits now prized by modern American kitchen gardeners. Whether a plant is a hybrid or an heirloom, it must be good tasting, disease resistant, and decorative. These Top 10 are just to get you started. As your garden expands, you'll want to look for the same qualities in whatever herbs and vegetables you grow.

Basil

Award-winning 'Siam Queen' basil is as beautiful as it is useful for cooking. It has a bushy habit, growing to 2 feet tall, with red stems, purple flowers, and dark leaves.

Basil, a tender perennial grown as an annual, loves hot, sunny weather. If you can give it that, along with plenty of water and elbowroom, it will grow from a spindly seedling to a knee-high bush in no time. Even in a spot that gets only 4 hours of full sun, you'll still have enough basil to enjoy pesto a few times a week—your plants just won't be huge.

I grow sweet basil in clay pots by the back door, which is convenient for the cook but not ideal for the plants, as they don't get quite as much sun as they'd like and the containers tend to dry out quickly. My plants have large, flat, green leaves, but there are small-leafed, ruffled, and purple varieties, too. 'Spicy Globe' basil has smaller, thicker leaves than sweet basil and grows naturally into a perfectly round bush. Some cooks prefer its spicier flavor for pesto. Thai basil 'Siam Queen' is a spectacular-looking plant with purple stems and deep bluish purple flowers. Though the rule of thumb for most vegetables and herbs—including basil—is deadhead, deadhead, deadhead, you'll want to enjoy this basil's gorgeous flowers awhile.

PEAK SEASON

Tasty leaves and attractive foliage from early summer to first frost

MY FAVORITES

'Genovese' is the classic sweet basil with glossy, large, bright green leaves.

'Purple Ruffles' has purple leaves with ruffled edges and pink flowers. 'Red Rubin' is another purple-leafed basil.

Lemon basil 'Citriodorum' has a citrusy flavor.

Cinnamon basil has a clovelike flavor.

'Siam Queen' (also known as Thai basil) has small, dark leaves and clusters of purple flowers. Its anise flavor is excellent in Asian dishes.

GARDEN COMPANIONS

Basil looks great with other herbs and can be used to edge a flower or kitchen garden. It also looks good with sweet alyssum and dusty miller. Plant 'Siam Queen' in a perennial garden with lavender, 'May Night' salvia, 'Silver Mound' artemisia, and 'Moonshine' yarrow.

When Basil is very frost-sensitive. Plant it outside a week after all danger of frost has passed, on a cloudy day if possible to reduce transplant shock. Sow seeds indoors 4 to 6 weeks before the last frost date. Germination takes 1 to 2 weeks.

Where Plant in full sun in average, well-drained soil. Rich soil produces lots of foliage, but leaves have reduced oil content and therefore less flavor and fragrance. Basil is attractive enough to be used in containers and in mixed plantings. Small-leafed types, such as 'Siam Queen', 'Spicy Globe', and lemon basil, make good edging plants.

How Loosen the soil to a depth of 10 to 12 inches and work in 2 to 3 inches of compost or other organic matter. Incorporate a controlled-release fertilizer before planting. Space garden plants about a foot apart. Water well and give each plant a half-cup of starter fertilizer solution.

TLC Water as needed to keep the soil evenly moist but not wet. Do not allow plants to dry out. After the soil has warmed in spring, mulch beds with 2 inches of chopped leaves, grass clippings, or other fine-textured organic material to retain moisture and control weeds. Fertilize every 2 weeks with a water-soluble fertilizer or use an organic equivalent. Pinch seedlings to encourage branching and bushy growth. Remove flower stalks as they appear. Rejuvenate plants by cutting them back by about half in midsummer. Pick leaves whenever you need them. For long-term storage, harvest leaves just before flowers appear, then dry or freeze them.

ABOVE: *'Genovese'*. LEFT: *'Red Rubin'*.

Beans

Hundreds of bean varieties are sold for the home garden. Don't know beans about them? No matter. All are grown similarly, and fall into one of three groups—snap, shell (or shelly or shelling), or dry—signifying the growth stage at which they taste best.

Snap beans, my favorites, are grown for their edible pods, which are tastiest when young. Most snap beans (also called string or green beans) are stringless and so tender you can eat the stem end. Shell and dry beans are grown for the edible seeds inside the pods. Shell beans are best when the seeds have just matured. Dry beans taste best after

the seeds have dried out in the pod. Lima, navy, pinto, and some kidney beans are dry beans.

Each of the three types is available in bush and vine (pole) forms. Pole beans are slower to mature but you plant them only once; picking beans off the vines stimulates the plants to produce more, so you get two to three times as many beans in the same space. Pods come in colors ranging from yellow to green to purple. They all turn green when cooked.

Scarlet runner beans will quickly scamper up several crisscrossed poles, as shown, or a tepee-style support with poles lashed together at the top.

TOP: *'Kentucky Wonder'.* BOTTOM: *'Royal Burgundy'.*

PEAK SEASON

Midsummer to first frost

MY FAVORITES

'Royal Burgundy' is a bright purple, bush-type snap bean that produces lots of pods and is good for freezing.

'Bountiful Stringless' is a bush-type heirloom that yields many 6-inch pods. It is the classic snap bean.

'Blue Lake' is a delicious string bean available as a compact bush or pole bean.

'Roc d'Or' is a bush-type yellow (wax) snap bean with a delicious buttery flavor. It matures early.

'Garden of Eden' has flat, green, sweet-tasting pods; a pole bean, it climbs to 6 feet.

'Scarlet Runner Bean' has long, green, meaty pods and brilliant orange-red flowers on a 6- to 8-foot vine; grow it on a support as you would a pole bean.

'Kentucky Wonder' is a very popular heirloom pole or bush bean. Pods are stringless and tender.

GARDEN COMPANIONS

Plant beans with other herbs and vegetables or surrounded by annuals such as verbena, zinnias, and marigolds. Pole beans grown on tepee–style supports look good in the center of round kitchen gardens or along the back row of rectangular gardens.

When Sow seeds outdoors a week or two after the threat of frost has passed, when soil temperatures are 55°F/13°C or higher. Seeds rot in cold, wet soil. To extend the harvest, sow successive crops every 2 weeks up to 12 weeks before the first expected fall frost.

Where Beans need a warm, sunny location and light soil that is well drained and rich in organic matter. Avoid saline soils. Place pole beans along the north side of the garden where they won't shade other sun-loving vegetables.

How Sow seeds 1 inch deep, 2 to 3 inches apart. Plant bush types in rows 3 feet apart. Pole beans need some sort of support, such as a trellis, string, or tepee-style poles, which should be set in place before planting seeds. To make a tepee, lash together five tall bamboo stakes at the top with twine.

TLC Beans need an even supply of water—about 1 inch a week. Thin seedlings of bush types to 5 to 6 inches apart, pole beans 6 to 8 inches apart. After plants have their second set of true leaves, mulch with 2 inches of chopped leaves, grass clippings, or other fine-textured organic material to conserve moisture and control weeds. Beans have the ability to "fix" nitrogen (pull it from the air), so avoid adding fertilizers high in nitrogen or plants will produce too much leaf growth at the expense of beans. Harvest snap beans when the pods are about 1/8 inch thick, before seeds begin to swell. Harvest shell beans when pods are plump and bright green. Harvest dry beans after pods have dried on the plant.

* Lima beans grow best in Zone 41 or warmer climates.

Dill

Dill poses a dilemma. The herb is so useful in cooking that you're going to want to keep it from going to seed—but that means snipping off its beautiful flowers, which are one of the delights of the kitchen garden. What to do? I grow lots of dill so I can have it both ways.

Willowy is the word for dill. It is tall and slender, like a ballet dancer, and wears an elegant, airy crown of minute flowers in clusters. I love the lime green color of the leaves. Be warned, however, that owing to its languorous nature, dill can get messy; it will sprawl all over its neighbors if you let it. Dill looks a lot like fennel, another tall, feathery-leafed herb, which if planted too close to dill will cross-fertilize and thereby wreak havoc. When I learned that, I immediately began thinking of these two as doomed lovers, the Romeo and Juliet of my herb garden.

Dill's feathery foliage and yellow flower clusters look good with colorful annuals like these tall orange zinnias.

Enough of that. I happen to like the look of dill's seed heads, too, and always save the seeds for cooking or sowing next spring. Wait until the seed heads are light brown before harvesting the seeds. Use fresh dill leaves or dried seeds to season fish, poultry, soups, and salad dressings.

PEAK SEASON

Tasty leaves early summer to first frost; seed heads in late summer. Feathery leaves and lacy yellow flowers are attractive in midsummer.

MY FAVORITES

'Bouquet' grows to 2¹/₂ feet tall. Its large seed heads make it the best for seed collecting.

'Dukat' is the sweetest dill. It grows to about 2 feet tall and stays leafy a long time.

'Mammoth' is the largest dill, growing to 5 feet, and is great for pickling.

'Fernleaf' is a dwarf, upright plant good for containers.

GARDEN COMPANIONS

Dill is a lovely filler that blends well with both hot and cool colors. Keep it away from its look-alike, fennel.

When Start sowing seeds outdoors in early spring and sow successive crops every 3 to 4 weeks to ensure a continuous supply. Dill does not like to be transplanted.

Where Dill does best in full sun and fertile, well-drained soil. It will tolerate afternoon shade. Dill's delicate foliage and tall flowers make it attractive enough for mixed plantings and containers.

How Loosen the soil to a depth of 10 to 12 inches and work in 2 to 3 inches of compost or other organic matter. Incorporate a controlled-release fertilizer before planting. Rake the seedbed smooth and scatter seeds on top of the soil. Seeds germinate better with some light, so cover minimally, if at all.

TLC When seedlings are 2 inches tall, thin to 6 to 8 inches apart. Water during dry weather. After the soil has warmed in spring, mulch beds with 2 inches of chopped leaves, grass clippings, or other fine-textured organic material to retain moisture and control weeds. Pick dill leaves as you need them, but do not remove more than one-fifth of the foliage or you will weaken the plant. Whole fresh leaves can be frozen. Cut flower heads for bouquets when they are half open. For seeds, harvest flower heads when they are brown and hang bunches upside down in paper bags to catch seeds and dried leaves. Dill will self-seed if you allow some seed heads to remain.

ABOVE: *Dill doesn't need staking when combined with mounding plants that it can lean on.* LEFT: *'Fernleaf' dill has an even softer, more feathery leaf texture than other dills.*

Parsley

Parsley is one of the prettiest plants for the kitchen garden—or any garden, for that matter. The deep green foliage naturally falls into perfectly sculpted waves, and the plant fills out quickly when its leaves and stems are regularly snipped for cooking.

Parsley may look like a feather bed from a distance, but up close its leaves are actually rather stiff and coarse. That's one reason it is often used as a garnish. A parsley sprig holds its shape for hours without wilting.

Italian parsley, also called flat-leafed or broadleaf parsley, has larger, flatter leaves than the more common curly parsley. Both are used in cooking. Curly parsley is identified with American

Curly parsley can be used as an edging for a kitchen garden or perennial border. Here it alternates with another low-growing annual, sweet alyssum.

dishes; it is chopped and sprinkled over everything from soups to mashed potatoes and is an essential ingredient in buttery sauces. Italian parsley is a bit more assertive in flavor and a staple of Italian cooking.

PEAK SEASON

Tasty leaves from early summer to early winter. Attractive green foliage all season.

MY FAVORITES

'Forest Green' is a finely curled parsley with a compact habit and long stems with very dark green leaves. It's extremely hardy.

'Gigante' is a tasty Italian parsley that grows to 2 feet tall.

'Moss Curled' is the curliest of the curly parsleys and makes a great garnish.

GARDEN COMPANIONS

Plant parsley as an edging for a kitchen or flower garden, or to fill in gaps between flowering perennials; its deep green color and rounded shape set off spiky plants like veronica and salvia, as well as annuals like pansies.

When A biennial grown as an annual, parsley does best in cool weather. Sow seeds outdoors several weeks before the last frost date. Mark the site by planting quick-germinating radish seeds, since parsley germination is slow. Seeds can be started indoors in individual pots 8 to 10 weeks before the last frost date. Soak seeds overnight in warm water to speed up germination, which can take 3 weeks. Cover seeds, since darkness aids germination. Plants mature 2 to 3 months from sowing.

Where Parsley grows best in full sun in rich, well-drained soil, but it tolerates partial shade. It's attractive enough to use as an edging plant in a flower border or in containers.

How Loosen the soil to a depth of 10 to 12 inches and work in 2 to 3 inches of compost or other organic matter. Incorporate a controlled-release fertilizer before planting. Rake the seedbed smooth and sow seeds $1/4$ inch deep. Use care if transplanting, as these plants resent being disturbed.

TLC Thin seedlings to 8 inches apart. Mulch with 2 inches of chopped leaves, grass clippings, or other fine-textured organic material to retain moisture, keep the soil cool, and control weeds. Water regularly in dry weather. Harvest leaves by cutting rather than pulling, as soon as they are large enough to use. Store leaves in bags in the refrigerator. For long-term storage, dry or freeze leaves. Plants will survive winter in most areas, but the flavor is not as good the second year.

Italian parsley (LEFT) *and curly parsley.*

Rosemary

This Mediterranean native looks like it might be related to sage or lavender, but don't let that fool you into thinking that rosemary *acts* like those herbs—which love nothing more than baking in the sun with nothing to drink for days on end. I found this out when I noticed the leaves of my rosemary were falling off. I thought some sort of bug had infested the plant, until a gardening friend tipped me off to the real problem. Rosemary needs regular watering. Mine was dying of thirst. I watered it twice a day for a week and it rebounded nicely.

Rosemary needs plenty of heat and sun, too, so overwintering this tender perennial is a dicey proposition. You can improve its chances of survival by growing it in pots so you can bring it indoors in winter and give it a few hours of artificial light every day. It's the only perennial herb for which I am happy to go to all that trouble, by the way. On a cold winter day, a big pot of rosemary on the kitchen counter is almost as comforting as a roaring fire in the fireplace.

When Plant rosemary plants outside after all danger of frost is past.

Where Select a site in full sun with good air circulation and poor to average, well-drained soil. Some gardeners grow rosemary in pots so they can bring it indoors at the end of the season. Although it's a challenge, rosemary can be grown year-round as a container plant.

How Loosen the soil to a depth of 10 to 12 inches and work in 2 to 3 inches of compost or other organic matter. Incorporate a controlled-release fertilizer before planting. Rosemary resents disturbance and should not be moved after planting.

TLC Water as necessary to keep the soil evenly moist but not wet. Wet soil can cause root rot. After the soil has warmed in spring, mulch with 2 inches of chopped leaves, grass clippings, or other fine-textured organic material to retain moisture and control weeds. Fertilize monthly and pinch and prune as needed to keep plants from getting gangly. The rigid, dense stems make rosemary one of the easiest herbs to snip into a topiary standard. Plants subjected to drought, overwatering, or frost will drop their leaves. Plants grown indoors are subject to houseplant insects such as aphids and spider mites. Harvest leaves or stem tips as needed and store in bags in the refrigerator. For long-term storage, freeze branches or dry by hanging them upside down in a warm, dark, dry place.

Upright rosemary types have a rigid bearing that is good for edging a kitchen garden. They also look great in pots and can be pruned to make a topiary standard.

OPPOSITE PAGE: Trailing rosemary (Rosmarinus officinalis 'Prostratus') looks great when planted along a stone wall. It will spread as much as 8 feet wide.

PEAK SEASON

Tasty leaves from early summer to early winter. Attractive gray-green, needlelike foliage all season. The small, lavender-blue flowers appear in summer.

MY FAVORITES

'Majorca Pink' has pink flowers.

'Albus' has white flowers.

'Benenden Blue' has blue flowers.

'Prostratus' is a trailing rosemary. It is a bit less cold-hardy than other rosemary types.

'Miss Jessup's Upright' is very hardy and has an erect habit.

GARDEN COMPANIONS

Rosemary looks good in an herb garden with plants like lavender, sage (try *Salvia officinalis* 'Tricolor' or 'Purpurascens'), catmint, parsley, and thyme. Or grow it in a flower garden; its gray-green leaves will harmonize with everything and lightly scent the air.

Sage

Sage is a member of the large and diverse salvia family. Common, or garden sage *(Salvia offici-nalis),* the culinary herb, is an attractive perennial with gnarled stems and velvety, oval-shaped leaves. Thanks to the efforts of plant breeders, we now have sage leaves in a rainbow of colors—from purplish gray to greenish yellow to variegated. I love them all and consider sage one of the showier specimens in my kitchen garden. It's fun to make a hedge of sage plants in all their different color combinations.

Green-leafed sage Salvia officinalis 'Berggarten' sets off purple 'Purpurascens' sage.

Given sun and dry heat, sage is almost self-sufficient in the garden. Rarely does it need watering; it scoffs at fertilizer, much preferring the poor to average soil of a well-drained, gravelly site. Even here in the far north, I've never lost mine in winter, but then I always cover it with leaves and straw. Sage can take a while to start putting on new growth in spring, so be patient before you give it up for dead.

Sage is used to season fish, meats, poultry, cheeses, marinades, and salad dressings.

PEAK SEASON

Tasty leaves from early summer to early winter. Attractive textured foliage all season.

MY FAVORITES

Salvia sclarea (clary sage) grows 2 to 3 feet tall and is an aromatic herb with pale purple flower spikes and small grayish green leaves. The flowers are edible, but the leaves are not. It can sometimes be invasive.

S. elegans (pineapple sage) grows to 6 feet tall and produces bright red flowers in late summer and fall. The green leaves have a fruity scent.

S. officinalis 'Tricolor' has green leaves with white borders; new growth is pink. 'Purpurascens' has purplish gray leaves. 'Icterina' has green-and-yellow leaves. All three grow 1 to 2 feet tall.

GARDEN COMPANIONS

In a kitchen garden, try combining different-colored sages with nasturtiums and dill. Plant pineapple sage along a path to enjoy its fragrance.

When Plant sage outside after all danger of frost has passed.

Where Choose a site in full sun with average, well-drained soil. In Zone 43, where garden sage doesn't always overwinter, grow plants against a south-facing wall for extra protection. Sage can be incorporated into a perennial border or used in containers.

How Loosen the soil to a depth of 10 to 12 inches and amend with organic matter before planting. Space plants 1 to 2 feet apart. Water thoroughly and keep the soil moist until plants are established.

TLC Water as needed to keep the soil evenly moist but not wet. After the soil has warmed in spring, mulch with 2 inches of chopped leaves, grass clippings, or other fine-textured organic material to retain moisture and control weeds. Cut plants back by one-third each spring to promote new growth. Even though garden sage is a perennial, plan to replace the woody plants every 3 to 4 years to keep them healthy and vigorous. Pinch off leaves as needed, but stop harvesting in early fall to harden off plants for winter. Store leaves in bags in the refrigerator. For long-term storage, dry leaves in a single layer in a dry location out of sunlight.

ABOVE: Salvia officinalis *'Purpurascens'*
LEFT: S. o. *'Icterina'*

Salad Greens

What goes into the salad bowl is no longer simple. We've come a long way from that flavorless wedge of iceberg lettuce slathered in Thousand Island dressing. The French practice of snipping tender leaves of young lettuces and other greens to make a "mesclun mix" has been widely embraced in this country. If you don't grow your own, you can pick up a packaged blend at the grocery store.

But why *not* grow your own? Salad greens are pretty in the garden and not difficult as long as you start early, leave off in midsummer (lettuce will bolt in hot weather), and resume as temperatures cool.

The most flavorful and attractive lettuces are loose-leaf, butterhead, and romaine. Once you're hooked on these, you'll want to spice up the salad with other leafy greens such as arugula, mustard, chicory, spinach, mâche, cress, endive, nasturtium, and radicchio.

When Salad greens like the cool, sunny conditions of late spring and early summer. Sow seeds as soon as the soil can be worked, as early as a month before the last frost date, and again in mid- to late summer for a fall crop. Make successive sowings every 10 days to extend your harvest.

OPPOSITE PAGE: Romaine and loose-leaf lettuces in red and green make a beautiful composition in the garden.

Where Plant salad greens where they'll get lots of sun. They are tolerant of most soil types, although they prefer fertile, slightly acidic soil that drains well. Many salad greens are very ornamental and great additions to a flower border or containers.

PEAK SEASON
Midspring to first frost

MY FAVORITES
Loose-leaf lettuce 'Lollo Rosso' has curly magenta leaves and great flavor.

'Red Salad Bowl' oakleaf lettuce (also called 'Red Oak Leaf') has deeply lobed green leaves with reddish edges and is slow to bolt.

Japanese mustard 'Osaka Purple', great for a salad of baby greens, has purple leaves with white veins.

'Red Sails' is a popular loose-leaf lettuce with crinkled maroon leaves. It is very slow to turn bitter.

'Buttercrunch' is an award-winning butterhead lettuce with a compact head and soft, cup-shaped leaves.

'Freckles' is an exquisite romaine lettuce with pale green leaves flecked with purple.

GARDEN COMPANIONS
Use lettuces to edge your herb or kitchen garden. They have a calming effect on the sometimes unruly behavior of herbs that like to spread or sprawl (thyme and dill leap to mind) and on vining vegetables.

How Add plenty of organic matter to the soil and rake it smooth before sowing seeds or planting. The small seeds should be scattered on the surface and pressed lightly into the soil. They need light to germinate.

TLC Salad greens require an even supply of water during their growing season. Weed carefully around plants to avoid damaging the shallow roots. Plants will benefit from regular applications of nitrogen fertilizer. Begin harvesting leaves from loose-leaf lettuce as soon as they're large enough to be used, cutting from the outside of the plant first. Pick head lettuces when their heads are firm and fully formed. Salad greens keep for a short time in the refrigerator. Once the hot weather of summer arrives, most lettuces will bolt (go to seed), and need to be ripped out. Salad greens' short lives mean they're safe from most insects and diseases, but overly moist soil can lead to rot. Rabbits and birds are especially attracted to salad greens and are hard to deter. Consider planting an extra row to accommodate them. Blood meal scattered around plants after every rain is sometimes effective at repelling rabbits and deer.

ABOVE: 'Buttercrunch' lettuce leaves have a soft yet crunchy texture. RIGHT: Because they put out fresh leaves after being snipped for salad-making, young loose-leaf lettuces like these are sometimes called "cut and come again" lettuces.

Squashes
Winter and summer squash, pumpkins, gourds

Some strange law of nature decreed that these particular vegetables must resemble oversize acorns, turbans, alien spaceships, or elongated balloons. Most squashes are large, flamboyant plants, with lovely blossoms in creamy yellow or pale peach from which the fruits emerge and swell into those amazing shapes. The bush types are more manageable, but vining types produce more fruit and can be quite beautiful when trained to grow on a fence or trellis.

Squashes are divided into two groups: Summer squashes—like the long, slender zucchini and the round, flat pattypan with scalloped edges—are harvested early and eaten while still tender (though some pattypans can be stored and eaten later like winter squash). Winter squashes are harvested late; their thick, shell-like skins have to be removed before eating. Pumpkins, the largest and most famous of the winter squashes, are really in a class by themselves—grown as much for ornamental as culinary uses.

'Small Sugar' ('Sugar Pie') is one of the sweetest pumpkins and among the best for pies. This heirloom has been grown in American gardens for more than a century.

If squashes aren't unusual enough for you, try your hand at ornamental gourds. These curvy, bell-shaped fruits make whimsical garden art.

PEAK SEASON

Midsummer to first frost

MY FAVORITES

'Yellow Crookneck', the best bush-type squash, is a yellow-skinned summer squash with a hooked neck.

'Black Beauty' is a glossy black-green zucchini with white flesh. Its open growing habit makes harvesting easy.

'Sunburst' is a space-saving, bush-type pattypan with small fruits that have a buttery flavor and color.

'Royal Acorn' is a high-yielding vine that produces deep green, ribbed winter squashes great for baking.

'Hokkaido' is a Japanese winter squash with rich orange flesh. It's good for storing.

'Green Hubbard' is an old-time favorite winter heirloom with orange flesh and fine-grained skin.

''Butternut' is a winter squash with bell-shaped fruit; smooth, tan skin; and moist flesh that's delicious for soups.

'Buttercup' is perhaps the tastiest of the winter squashes, with a buttery, sweet flavor.

'Howden' pumpkins may be the best for jack-o'-lanterns, thanks to their sturdy handles.

GARDEN COMPANIONS

Vining squashes trained to a fence or trellis make an interesting backdrop for a kitchen garden.

TOP TO BOTTOM: *acorn-type 'Carnival' squash; bell-shaped 'Waltham' butternut squash; 'Gold Rush' summer squash*

When Plant seedlings or sow seeds directly in the ground after all danger of frost has passed. Start seeds indoors in individual pots 2 to 3 weeks before you plan to plant them outside. Acclimatize seedlings to outdoor temperatures over a period of 7 to 10 days before planting them outdoors.

Where Squashes need all-day sun and plenty of water. Soil should be rich in organic matter to retain moisture. Grow the bigger squashes and pumpkins in a large patch where there's no competition for sun or nutrients. Bush types can be grown in large containers. Small-fruited vining types can be grown on trellises.

How Loosen the soil to a depth of 10 to 12 inches and work in 2 to 3 inches of compost or other organic matter. Incorporate a controlled-release fertilizer before planting. Space plants 3 to 5 feet apart in rows 4 to 6 feet apart.

TLC Squashes need an even supply of water—about 1 inch a week. Once plants are established, mulch soil with 2 inches of chopped leaves, grass clippings, or other fine-textured organic material or cover soil with black plastic to retain moisture and control weeds. Squashes are heavy feeders, requiring regular applications of fertilizer throughout the growing season. Harvest summer squashes while they're still young and tender. Winter squashes, pumpkins, and gourds must be fully mature before harvesting.

Thyme

Thymus vulgaris, common thyme, is both herb and ground cover. Its usefulness in the kitchen needs no elaboration, as it seasons everything from stews to salad dressings. In the garden its tiny leaves form a dense, low mat that can spread quite a distance. It gives off a wonderful fragrance when stepped on and doesn't mind the foot traffic a bit.

Thyme needs almost no care and keeps very busy beautifying everything it touches, filling cracks and crevices with fetching aplomb, and draping itself over stone walls or the edges of containers. There are thymes with variegated leaves, green-and-yellow-striped leaves, even woolly gray leaves. Depending on the variety, it may trail or mound or hug the ground. Tiny flowers of white, pink, mauve, lavender, or deep purple bloom in spring and early summer. It's fun to combine several different varieties to create a tapestry effect.

Technically, thyme is evergreen, but don't be alarmed if it loses its foliage in winter. It always bounces back.

OPPOSITE PAGE: *Thymus × citriodorus 'Gold Edge' has a delightful citrusy fragrance and pretty purple summer flowers.*

PEAK SEASON

Tasty leaves from early summer to fall. Attractive foliage all season. Tiny flowers appear from late spring into summer.

MY FAVORITES

Thymus × citriodorus (lemon thyme) has a lemony scent and grows 4 to 12 inches tall. It has green-and-yellow leaves and pale lilac flowers.

T. serpyllum (mother-of-thyme) is a woody, shrublike perennial that grows to 3 inches tall and has purple or rose flowers that bloom from June through September. 'Annie Hall' has pinkish purple flowers. 'Coccineum' is a purplish red creeping thyme.

T. pseudolanuginosus (woolly thyme) has minute, fuzzy gray leaves that are covered with pinprick-size lavender flowers in early summer.

GARDEN COMPANIONS

Thyme is one of gardening's great peacemakers. Use it to knit a busy scheme together and give it harmony. It looks good with other herbs, evergreens like juniper, and shrub roses. Combine 'Annie Hall' with the purple-leafed *Salvia officinalis* 'Purpurascens'.

When Thyme is difficult to start from seed. Start with nursery-grown plants in late spring to early summer. They can tolerate light spring frosts.

Where Plant in full sun in average, well-drained soil. These attractive plants can be incorporated into a perennial border or rock garden or used in containers. The low-growing types make attractive ground covers and can take light foot traffic, which releases their heady fragrance. In Zone 43, where garden thyme doesn't always overwinter, grow plants against a south-facing wall for extra protection.

How Loosen the soil to a depth of 10 to 12 inches and amend with organic matter before planting. Space plants 6 to 12 inches apart. Water thoroughly and keep the soil moist until plants are established.

TLC Water during dry weather. After the soil has warmed in spring, mulch beds with 2 inches of chopped leaves, grass clippings, or other fine-textured organic material to control weeds. Cut plants back after they flower to encourage bushiness. Harvest leaves by cutting as needed. For long-term storage, hang them upside down in a dry location out of sunlight. Strip off dried leaves and flowers and store them in a cool, dark place. In Zone 43, apply a winter mulch after the ground has frozen. After 3 or 4 years, thyme becomes woody and less productive and should be renewed if you are using it for culinary purposes. Either replace plants or divide them in spring or fall.

Mother-of-thyme blooms all summer, making it one of the best ground covers for sunny locations.

Tomatoes

'Sweet 100' is a vigorous indeterminate vine that matures quickly (in 60 days), grows to 10 feet, produces an awesome amount of fruit, and has as sweet a flavor as you'll find.

Every fall after the last of the tomatoes has been harvested, I announce that next year I'm going to give tomatoes a break. They're so much work, I complain, and I can buy them at the produce stand down the street. But every year at the garden center, I load my cart with the first tomato plants I see. I must have early tomatoes and cherry tomatoes, tomatoes for canning and cooking, big beefsteaks for sandwiches, luscious heirlooms.

Tomatoes actually aren't hard to grow if you plant in moderation. The bush (determinate) types get to a certain size and stop growing, then produce tomatoes for a 10-day period. The vining (indeterminate) types are a little more trouble, as they continue to grow and produce until the frost kills them. They need staking and a lot of space.

Tomatoes are quite attractive, especially the multicolored ones. Colors range from white to yellow to red to purple to almost black.

When Plant tomato plants outside after all danger of frost has passed, on a cloudy day if possible to reduce transplant shock. Sow seeds indoors 6 to 8 weeks before the last frost date.

Where Tomatoes need all-day sun and lots of water. Soil should be fertile and rich in organic matter. Compact bush types can be grown in large containers.

How Harden off seedlings before planting them outside by gradually exposing them to outdoor conditions. Loosen the soil to a depth of 10 to 12 inches and work in 2 to 3 inches of compost or other organic matter. Incorporate a controlled-release fertilizer before planting. Space plants 6 feet apart if allowed to sprawl, 3 feet apart if staked (stake at planting time). Water well and give each plant a half-cup of starter fertilizer solution.

TLC Tomatoes need an even supply of water—about 1 inch a week. Cracked and deformed fruits and blossom-end rot are the result of an uneven water supply. Once plants are established, mulch beds with 2 inches of chopped leaves, grass clippings, or other fine-textured organic material, or cover soil with black plastic to retain moisture and control weeds. Tomatoes are heavy feeders, requiring regular applications of fertilizer throughout the growing season. Don't overdo the nitrogen, however, or you will have all vines and no fruit. All tomatoes grow best if they're staked or caged to keep their fruits off the ground, increase air circulation around plants, and reduce the chance of infection from soilborne diseases. Harvest fruits when they are evenly colored and slightly firm or soft. Store at room temperature. To ripen green tomatoes, place them in a warm place away from sunlight.

PEAK SEASON
Midsummer to first frost

MY FAVORITES
The heirloom 'Black Krim' is purplish black in color and delicious, with a hint of saltiness. 'Brandywine', another heirloom, is large and luscious, reddish purple, and a great slicing tomato.

'Lemon Boy' is the first true yellow hybrid tomato.

The heirloom 'Green Zebra' is an early-maturing, green-and-chartreuse-striped tomato about 3 inches in diameter with a zingy flavor.

'Micro-Tom' bears tiny fruit on a 5- to 8-inch plant. It's great for containers.

GARDEN COMPANIONS
Give sprawling tomato plants their own corner of the garden, or grow them on tall supports at the back of a flower garden. Plant multicolored cherry tomatoes in pots with ornamental peppers.

ABOVE: *'Green Zebra'.* LEFT: *This collection of heirloom tomatoes shows the wide variety of shapes and colors available.*

Ornamental Grasses

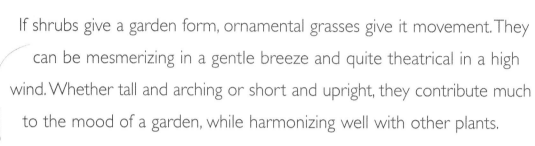

If shrubs give a garden form, ornamental grasses give it movement. They can be mesmerizing in a gentle breeze and quite theatrical in a high wind. Whether tall and arching or short and upright, they contribute much to the mood of a garden, while harmonizing well with other plants.

Grasses come in many forms and colors. Leaves may be upright or arching, strappy or tasseled. Foliage colors include a range of silvers, reds, greens, grays, and blues. The wildly popular 'Aureola' hakone grass is a brilliant gold with a hint of chartreuse. Another one of my favorites, *Miscanthus sinensis* 'Zebrinus', has slender green leaves banded with yellow. Blue fescue is a cool grayish blue color.

Tall, willowy grasses also make a wonderful foil for plants that have a horizontal branching habit. The rounder, billowy types can be grouped together or planted singly in mixed borders. If you have a small garden, choose dwarf varieties and use them as individual focal points or to fill in gaps. The short, compact types can be used as edging plants. Plant a statuesque feather reed grass in a formal urn beside the front door.

VARIED AND VERSATILE

You'll find that there is an ornamental grass for just about every site and design challenge. If you have a large garden, plant tall grasses in masses and enjoy their beauty from a distance.

Most perennial grasses turn gold or silver in late fall and hold their color and form through the winter. If you like the look of grasses or their feathery plumes poking up through the snow, you can leave them standing until early

spring; at that time they're easily cut to the ground with hedge shears.

HOMEGROWN TENACITY

Grasses adapt exceptionally well to midwestern soils and weather. They are resistant to pests and diseases and usually able to tough it out through a drought, thanks to their long roots.

Grasses aren't perfect, though. Remember, many of these plants' ancestors freely roamed across hundreds of miles of open plains. Only the most tenacious were able to survive the heavy soil, extreme temperatures, and gale-force winds. Perennial grasses that spread in clumps aren't as invasive as those that spread by putting out underground roots called runners, but both kinds must be carefully monitored to prevent them from muscling in on their neighbors.

I've chosen grasses that are generally well behaved but hardy and resilient. Since grasses most likely won't play quite as significant a role in your overall scheme as plants in our other

ABOVE: *A mixed planting of tall ornamental grasses makes a dramatic backdrop in a large garden.* OPPOSITE PAGE: *The silver tassels of feather reed grass shimmer in the bright sunshine.*

categories, I've limited the list to six. Each of them is unique in form and color, and excellent in mass plantings. These grasses also look good together; try a mixed planting of two or three varieties.

187

Big and Little Bluestem

Andropogon gerardii, Schizachyrium scoparium (Andropogon scoparius)

There are lots of great ornamental grasses, but I wanted to start off with a plant that ranks among the best in the Midwest by virtue of birthright. Hundreds of years ago, big bluestem *(Andropogon gerardii)* dominated the tallgrass prairie that covered much of the Central Plains. By many accounts, it grew as tall as a horse, and its silvery blue leaves set off tall purple and yellow coneflowers, rattlesnake masters *(Eryngium yuccifolium)*, asters, liatrises, and other flowering plants.

Big bluestem's height puts it off-limits to the average gardener. That's why I grow little bluestem, the miniature version, which grows to about 3 feet tall. Like its larger sibling, little bluestem is handsome, rugged, hardy, and pest free. Both grow best in rich, loamy, well-drained soil, though big bluestem will tolerate heavy clay. The purplish seed heads that form in fall resemble turkeys' feet.

Feathery clumps of little bluestem will turn reddish bronze in fall and stand erect through winter. They'll poke right up through the snow cover.

PEAK SEASON

Spring through fall

MY FAVORITES

Schizachyrium scoparium (little bluestem) gets its common name from the silvery blue color at the base of its leaves. Foliage turns light bronze with the onset of frost. Plants stay upright all winter and provide food and shelter for birds. They grow to about 2 feet wide.

Andropogon gerardii (big bluestem) grows to 8 feet tall and 5 feet wide. 'Champ' is a bit shorter. 'Pawnee' has a more exaggerated arching habit, causing it to "weep."

GARDEN COMPANIONS

Plant big bluestem in a large meadow or prairie landscape with coneflowers and other flowering natives and grasses. Little bluestem is more versatile in the garden, and works well in a mixed border setting off flowering perennials like upright sedums, salvias, and daylilies. It can also be massed.

When Spring is the best time to plant.

Where Grow in full sun in average soil. Little bluestem must have excellent drainage; big bluestem tolerates heavy soils. Use little bluestem as an accent plant in a mixed border or in massed plantings. Use big bluestem as an accent plant or, if you have space, in groups of three in the back of a border.

How Amend the soil with organic matter before planting. Plant bluestem at the same depth as it was in the container, spacing little bluestem plants 1 to 2 feet apart, big bluestem plants 2 to 3 feet apart. Water well and give each plant a half-cup of starter fertilizer solution.

TLC After the soil has warmed, apply a 2-inch layer of organic mulch to retain moisture, improve the soil, and reduce weeds. Water as needed during dry periods. Cut plants to the ground in late winter before new growth appears.

ABOVE: Schizachyrium scoparium
LEFT: Andropogon gerardii

189

Blue Fescue
Festuca glauca (or *Festuca ovina* 'Glauca')

Low-growing blue fescue and reddish pink-flowered Sedum spurium 'Dragon's Blood' make a great combination for a curbside planting or to edge a walk or perennial border.

Lots of beginning gardeners figure that if you've seen one ornamental grass, you've seen them all. They haven't seen blue fescue. It's short and squat. And blue. Its angel hair–thin leaves shoot outward to form a round clump that some people think looks like a porcupine. In early summer, flower stalks rise out of the clump as high as 1½ feet (the clump itself gets only about a foot tall). If you decide the flowers spoil the formal effect you've achieved by planting this ornamental grass instead of, say, a low boxwood hedge to enclose a flower border, it's okay to snip the flowers off.

Blue fescue also works well as a filler; its simple round shape is tidy and calming, and its cool color sets off more vivid flower colors, such as lime green, lavender, and pale pink. In late summer, blue fescue is tinged with gold but it holds it bluish color and shape all through winter.

PEAK SEASON

Best in spring and fall, but holds its foliage through winter

MY FAVORITES

'Elijah Blue' grows to just 8 inches tall. Its bright blue leaves are very fine textured.

Silvery-leafed 'Sea Urchin' grows 6 to 12 inches tall.

'Blaufuchs' is a tough, reliable blue fescue that grows 6 to 12 inches tall.

GARDEN COMPANIONS

Plant blue fescue with other plants that must have excellent drainage, such as alpines, sedums, dianthus, and hardy geraniums. It makes a fine rock garden plant, especially 'Elijah Blue'. It's also effective massed in groups of six or more.

When Plant from seeds or set out nursery-grown plants in spring. Nursery-grown plants can also be planted in early fall if they are watered well. Plants self-sow, but only the species produces identical offspring; varieties do not grow back true.

Where Grow in full sun to light shade. Good soil drainage is crucial. Blue fescue does not grow well where summers are hot and humid, but a site with afternoon shade helps. Blue fescue is suitable for use as a ground cover, in a mixed border, or in a rock garden.

How Amend the soil with organic matter before planting. Plant nursery-grown plants at the same depth as they were in the containers, spacing plants 8 to 15 inches apart. Water well and give each plant a half-cup of starter fertilizer solution.

TLC After the soil has warmed, apply a 2-inch layer of organic mulch to retain moisture, improve the soil, and reduce weeds. Cut plants back to a height of 3 or 4 inches in early spring or fall to keep them looking neat. Many gardeners clip off seed heads to focus attention on foliage. Divide clumps every 3 years to keep plants vigorous.

ABOVE: Festuca glauca 'Elijah Blue' surrounded by hot pink petunias. LEFT: Festuca glauca with purple coral bells (Heuchera micrantha).

Eulalia Grass
Miscanthus sinensis

This ornamental grass goes by so many different common names that it can confuse the beginning gardener. The expert, too, for that matter. In addition to eulalia grass, you might find *Miscanthus sinensis* labeled maiden grass, porcupine grass, Japanese silver grass, flame grass, or zebra grass, just to name a few of the many possibilities. All varieties have feathery blooms that open as tassels and slowly swell to form those big, soft plumes of shimmering, reddish bronze or pinkish silver color. They always remind me of conquering Romans wearing plumed helmets.

M. sinensis has graceful foliage clumps at the base that come in a wide range of colors and color combinations. Leaves may be broad or slim, some striped lengthwise or banded. They may turn yellow, orange, or reddish brown as winter nears, and they look good against snow.

Gardeners in Zone 43 should grow hardy varieties such as 'Purpurascens' (flame grass) or 'Silberfeder' (silver feather grass).

Miscanthus sinensis 'Gracillimus' shows off the distinctive white-gold tassels that will swell to plumes as winter approaches.

PEAK SEASON

Midsummer through winter

MY FAVORITES

'Gracillimus' (maiden grass) grows 4 to 6 feet tall with slender, upright, dark green blades that have silver stripes down the middle. Coppery plumes turn a soft beige color in winter.

'Morning Light' grows to 5 feet tall with wispy, fine-textured green leaves edged in white and plumes that are reddish bronze.

'Purpurascens' (flame grass) grows in 3- to 4-foot-tall clumps that turn reddish in fall. Plumes are silver.

'Zebrinus' (zebra grass) grows 4 to 6 feet tall with arching leaves that are banded crosswise with yellow stripes; plumes are coppery pink.

'Silberfeder' (silver feather grass) grows to 6 feet tall with showy silver plumes. Use it as a screen or focal point.

'Strictus' (porcupine grass) is an improved zebra grass, with banded leaves and a more upright, fountain-like shape. Its feathery plumes grow on 6-foot stems.

GARDEN COMPANIONS

M. sinensis looks good in a prairie-style garden with upright sedums, yarrows, and rudbeckias; or in a more formal perennial garden as a background for lilies and daylilies. Pair 'Strictus' with oakleaf hydrangea.

When The best time to plant *Miscanthus sinensis* is spring.

Where Plant in full sun in average, well-drained soil. *M. sinensis* makes a good single specimen in a mixed border, or it can be mass-planted for use as a screen. Plant larger varieties in a landscape where their feathery plumes can be viewed from a distance.

How Amend the soil with organic matter before planting. Plant at the same depth as it was in the container. Give plants plenty of room, as mature clumps can be 6 feet across. Water well and give each plant a half-cup of starter fertilizer solution.

TLC After the soil has warmed, apply a 2-inch layer of organic mulch to retain moisture, improve the soil, and reduce weeds. Saturate the soil to at least a foot deep to accommodate the extensive root system. Once mature, *M. sinensis* is fairly drought tolerant, but it will need watering during hot, dry weather. Gardeners in Zone 43 should apply a winter mulch after the ground has frozen. Cut plants to the ground in late winter before new growth appears. When crowns start to die out and plants become floppy, divide plants in spring to rejuvenate them. *M. sinensis* can become invasive in some situations because of its prolific self-sowing.

ABOVE: Miscanthus sinensis *'Variegatus'*. RIGHT: M. s. *'Zebrinus'*.

Feather Reed Grass

Calamagrostis × acutiflora

Feather reed grass looks just as you'd imagine it would, with stiff, reedlike blades holding aloft thin, feathery, 2- to 3-foot plumes. The plumes bloom soft and pink, then gradually deepen to a pale purple in summer; by fall they resemble golden chaffs of wheat.

Feather reed grass is one of the earliest-blooming ornamental grasses, and it looks good all season and even in winter. It is probably the neatest and most contained of the ornamental grasses, with perfect posture on a still day, and primly graceful when tossed by a gentle breeze. It is handsome enough to be used in small formal gardens as an accent plant or

Feather reed grass shoots up like a geyser from a sea of black-eyed Susans and Sedum 'Autumn Joy'.

focal point or planted single file along a walk or foundation as a hedge. It also makes an excellent addition to a perennial border, filling in gaps and complementing other plants, especially those gaudy and rambunctious types that could use some discipline. In a large garden or low-maintenance landscape or near a pond, feather reed grass is very effective planted in masses.

PEAK SEASON
Mid-June through winter

MY FAVORITES
'Karl Foerster' ('Stricta') is an award-winning early bloomer that grows 5 to 6 feet tall.

GARDEN COMPANIONS
Plant in masses (for blocks of color), alternating feather reed grass with blue-flowered, gray-leafed Russian sage, and a pink-flowered upright sedum. In a formal border it contrasts well with colorful mounding plants like hardy geraniums.

When The best time to plant feather reed grass is spring, but it can be planted all season if it is watered well.

Russian sage (Perovskia) and feather reed grass both require little water.

Where Grow in full sun to light shade in average to rich, well-drained soil. Plants tolerate a wide range of soil conditions, including heavy clay and drought. Mature clumps add strong vertical components to mixed borders. Plants can also be used as a hedge or in containers.

How Amend the soil with organic matter before planting. Plant feather reed grass at the same depth as it was in the container, spacing plants 2 feet apart. Water well and give each plant a half-cup of starter fertilizer solution.

TLC After the soil has warmed, apply a 2-inch layer of organic mulch to retain moisture, improve the soil, and reduce weeds. Saturate the soil to at least a foot deep to accommodate the extensive root system. Once mature, feather reed grass is fairly drought tolerant, but it will need watering during hot, dry weather. Cut plants to the ground in late winter before new growth appears. Clumps expand slowly. When crowns start to die out and plants become floppy, divide plants in spring to rejuvenate them.

195

Fountain Grass

Pennisetum

Fountain grass sends up slender, arching stems with long flower spikes that look like sprays of water when the sun catches them. These plumes (called foxtails) grow as long as 9 inches, turning from green to rosy silver or white in late fall. The flowers don't last through the winter, but the leaves hold up well and change from green to rose, apricot, or gold before bleaching to pale tan in winter.

The arching plumes of fountain grass steal the show from everyday annuals white nicotiana and pink petunias.

Fountain grass forms a symmetrical mound 2 to 4 feet wide and tall. Its compact shape makes it quite useful as a single specimen in a mixed border. It can also be massed for a formal effect beside a pond or pool. Perennial fountain grasses are not reliably hardy in my garden, so every year I replant the less-expensive annual fountain grass (*Pennisetum setaceum* 'Atropurpureum'), which has burgundy-bronze leaves and foot-long foxtails. It combines well with most colors in a flower garden and in large containers, and makes an excellent cut flower.

PEAK SEASON

Perennial fountain grasses have foxtail-like pinkish flower spikes mid-summer to fall and clumps of green foliage that turns straw-colored in winter. Annual fountain grass has pink-purple flower spikes and attractive green or purple foliage spring through fall.

MY FAVORITES

Perennial *Pennisetum alopecuroides* 'Hameln' is a more compact version of the species, with 1½-foot-tall mounds of fine, green foliage and 3-foot-tall white flower spikes. The miniature 'Little Bunny' grows to just 1 foot tall and wide.

P. orientale, another perennial, has fine-textured green leaves that form a dense clump 1 to 2 feet tall and wide, covered with silky, 4-inch-long foxtails in late summer and fall.

P. setaceum 'Atropurpureum' is a tender perennial grown as an annual in the Midwest. Its reddish purple foxtails are almost a foot long, and its leaves are burgundy-bronze. It can be a vigorous self-seeder.

GARDEN COMPANIONS

Grow large fountain grasses in a mixed border with hydrangeas, dogwoods, and hostas. The smaller varieties are excellent fillers in a perennial garden, especially with salvia, veronica, and hardy geraniums and with all flowering annuals.

When The best time to plant fountain grass is in spring after all danger of frost is past.

Where Choose a site in full sun with average to rich, well-drained soil. Perennial fountain grasses can be massed or used as single specimens in mixed borders. Plant annual fountain grass in a border or in containers.

How Amend the soil with organic matter before planting. Plant fountain grass at the same depth as it was in the container, spacing perennial plants 3 feet apart and annual plants 2 feet apart. Water well and give each plant a half-cup of starter fertilizer solution.

TLC After the soil has warmed, apply a 2-inch layer of organic mulch to retain moisture, improve the soil, and reduce weeds. Water as needed during dry periods. Gardeners in Zone 43 should apply a winter mulch to perennial types after the ground has frozen. Cut perennials to the ground in late winter before new growth appears. When the crowns start to die out and plants become floppy, divide plants in spring to rejuvenate them.

ABOVE: Pennisetum alopecuroides 'Hameln'. BELOW: P. setaceum.

Hakone Grass

Hakonechloa macra 'Aureola'

Every now and then a plant is pulled out of obscurity and into the limelight, becoming an overnight sensation. *Hakonechloa macra* 'Aureola' is a classic example. A few years ago someone noticed that the yellow-gold leaves of this otherwise ordinary plant make everything else in the garden look fabulous. Hakone grass is now officially trendy, following in the footsteps of the gray-leafed *Artemisia schmidtiana* 'Silver Mound' and the chartreuse sweet potato vine *(Ipomoea batatas* 'Margarita', page 74), both of which achieved fame and fortune as accent plants.

The species, *Hakonechloa macra,* has solid green leaves. Look for 'Aureola' to really perk up a garden. Its green-and-gold leaves look chartreuse in dense shade, and the foliage takes on a pinkish hue in fall.

Hakonechloa macra 'Aureola' makes an eye-catching addition to a semishady perennial border with lady's-mantle (lower left).

'Aureola' grows in clumps to about 1½ feet tall with arching stems and looks a little like a miniature bamboo. It spreads slowly by underground runners but is not invasive. It dies back in winter but will return if it's given a sheltered site and is heavily mulched in winter.

PEAK SEASON

Spring through fall

GARDEN COMPANIONS

'Aureola' lights up a dark corner and complements all colors in a flower garden. Plant with other partial- or full-shade lovers, such as

- Japanese maple
- dogwood
- hosta
- lady's-mantle
- Solomon's seal
- Japanese painted fern *(Athyrium nipponicum)*
- pulmonaria
- epimedium
- wild ginger *(Asarum)*

ABOVE: Hakonechloa macra *'Aureola' with* Hosta *'So Sweet'.* BELOW: Hakone grass planted at intervals along a path draws the eye forward.

When The best time to plant hakone grass is spring, but it also can be planted in early fall if it is watered well and heavily mulched.

Where Choose a site in partial shade with rich, well-drained soil. In cooler areas, hakone grass can be grown in full sun, but variegation will not be as pronounced. Use it to brighten up darker areas of any garden, beside a garden pond or waterfall, or in a woodland setting. It's also a great container plant.

How Amend the soil with organic matter before planting. Plant hakone grass at the same depth as it was in the container, spacing plants 1½ to 2 feet apart. Water well and give each plant a half-cup of starter fertilizer solution.

TLC After the soil has warmed, apply a 2-inch layer of organic mulch to retain moisture, improve the soil, and reduce weeds. Keep the soil evenly moist from spring until the ground freezes, watering when the top 2 inches of the soil has dried out. Gardeners in Zone 43 should apply a winter mulch after the ground has frozen. Cut back foliage in spring before new growth appears. Divide clumps every 3 years in spring.

Bulbs

Mention "bulbs" and most people picture tulips and daffodils popping up in April or May. Hyacinths are also spring bulbs—you knew that—but does fritillaria ring a bell? Maybe you also didn't know about summer bulbs. Lilies are bulbs. So are onions, a.k.a. alliums.

Bulbs provide bursts of color, often just when our gardens need it most. In this chapter you'll learn about bulbs that bloom in spring, summer, and fall, and you'll discover, too, that not all the plants we call bulbs are technically bulbs.

Crocuses are corms, some begonias are tubers, dahlias are tuberous roots, and daylilies are rhizomes. These terms all refer to the underground parts of the plants. Corms, tubers, and rhizomes are thickened stems; tuberous roots are swollen roots. True bulbs, such as daffodils, are round or oval embryos containing the minute beginnings of stems, roots, leaves, and flowers—compact packages that lie dormant underground until Mother Nature tells them to wake up and realize their full potential.

A BULB'S LIFE

For the most part, all bulbous plants are grown the same way: you dig holes, plant the bulbs, then wait several months for some sign of life to appear aboveground, crossing your fingers and hoping your bulbs don't rot or attract the attention of hungry rodents. Most blooms last anywhere from 2 to 4 weeks, though some, like tuberous begonias, bloom continuously all summer. Time your planting right and bulbs can supply color when your garden is desperate for it. Daffodils, crocuses, and the early fritillarias *(F. meleagris)* are especially lovely in spring carpeting a woodsy area before the trees have leafed out. Dahlias bloom in mid- to late July, when most gardens are in the doldrums.

Bulbous plants store energy for the next year in their leaves, so don't remove them until they're withered. This is where companion planting really helps. In spring, clumps of forget-me-nots easily hide the yellowing leaves of daffodils, hyacinths, lily-of-the-valley, and crocuses. Tulip leaves are more troublesome because their large size makes them difficult to disguise. Alliums, lilies, and the giant fritillarias *(F. imperialis)* bloom in early to midsummer, when the garden has filled out and withering leaves aren't so obvious.

ABOVE: *'World's Favorite' daffodils tower over tiny 'Tete-a-Tete' daffodils.* OPPOSITE PAGE: *Multicolored parrot tulips.*

AFTER-BLOOM CARE

After flowering, some bulbs can be left in the ground indefinitely. Daffodils, crocuses, some alliums, and the early fritillaria are enthusiastic "naturalizers," meaning they come back more plentifully each year. Other bulbs must be dug up and replanted the following season. In colder parts of the Midwest, dahlia roots and begonia tubers must be dug up and shel-

tered in a cool garage or basement. You may decide to dig up your tulips as well, depending on the variety, as some decline noticeably from year to year.

Bulbs may seem like push-button plants, programmed to perform on schedule, but designing with them takes planning. I'll help you time your planting so your bulbs will add color and vigor to your garden not just in spring but all summer long.

Allium

Alliums belong to the onion family, but they don't look anything like onions. They actually look like lollipops. Their pinkish purple flowers perch on top of erect blue-gray stems; the leaves grow out of the base of the plant.

Allium giganteum, with its distinctive spherical flowers on tall stems, adds color and drama to an otherwise serene, mostly green garden.

Small alliums are quite delicate and most effective in groups. They bloom in mid- to late summer, depending on the variety, and may spread by reseeding. The leaves are sometimes deep green and brushlike, sometimes gray-green and swirly, like mop heads frozen in motion. The large alliums top out at about 2 feet, with leaves that are pointed and a bit like tulip leaves. With their strong architecture and perfect symmetry, they're beautiful in a formal garden. They are quite striking when planted in groups of three or five.

After the flowers of larger alliums are spent, their seed heads are attractive enough to leave standing. Fading foliage, however, is best hidden from view. A clump of softly textured, lime green lady's-mantle is a perfect screen for it.

PEAK SEASON

Various species provide flower color from late spring through summer, some into fall.

MY FAVORITES

Allium giganteum grows to about 4 feet tall and has purple globes (composed of tiny "florets") 6 inches across. It blooms in June or early July.

A. 'Globemaster' is similar to *A. giganteum* but shorter (2 to 3 feet tall) with flowers that are 10 inches in diameter. It blooms in June.

A. christophii (Star of Persia) grows to 1½ feet tall and has lavender flowers that are 10 inches in diameter. It blooms in late spring or early summer.

A. sphaerocephalum grows to 2 feet tall, with dark red, egg-shaped flowers that bloom in midsummer. It is commonly called drumstick allium.

GARDEN COMPANIONS

Plant big-flowered alliums in a perennial border with yellow daylilies, lady's-mantle, foxtail lilies *(Eremurus)*, and Siberian irises. Alliums also look good poking through hosta leaves. Plant *A. moly* with blue muscari or scilla, under a lavender-flowered dwarf Meyer's lilac.

When Plant dormant allium bulbs in early fall. Nursery-grown plants are best planted in spring.

Where Alliums grow well in full sun and well-drained soil. Choose a site where the dying foliage will be hidden by neighboring plants. Some smaller alliums, such as yellow-flowered, spring-blooming *A. moly,* and the summer-blooming drumstick allium, *A. sphaerocephalum,* are suitable for naturalizing in informal or woodland gardens.

How Amend the soil with organic matter and plant each bulb at a depth two to three times its diameter. Space bulbs 4 to 18 inches apart, depending on the variety.

TLC Keep alliums well watered during the growing season, but stop watering once the foliage begins to turn yellow. (Most alliums are tolerant of dry conditions once established.) Do not remove foliage until it is withered and brown. Fertilize with a controlled-release 10-10-10 or an organic equivalent in spring just after shoots emerge. A light summer mulch will help suppress weeds. To prevent alliums from reseeding throughout the garden, remove flower heads as soon as they have finished flowering. Alliums are rodent proof.

ABOVE: Allium giganteum *blooms are made up of hundreds of tiny florets.* BELOW: *The spring bloomer* A. moly, *which grows to about 1 foot tall, has a more relaxed, open look.*

Crocus

Crocus, Colchicum autumnale

Purple and yellow is a classic color combination for Dutch crocuses. They also come in white, blue, and lavender.

Legend has it that my neighborhood used to be carpeted in wild crocuses, which is why it is called Crocus Hill. The crocuses are long gone, but several years ago I decided to restore a bit of the past in my small corner lot. I planted crocus corms—hundreds of them—on a broad slope along the east side of the house. Every year the clumps swell a bit more. I look forward to seeing their grassy dark leaves poking up through the snow in February or March, followed by the fat buds in early April, and finally the vivid purple, yellow, and white flowers in late April.

My neighbors liked the idea and started planting crocuses, too. Now people passing by can't help noticing all the crocuses popping up beside mailboxes, along sidewalks, and in flower beds. I always enjoy it when someone makes the connection to Crocus Hill and says, "Not hard to figure out how this neighborhood got its name."

TOP: *Fall-blooming colchicums resemble crocuses but are actually members of the lily family.* BOTTOM: *Dutch crocuses flower in spring.*

PEAK SEASON

Most crocuses have showy flowers from late winter to early spring. *Crocus speciosus* and colchicums bloom from late summer into autumn.

MY FAVORITES

Crocus flavus is the earliest spring bloomer and has yellow flowers.

C. biflorus 'Miss Vain' is pure white. It blooms in March or April.

C. sieberi 'Firefly' is pale lavender. 'Tricolor' is lilac blue, white, and yellow. Both bloom in March or April.

C. vernus (often called Dutch crocus) is the most common crocus, with large white, yellow, purple, blue, or lavender flowers. It blooms in April.

C. speciosus is a purplish fall bloomer and very easy to grow.

Colchicum autumnale leafs out in early summer but the flower clusters don't appear until fall. Flowers are lavender, white, and rose.

GARDEN COMPANIONS

Crocuses look best massed, and are pretty when mixed with early daffodils, which help deter squirrels (they avoid daffodils as much as they love crocuses). Crocuses can also be combined with a ground cover like myrtle (*Vinca minor*) that isn't too dense to allow them to poke through.

When Plant spring-blooming crocus corms as early in fall as possible. Fall-blooming *Crocus speciosus* and colchicums should be planted in spring or late summer.

Where Crocuses prefer full sun to partial shade and well-drained, sandy loam with abundant organic matter. Colchicums grow in sun or partial shade in fertile soil. Both must be planted where the unattractive leaves can be left to die throughout summer. All crocuses and colchicums can be naturalized in lawns.

How Dig a bed or individual holes to a minimum depth of 8 inches, setting the soil aside. (Space holes for crocuses 4 inches apart, for colchicums 6 to 8 inches apart.) Sprinkle a bulb fertilizer (9-9-6) or bonemeal in the bottom. Mix enough organic matter with the loosened soil to make it light and fluffy, and fill the bed or holes about half-full with the soil. Plant crocuses root end down, 3 inches deep. Plant colchicums 3 to 4 inches deep. Cover with the remaining soil and water well.

TLC Water newly planted corms frequently right after planting. Water established crocuses in the spring only if the season is dry, and avoid excessive watering in summer, when plants are dormant. Colchicums require water during prolonged dry periods. Fertilize all crocuses and colchicums with a bulb fertilizer or an organic equivalent in early spring just as tips poke above the soil. You may remove spent flower stalks, but do not remove foliage until it is completely withered and brown. (Colchicums' leaves show for about 2 months in spring to early summer, then die out, long before their flower clusters appear in fall.) Crocuses and colchicums are a favorite food of squirrels, chipmunks, and mice. To deter them line the bottom, sides, and top of the planting bed with hardware cloth. Remove the top lining in spring before growth starts.

Colchicums can be planted in Zones 2 and 33–41.

Daffodil

Narcissus

Their bright color and perky shapes make daffodils the most ebullient of plants, the perfect antidote to winter doldrums. In addition to yellow, daffodils come in orange, pale pink, peach, white, and combinations thereof, and in many shapes, sizes, and bloom times. The classic flower form has a cuplike center surrounded by petals, but there are also double-flowering daffodils as well as varieties with multiple flowers on each stem. The slender, strappy leaves are more attractive than tulip foliage, and thus more palatable to people who hate to look at withering leaves.

Daffodils are quite fragrant and amazingly tough and reliable. They come back year after year without fail. One year some daffodils in my garden swallowed their pride and came back even after being dug up and tossed on the compost heap—accidentally dug up, of course. If that's not enough to win our hearts, many varieties naturalize, meaning their clumps spread significantly every year.

Narcissus 'February Gold' is one of the better daffodils for naturalizing and especially effective in a woodland setting.

PEAK SEASON

Early to midspring

MY FAVORITES

Good varieties for naturalizing are yellow 'February Gold' and 'King Alfred'; white 'Mount Hood'; and 'Barrett Browning', which is white with orange-red cups.

I love 'Actaea' for its delicate orange center in a circle of white petals, and the sculpted flowers of 'Jack Snipe', which has white petals and yellow trumpets. Both are also excellent for naturalizing.

GARDEN COMPANIONS

Masses of yellow and blue are striking. Plant early daffodils with other early bloomers like blue scilla. Combine later bloomers with grape hyacinths or hyacinths. Daffodils planted with blue forget-me-nots have a more practical attribute: the forget-me-nots mask the daffodils' foliage. Tulips and daffodils also look good together.

When Plant bulbs in fall as early as you can get them. Daffodils need 10 to 12 weeks of growing time to form roots properly.

The exquisite N. poeticus 'Actaea' (LEFT) and the bold 'King Alfred' (RIGHT).

Where Daffodils do best in full sun, although they tolerate light shade. They require loamy, well-drained soil (soggy soil leads to rot). Daffodils can be naturalized in lawns.

How Dig a bed to a minimum depth of 1 foot or dig individual holes spaced 5 to 8 inches apart, setting the soil aside. Sprinkle a bulb fertilizer (9-9-6) or bonemeal in the bottom. Mix organic matter with the loosened soil and fill the bed or holes to about 8 inches from the surface. Plant each bulb with the fat end down at a depth three times its diameter (bulbs planted too shallowly may not survive cold winters). Cover with the remaining soil and water well.

TLC Water newly planted bulbs frequently the fall they are planted. Bulbs planted late in the season should be protected with a 6-inch layer of winter mulch. Remove mulch as soon as the weather begins to warm in spring, before the bulb foliage comes up. Start watering generously again. Fertilize with a bulb fertilizer or an organic equivalent before growth appears. An organic mulch such as shredded leaves or bark can be placed around plants when they are 3 to 4 inches tall, but keep it away from the leaves. Cut back on watering as foliage dies down after blooming. Do not remove daffodil foliage until it begins to turn yellow and unsightly. If you have naturalized daffodils in the lawn, do not mow until the leaves have died back, at least 7 weeks after the last flowering. Begin regular watering again in late summer, when flower buds form for next year. A fall application of fertilizer also is beneficial.

Dahlia

Dahlia

I admit I wasn't a huge fan of dahlias until a professional dahlia grower asked me to try out three of her favorites in my garden. How could I refuse? I planted them and then left for a 3-week vacation, convinced I'd never see the dahlias again. On my return I was amazed that they had survived a regimen of neglect exacerbated by a dry spell. I'd always thought they had to be coddled, but dahlias are strong plants if given a good start in rich soil.

They're also remarkably varied. Dahlias come in just about every flower color (and color combination), shape, and size you can imagine, including small pom-poms; spiky, cactus-style flowers; and blooms as big across as a dinner plate. They have attractive, bushy foliage, and generally only the giant-flowering types need staking.

Dahlias can't take temperatures much below 30°F/-1°C; where I live, they must be dug up in October and overwintered in a cool place, then carefully potted up in early spring and transplanted into the garden in late May. They are worth the effort, as dahlias are about as showy a plant as you can grow, and so welcome in late summer when most flowering plants have long since peaked.

One of the delights of dahlias is their many flower types. Among them is the small, tightly petaled pom-pom.

PEAK SEASON

Midsummer to frost

MY FAVORITES

'Pooh' is the dahlia I love best. It grows 5 feet tall and bears orange-and-yellow-ringed, daisylike flowers.

'Kelvin Floodlight' has giant yellow flowers that more than live up to the plant's comic name, and grows to about 5 feet tall.

'Eveline' has ball-shaped flowers that are white with a dab of purple at the center. It grows 3 to 4 feet tall.

'Awaikoe' is among the hardiest and most unusual dahlias. It has reddish mahogany petals with white collars and an orange button center. It grows to 3 feet tall. This half-hardy perennial often makes it through the winters in warmer parts of the Midwest if covered.

GARDEN COMPANIONS

Large-flowered dahlias will steal the show. I grow them as accent plants. The smaller varieties look good in a colorful flower bed or in containers with sun-loving annuals like nicotiana, verbena, petunias, and zinnias. Plant 'Eveline' in a cutting garden with tall, white 'Casablanca' lilies and tall annuals like *Verbena bonariensis* and *Nicotiana sylvestris.*

When Plant dahlias outdoors after all danger of frost has passed.

Where Dahlias grow and flower best in full sun but will tolerate partial shade. Plant them in well-drained soil liberally enriched with peat moss or well-rotted compost or manure. They are suitable for pots, flower beds, and cutting gardens.

ABOVE, LEFT: *The most common dahlia flower type has multiple pointy petals.* TOP, RIGHT: *The ball-flower type is flat and larger than a pom-pom.* BOTTOM, RIGHT: *The cactus-type dahlias resemble the blooms of many real cactuses.*

How Space plants 1 to 5 feet apart, depending on the variety. For each plant, dig a hole 1 foot wide and 1 foot deep for taller dahlia varieties, 6 inches deep for shorter varieties. Work a half-cup of bulb fertilizer into the bottom of the hole. If you're planting a taller variety, drive a stake into the hole. Set one root in the bottom, with the stem end facing up. Spread out the roots. Cover taller varieties with 3 inches of soil, shorter ones with 2 inches. Water thoroughly. As the shoots grow, gradually fill the hole with more soil. When they are 6 inches tall, thin out all but one or two of them.

TLC Keep dahlias well watered all season. Place a 2-inch layer of organic mulch around the plants to conserve moisture and suppress weeds. When plants have two or three sets of leaves, you can pinch out the growing tips just above the upper set of leaves to encourage bushy growth. A light application of bulb fertilizer in midsummer is beneficial. See page 30 for how to dig up and store dahlias over the winter.

Fritillaria

Fritillaria imperialis, F. meleagris

I once read this description of fritillarias in a gardening book: "small, nodding, bell-shaped flowers with a plaid maroon-and-white pattern." I was so intrigued that I looked up the plant in an illustrated gardening encyclopedia. Stripes, speckles, and swirls I could visualize, but plaid? Sure enough, *Fritillaria meleagris* turned out to have flowers that perfectly fit that description. There was no other word for them. They were, in fact, plaid.

I planted some bulbs in fall—alas, too late for them to get established. My little fritillarias didn't make it through an unusually hard winter, but another fritillaria that I bought by accident did: *F. imperialis,* which is so unlike its delicate, plaid cousin that I keep forgetting they're kin. A tall, erect plant with pointy leaves, it looks a little like a toilet plunger or a mop, the business end being the flower, which is a brilliant orange, shaggy affair that can be extremely effective when planted in masses.

Fritillaria imperialis looks like one of the taller alliums, but only from the neck down. On top, a crown of leaves tops bell-shaped flowers.

When Plant bulbs in the fall as early as you can get them.

Where Fritillarias grow best in partial shade and rich soil. Plant *F. meleagris* where its subtle beauty can be appreciated, such as in the cracks in a stone terrace or in a container.

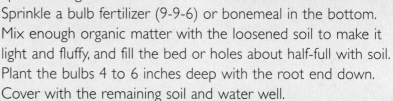

How Dig a bed to a minimum depth of 1 foot or dig individual holes 4 to 8 inches apart, setting the soil aside. Sprinkle a bulb fertilizer (9-9-6) or bonemeal in the bottom. Mix enough organic matter with the loosened soil to make it light and fluffy, and fill the bed or holes about half-full with soil. Plant the bulbs 4 to 6 inches deep with the root end down. Cover with the remaining soil and water well.

TLC Water newly planted bulbs frequently the fall they are planted. Cover the bed with 6 inches of winter mulch when the top 2 inches of the ground has frozen. Remove mulch as soon as the weather begins to warm in spring, before the bulb foliage comes up. Begin watering generously again. Fertilize with a bulb fertilizer or an organic equivalent just as tips poke above the soil. An organic mulch such as shredded leaves or bark can be placed around plants when they are 3 to 4 inches tall, but keep it away from the leaves. Cut back on watering as foliage dies down after blooming. You may remove spent flower stalks, but do not remove foliage until it is completely withered and brown. Begin regular watering again in late summer, when flower buds form for next year. Rodents hate the skunklike smell of fritillaria bulbs and leave them alone.

PEAK SEASON

Midspring

MY FAVORITES

Fritillaria meleagris is a 1-foot-tall, plaid spring bloomer. 'Alba' is pure white.

F. imperialis (crown imperial) is the orange-flowered 3-footer that blooms in early summer. It also comes in yellow ('Lutea Maxima') and reddish orange ('Rubra Maxima').

GARDEN COMPANIONS

My *F. imperialis* plants grow in masses along with blue-flowered 'Johnson's Blue' geraniums, 'Blue Wonder' catmint, and 'Sunny Border Blue' veronica, and the large purple pom-poms of *Allium giganteum*. Chartreuse euphorbia and silver-gray artemisia harmonize with these strong colors.

LEFT: Fritillaria meleagris *is sometimes called the checkered lily or described as looking like a plaid lampshade.* ABOVE: *Its unusual coloring makes* F. acmopetala *an eye-catching addition to the spring border when planted in small groups.*

Hyacinth

Hyacinthus orientalis

For some reason, hyacinths strike me as quintessentially Dutch. Of course, Holland is the home of the bulb industry and most famous for its tulips. But something about the hyacinth's tidy, upright domesticity makes me imagine them in every window box in Amsterdam.

Hyacinths are extremely fragrant and come in blue, purple, pink, yellow, and white. They are well suited to containers and among the best bulbs for forcing (that is, coaxed out of dormancy early to bloom as indoor houseplants). Their rigid shape and waxy blooms have an almost plastic primness that makes them more challenging to design with in the landscape; they benefit from the softening influence of ground covers like

'Delft Blue' hyacinths look great planted in masses, as their penetrating color is their best feature.

myrtle *(Vinca minor)* and pachysandra. They should be planted in groups of three or more, but don't expect them to naturalize as well as the grape hyacinth *(Muscari)* or wood hyacinth *(Hyacinthoides hispanica),* two bulbs that are often mistaken for common hyacinth.

PEAK SEASON
Early to midspring

MY FAVORITES
I love blue hyacinths best, and my favorite is 'Delft Blue', with bluish purple 'Blue Jacket' a close second.

'City of Haarlem' is a charming yellow.

'Anna Marie' (also sold as 'Anne Marie') is light pink.

'Carnegie' is white.

GARDEN COMPANIONS
Hyacinths look good in groups of three or more. They are also excellent combined with other bulbs in pots and window boxes. In the garden, soften their rigid formality with clumps of forget-me-nots or ground covers like myrtle *(Vinca minor).*

When Plant bulbs in fall as early as you can.

Where Hyacinths require full sun or partial shade and well-drained, normal garden soil. Plant them in pots or in a flower bed or ground cover near a doorway or sitting area, where you can enjoy their heady fragrance.

How Dig a bed to a minimum depth of 1 foot or dig individual holes 4 to 6 inches apart, setting the soil aside. Sprinkle a bulb fertilizer (9-9-6) or bonemeal in the bottom. Mix enough organic matter with the loosened soil to make it light and fluffy, and fill the bed or holes about half-full with soil. Plant bulbs 5 to 6 inches deep with the root end down. Cover with the remaining soil and water well.

'Queen of the Pinks' hyacinth is a deep pink, late-spring bloomer.

TLC Water newly planted bulbs frequently the fall they are planted. Cover the bed with 6 inches of winter mulch when the top 2 inches of the ground has frozen. Remove mulch as soon as the weather begins to warm in spring, before the bulb foliage is up. Begin watering generously again. Fertilize with a bulb fertilizer or an organic equivalent just as tips poke above the soil. An organic mulch such as shredded leaves or bark can be placed around plants when they are 3 to 4 inches tall, but keep it away from the leaves. Cut back on watering as foliage dies down after blooming. You may remove spent flower stalks, but do not remove foliage until it is completely withered and brown. Begin regular watering again in late summer, when flower buds form for the next year. Rodents are not attracted to hyacinth bulbs.

Lily
Lilium

Asiatic lilies are remarkably hardy and pest free, and will quickly spread to fill a large space with brilliant color.

Lilies are like dahlias in that they are grown for their large, showy flowers, which are often quite fragrant. The most common lilies for gardens are the early-blooming (June) Asiatic varieties and the later (July and August) oriental lilies.

Asiatic lilies have slightly smaller blooms in vivid shades ranging from white to yellow, pink, red, and orange. The flowers grow on stems that rise out of attractive clumps of slender leaves. Oriental lilies have large white or pink flowers often spotted with gold or banded with red. They are so aromatic and painterly, they always remind me of prom night. They are the perfect corsage flower. The orientals grow on tall stems whose leaves fan out from top to bottom; they sometimes need staking.

These lilies are best in the back of the border, where their flowers have no trouble attracting attention and their less appealing features are kept in the background. Newer hybrids of both types have much improved hardiness and disease resistance, making lilies among the easiest garden plants.

When Plant bulbs in fall as early as you can get them. Some lily bulbs are available in spring; plant these as soon as you get them home. Nursery-grown lilies can be planted anytime if they are given ample water.

Where Most lilies do best in full sun in well-drained, slightly acidic to acidic soil. Heavy or compacted soils can lead to rot. Lilies will tolerate partial shade. They look best planted in groups of three or more and are excellent in a perennial border, where other plants can soften their leaves and stems.

How Loosen the soil to a depth of 1 to 1¹/₂ feet. Mix in peat moss. For each bulb, dig a hole to a depth three times the bulb's diameter. Space the holes at least 8 inches apart. Add bonemeal or a controlled-release 10-10-10 fertilizer to the bottom of each hole, then fill halfway with soil. Plant the bulbs with the fat end down. If your variety will need staking, install the supports now to avoid damaging the bulbs. Cover with the remaining soil and water well. Nursery-grown lilies should be planted at the same depth they were growing in the pots. It's best to remove all blooms and buds to help plants become established. Stake taller varieties.

TLC Water regularly to keep the soil evenly moist. Bulbs planted in late fall in cold climates should be covered with a thick layer of organic mulch after planting to keep the soil warmer and delay warming of the bed in spring. (After the first year, only oriental lilies should require winter protection in cold climates.) An organic mulch such as shredded leaves or bark can be placed around plants when they are 3 to 4 inches tall, but keep it away from the leaves. Every spring after planting, fertilize with 10-10-10 or an organic equivalent. Avoid getting chemical fertilizer on the leaves, as it may burn them. After the flowers fade, cut the main stem just below the lowest bloom.

TOP TO BOTTOM: *Asiatic lily 'Dawn's Delight', the oriental lily 'Casablanca', and the oriental lily 'Stargazer'.*

PEAK SEASON
Early summer to early fall

MY FAVORITES
'Red Night' (cherry red flowers on 3- to 4-foot stems) and 'Enchantment' (orange flowers on 4-foot stems) are both attractive Asiatic lilies.

'Casablanca' (white flowers on 4- to 5-foot spikes) and 'Stargazer' (deep pink, speckled flowers on 3-foot spikes) are two of the more spectacular orientals.

Other excellent lilies are the martagon or Turk's cap lily (*Lilium martagon*), which has pendant, often purplish flowers; and trumpet or Easter lily (try *L. longiflorum* 'White Elegance', with fragrant white trumpets on 3-foot stems). Plant and care for these as you would Asiatics and orientals.

GARDEN COMPANIONS
Asiatic lilies can be planted in the middle of a border behind bushy plants like catmint and cranesbill geraniums. Oriental lilies need their leaves masked and may also need other plants to lean on; they do well in the back of a border. White lilies like 'Casablanca' are exquisite in an all-white garden with other white-flowered plants such as cimicifuga, Japanese anemones, astilbe, phlox, and meadow rue. All midsummer-blooming lilies go well with purple coneflower, liatris, and phlox.

Siberian Squill

Scilla siberica

If I had to pick one time for out-of-town guests to go on a garden tour, I'd choose the first of May and take my guests to see a garden that is, for one week only, a virtual sea of blue. Minnesota is the land of 10,000 lakes, after all, and this front yard could almost qualify as number 10,001. The watery effect is the work of scilla, a little spring bulb that naturalizes in lawns as eagerly as any bulb I know of. The effect is made all the more dazzling by the presence of four massive oak trees, which filter sunlight in a way that suggests a gentle breeze rippling the surface.

The owner of this glorious display takes care not to cut her lawn before the scilla bulbs have absorbed all the energy stored in the leaves for next year's bloom. Only when the

Scilla siberica 'Spring Beauty' spreads quickly to turn the springtime landscape a glorious shade of blue. The nodding, bell-shaped flowers cluster at the top of 3- to 6-inch stems.

weeds and grass are as high as her calf, when her yard is as much an eyesore as just weeks earlier it was a thing of transcendent beauty, does she deem it safe to get out the mower. After a few passes her scilla is finished, and the grass takes over until next spring.

Note that scilla blooms as early as February in warmer parts of the Midwest.

PEAK SEASON
Early spring

MY FAVORITES
Scilla siberica 'Spring Beauty' spreads quickly. If you prefer white flowers, plant 'Alba'.

S. bifolia is a bit shorter with blue, star-shaped flowers.

Puschkinia scilloides is a close relative with fragrant, pale blue flowers.

GARDEN COMPANIONS
Scilla blooms at the same time as white snowdrops (*Galanthus nivalis*), and they make ideal companions.

When Plant scilla bulbs as early in fall as possible.

Scilla campanulata, or Spanish bluebell (recently reclassified as Hyacinthoides hispanica), does best in warmer regions of the Midwest.

Where Scilla prefers full sun to partial shade and well-drained soil. It is ideal planted in drifts among shrubs or perennials or under deciduous trees. Scilla is the best bulb for naturalizing in lawns.

How Dig a bed to a depth of 6 inches or dig individual holes about 3 inches apart, setting the soil aside. Mix enough organic matter with the loosened soil to make it light and fluffy, and fill the bed or holes about half-full with the soil. Plant the bulbs 2 to 3 inches deep with the root end down. Cover with the remaining soil.

TLC Water newly planted scilla bulbs right after planting. Water in spring only if the season is dry, and avoid excessive watering in summer, when plants are dormant. You may remove spent flower stalks to help prevent the plants from self-sowing, but do not remove foliage until it is completely withered and brown. Scilla can be divided after the foliage has died in summer, but because the small bulbs are so inexpensive, it's easier to just plant new ones in fall. Rodents are not attracted to scilla bulbs.

Tuberous Begonia

Begonia

egonia is a big family. It includes annuals often massed in flower beds, tender perennials grown

With its compact growth habit, Begonia multiflora *is excellent for formal planters.*

as houseplants for their beautiful foliage, and tuberous begonias, so-named because they grow from underground tubers but most notable for their spectacular flowers, which are often compared to camellias.

Tuberous begonias' fuzzy, pointy leaves make an excellent cushion for the heavy, colorful blooms, but the plants are difficult to fit into a perennial border. The blooms are too large and showy for the front of the border, and the plants are too short to go farther back. They are best planted in containers. Container-planting also lets you keep your begonias close to the house, perhaps on the porch, as they prefer shade to sun. The trailing type is ideal for hanging baskets. Growing tuberous begonias in pots also makes digging up the tubers in the fall a fairly simple procedure.

PEAK SEASON

Early summer to frost

MY FAVORITES

Begonia tuberhybrida has flowers as large as 10 inches wide and grows 2 feet tall.

B. multiflora is shorter and bushier, with smaller flowers.

'Non-Stop' varieties are hybrids of *B. tuberhybrida* and *B. multiflora* that do indeed bloom nonstop from spring to frost. They are fairly short, squat plants (growing to about 8 inches tall), with flowers 3 to 4 inches across.

B. pendula is a trailing-type begonia.

All these begonias may have ruffled flowers and come in just about every color except blue.

GARDEN COMPANIONS

In the garden, plant tuberous begonias in groups of three or more among plants with great foliage, like hosta, wild ginger *(Asarum),* and Japanese painted fern *(Athyrium nipponicum* 'Pictum'). Clusters of impatiens whose colors complement or match those of the begonias add a charming touch.

When Start tubers indoors about 8 weeks before the last frost date. Plant outside after all danger of frost has passed.

Where Tuberous begonias prefer light to medium shade and average soil fortified with peat moss or well-rotted compost. They will not grow well in full sun or strong winds. They adapt well to containers, and the pendulous types are especially nice in hanging baskets.

How To start tubers indoors, plant them indented side up in 4-inch pots filled with a soilless potting mix. Barely cover with the mix. Grow on a warm, sunny windowsill or under fluorescent lights, watering sparingly until top growth commences, which may take up to 6 weeks. Once shoots emerge, continue to provide bright light, but shade from strong midday sun. After all danger of frost has passed, transplant the tubers outdoors, planting them just deep enough so they're covered lightly with soil. Space them 10 inches apart in the ground, closer in containers.

TLC Keep the soil moist throughout the growing season. Fertilize plants every 2 to 3 weeks with bulb fertilizer or an organic equivalent until foliage starts to wither in fall. A light summer mulch will help suppress weeds and retain moisture. When plants die back to the ground but before the first frost, dig up the tubers. Do not remove soil from them. Allow the tubers to dry in an airy, shady, frost-free place for several weeks until the stems break away easily. Divide and store as for dahlias (see page 30), until it is time to pot up plants in spring.

ABOVE: 'Non-Stop' begonias are profuse bloomers. RIGHT: Begonia tuberhybrida shows off its large flowers.

Tulip

Tulipa

Tulips bloom early and late in spring, depending on the variety, marking that wonderfully heady transition from winter to summer. The earliest tulips are the species types, with short stems and flowers that open and close. Later come the aristocrats, like the Darwins and the Darwin hybrids, with their elegant simplicity, and the parrot tulips, which are just the opposite, all ruffles and cacophonous color. Later still, 'Angelique' makes her entrance; this feminine tulip has a soft pink, ruffled, peony-like flower.

Alas, tulips are as common as crabgrass in spring. After a while I stop seeing them. But last May, I drove by a tulip bed that was so tastefully designed I stopped my car and got out for a closer look. The planting was small—no more than 50 tulips, arranged in an oval beneath a small pruned hydrangea tree, and backed by low, orblike shrubs in shades of green and crimson. The tulips were all pale pink—a tall, slender variety at the back, and a shorter, showier, deep pink tulip with a horizontal winged flower in front. I was so impressed, I left a thank-you note in the mailbox.

The contrasting color and shape of orange-red 'Ad Rem' Darwin tulips and deep pink 'Primavera' tulips, both late-spring bloomers, make a pleasing formal composition.

TOP TO BOTTOM: *A bicolored Darwin tulip, the species tulip* T. greigii *'Red Riding Hood', and the species tulip* T. tarda.

PEAK SEASON

Early to late spring

MY FAVORITES

I have a special fondness for the early species tulips: *Tulipa greigii, T. kaufman-niana, T. tarda,* and *T. fosteriana.* They usually have pale yellow or white flowers on short stems. *T. greigii* may also be red or orange.

Midseason tulips include the taller Darwin hybrids and Apeldoorn varieties, which come in many colors and grow 1½ to 2½ feet tall.

The Darwin tulips arrive later. They are a bit taller and extremely elegant. 'Black Diamond' has striking purplish black flowers.

Other favorite late bloomers are *T. viridiflora* 'Greenland', which has fringed, pale pink petals with green stripes, and *T.* 'Angelique', which resembles a peony.

GARDEN COMPANIONS

Tulips' big, strappy, gray-green leaves can be lovely when the flower is blooming, but they quickly get floppy and tattered as they turn yellow. Plant tulips behind perennials such as forget-me-nots and hostas that will fill out just as the spring bulbs are fading. Tulips are natural companions for daffodils, hyacinths, and crocuses.

When Plant bulbs in fall as early as you can.

Where Tulips do best in full sun, but they tolerate late-day shade. They require well-drained soil. Choose a site with good overhead light to prevent stems from leaning toward the light source. They look best massed in beds or pots.

How Dig a bed to a minimum depth of 12 inches or dig individual holes 4 to 6 inches apart, setting the soil aside. Sprinkle a bulb fertilizer (9-9-6) or bonemeal in the bottom. Mix enough organic matter with the loosened soil to make it light and fluffy, and fill the bed or holes to about 8 inches from the surface. Plant each bulb at a depth three to five times its diameter, with the pointed end up. Cover with the remaining soil and water well.

TLC Water newly planted bulbs frequently the fall they are planted. Cover the bed with 6 inches of winter mulch when the top 2 inches of the ground has frozen. Remove mulch as soon as the weather begins to warm in spring, before the bulb foliage comes up. Begin watering generously again. An application of bulb fertilizer or an organic equivalent just as the tiny tips poke through the soil is beneficial, but do not fertilize during or right after bloom, as this can lead to disease problems. An organic mulch such as shredded leaves or bark can be placed around plants to retain moisture and reduce weed growth. Cut back on watering as foliage dies down after blooming. Do not remove tulip foliage until it dies completely. Begin regular watering again in late summer when flower buds form for the next year. Fertilize again in fall. To deter rodents, line the bottom, sides, and top of the planting bed with hardware cloth. Remove the top lining in spring before growth starts.

221

Roses

My brother-in-law can't understand my devotion to roses. I grow lots of them—climbers, ramblers, ground covers, and bushes—tending to them in protective goggles and leather snowmobiling gloves. "Why would you want to grow plants that hurt you?" he asks every time he sees me suited up for another pruning session.

Why? I'll tell you why. Giving them all that attention (for shape, to encourage reblooming, to prevent disease), at great personal risk, forges a bond: These plants need me. I can really be there for my roses. And I have to say that the payback is awesome. Like peonies, which take patience in the early going and are prone to some nasty illnesses, roses—once established—possess remarkable longevity. And though most roses don't bloom all the time, they flower abundantly. Even the types that bloom just once and then quit for the season produce such a bumper crop of flowers during their peak that you'll spent the rest of the summer getting your breath back.

Most roses can be coaxed to rebloom, at least intermittently, if you fertilize and deadhead. (And prune.) A few are everblooming, meaning they bloom their heads off from spring to fall.

IN SICKNESS AND IN HEALTH

Generally speaking, roses are more disease-prone than the average plant. To stay healthy, they must have full sun; rich, loamy soil; even moisture but excellent drainage; and lots of elbowroom. Roses are particularly susceptible to black spot, a pernicious fungal disorder that turns leaves yellow, then black, before they drop off. Eventually there are no more leaves and the infected

plant expires unless you put it out of its misery first, not just because you feel sorry for it but to protect other plants in your garden, as black spot can be contagious.

Pruning to remove older canes and open up the center of the plant lets in sunlight and improves air circulation, reducing the risk of illness. Pruning also helps control the sometimes unruly growth habit that is another of the rose's dubious distinctions. Pruning is essential if you want your rose to climb. Climbing roses are really just shrub roses with long canes. They don't naturally adhere to a support as vines do, but must be trained. This means pruning out aging canes, as flowers prefer to grow on new

ABOVE: *The floribunda rose 'Bonica' is at its peak of beauty in early summer but blooms on and off until fall.* OPPOSITE PAGE: *'Graham Thomas' blends the best traits of old-fashioned and modern roses. It was bred by David Austin and named after the legendary English rose breeder who brought old roses back into fashion.*

wood, and tying the young canes to the support so they don't flop over.

Our midwestern winters pose real challenges for roses. Some are hardier than others, but only those roses bred in places like Manitoba can be relied on to survive without winter protection. Even the super-hardy varieties often suffer dieback, leaving their roots with the task of regenerating new stems and leaves come spring. None of the roses on my list is off-limits to northern gardeners, but some of you may want to provide winter protection, at least by covering plants with plastic cones or mulch. The best way to protect a tender rose is with the "Minnesota tip" method: At the end of the growing season, tie the canes together; loosen the roots on one side of the plant, gently tip the canes over into a 6- to 8-inch-deep trench on the opposite side of the plant, and bury them with soil. After the ground freezes, cover the buried plant with 4 to 6 inches of leaves.

OLD ROSE REVIVAL

Much rose-breeding in recent decades has focused on hybrid tea roses, which produce long-budded flowers on strong, slender stems and bloom all sum-

ABOVE: 'John Cabot' is a member of the super cold-hardy Explorer series bred in Canada, and able to withstand subzero winter temperatures without being buried or even mulched. It can be trained to climb an arbor or trellis. RIGHT: The Explorer rose 'Jens Munk'.

mer. But hybrid teas are relatively difficult to grow. They are prone to black spot and don't survive the winter in cold climates. They are usually grown in a bed by themselves because their leggy habit doesn't work for hedges or ground covers. Nor does it belong in a perennial border. Their fragrance has often been sacrificed in the breeders' zeal to produce the most floriferous plants.

Hoping to recapture the charm of old garden roses, along with their toughness and versatility, many gardeners are now growing

varieties that were popular early in the last century, as well as modern "landscape" types such as the English roses popularized by breeder David Austin. Landscape roses have enough mass because of their foliage density and growth habit to make them useful in the same way shrubs and ground covers are useful. You can place them in a landscape (not just in a flower border) as structure plants; for example, as foundation plants, hedges, or ground covers. They can be massed or used alone as specimen plants.

All the roses I'm recommending are either old or modern landscape roses that are widely recognized for their beauty, hardiness, and vigor. Many are award winners. Some are more shade tolerant. Some are more finicky about drainage. I've tried to select a range of flower colors, though I should tell you that given its druthers, a rose would choose to be pink. Wild roses are almost always that color. It's up to you to factor in your own soil, sun, and weather, as well as your preferences for growth habit and color, and choose the perfect rose for your garden. All will thrive given the right conditions.

If you're not passionate about roses yet, you will be. But do get yourself a good pair of pruning gloves—mine go up to my elbows.

ABOVE: *'Carefree Beauty', bred by Griffith Buck, is as cold-hardy as it is beautiful.* BELOW, LEFT: *'Aunt Honey', another Buck rose.* BELOW, RIGHT: *'Sea Foam' blooms from mid-June into fall.*

'Angel Face'

A re you the kind of person who loves elaborate curtains and canopy beds? 'Angel Face' is the rose for you. Its ruffled double flowers are often compared to hybrid tea roses. Even more remarkable than their voluptuous shape is the color, which varies from a pale pink tinged with violet at the top of the blossom to deep lavender where it gets less sun exposure. The effect is seductive, to say the least.

'Angel Face' is a floribunda rose—one of several I'm recommending in this chapter. While not the hardiest of roses, floribundas are the most floriferous (with the exception of hybrid teas), producing masses of flowers in clusters on vigorous and bushy plants.

'Angel Face' blooms heavily in early summer and again later in the season on a compact plant, growing just 2 feet tall and 3 feet wide. Its gorgeous flowers give off a strong citrusy fragrance. Their beauty—and the plant's reputation as the perfect rose for beginners—has made 'Angel Face' a popular choice for the past 30 years.

'Angel Face' blooms in early summer, perfuming the air with a citrusy fragrance. Its flowers are unusually large and frilly for a hardy shrub rose.

When The best time to plant 'Angel Face' is early spring. Bare-root roses should be planted as soon as the soil can be worked. Nursery-grown plants should be planted after all danger of spring frost has passed.

Where 'Angel Face' thrives in full sun and rich, well-drained soil. Its bushy, compact growth habit makes it a good choice in flower borders or mass plantings.

How Amend the soil with abundant organic matter before planting. Clay or rocky soil should be replaced with loam soil. Soak bare-root roses in water overnight before planting. Plant so the bud union is half-buried in the soil, deeper if you live in the far north. Space plants 2 to 3 feet apart.

'Angel Face's' flowers turn deep lavender in semishade.

TLC Keep the soil evenly moist throughout the growing season. Deep watering is more effective than frequent sprinkling. After the soil has warmed up in late spring, apply a 3- to 4-inch layer of organic mulch such as shredded leaves or bark around plants. Mulch should come close to but not touch canes. Feed established plants as early as possible in spring, sprinkling a controlled-release 10-10-10 fertilizer or an organic equivalent around the base of each plant. Water immediately to dissolve granules and carry nutrients to the roots. Additional applications of a water-soluble fertilizer should be given throughout the summer. Remove faded blossoms to encourage more blooms. Careful pruning greatly reduces the risk of black spot, to which 'Angel Face' is susceptible. In early spring, remove dead or diseased canes and prune to maintain outward growing, vase-shaped plants. Remove any suckers growing from the roots. 'Angel Face' will need winter protection in the far north.

PEAK SEASON

Blooms from June intermittently until frost.

GOOD ALTERNATIVES

Profuse-blooming floribundas come in just about any color you could ask for. The following are disease resistant and trouble free.

'Sunsprite' has yellow flowers that bloom from spring through August. It grows to 3 feet tall.

'Iceberg' has white flowers, is a repeat bloomer, and grows 4 to 5 feet tall.

'Showbiz' is an award-winning red rose. It grows to 3 feet tall with a bushy habit.

'Marmalade Skies' is an award-winning new floribunda with orange flowers and a compact form. It grows to 3 feet.

GARDEN COMPANIONS

Plant 'Angel Face' in the front of a perennial border with 'Silver Mound' artemisia or lamb's ears to set off its lavender blooms. Grow lady's-mantle and blue catmint nearby. Other good companions are white-flowered and gray-leafed snow-in-summer, and white or blue salvias, veronicas, and delphiniums.

'Betty Prior'

This floribunda, a long-time sentimental favorite especially with northern gardeners, was introduced in England in 1935. For decades gardeners have enjoyed its delicate, upright form and prolific blooming. 'Betty Prior' just doesn't stop. Its single, medium-pink flowers are simple but fragrant, smelling of exotic spices, and very charming against the plant's shiny green leaves.

'Betty Prior' combines the tenacity of a wild rose with the obliging good manners of a hedge or bedding plant. Its compact habit never exceeds 4 feet.

'Betty Prior' is exceptionally hardy for a floribunda—more so than 'Angel Face'—though in the far north it will need some protection. To be safe bury your roses according to the "Minnesota tip" method (see page 224). One northern gardener I know loves this rose so much she grows several where her tall brick house can offer shelter on two sides, and covers them in winter with a 6-inch layer of leaves. She replants the roses that don't make it, and usually some don't.

PEAK SEASON

Blooms June through frost.

GOOD ALTERNATIVES

The following are both excellent landscape roses, trainable and useful as ground covers or hedges. 'Simplicity' is not as hardy as 'Schneekoppe'.

'Simplicity' has beautifully formed, soft pink flowers and glossy, dark green leaves. It is a small shrub rose and quite disease resistant, but it needs winter protection. It is wonderful planted as a hedge against a white picket fence.

'Schneekoppe' is a low-growing rugosa rose developed in Germany. Rugosas are extremely tough, hardy plants with good disease resistance. If you think this rose's original name is unfortunate, listen to the name it was given for marketing in the United States: 'Snow Pavement'. It is part of the Pavement series of roses, all of them more attractive than their names. 'Schneekoppe' has exquisite semidouble flowers that open violet and fade to blush and then white. It has a sweet fragrance.

GARDEN COMPANIONS

Grow 'Betty Prior' in masses in front of a fence covered with clematis and enclosed in a border of pale blue lavender.

When The best time to plant 'Betty Prior' is early spring. Bare-root roses should be planted as soon as the soil can be worked. Nursery-grown plants should be planted after all danger of spring frost has passed.

Where 'Betty Prior' thrives in full sun and rich, well-drained soil. Its bushy, compact growth habit makes it a good choice for a landscape or bedding plant.

How Amend the soil with abundant organic matter before planting. Clay or rocky soil should be replaced with loam soil. Soak bare-root roses in water overnight before planting. Plant so that the bud union is half-buried in the soil, deeper in colder climates. Space plants 2 to 3 feet apart.

TLC Keep the soil evenly moist throughout the growing season. Deep watering is more effective than frequent sprinkling. After the soil has warmed up in late spring, apply a 3- to 4-inch layer of organic mulch such as shredded leaves or bark around plants. Mulch should come close to but not touch canes. Feed established plants as early as possible in spring, sprinkling a controlled-release 10-10-10 fertilizer or an organic equivalent around the base of each plant. Water immediately to dissolve granules and carry nutrients to the roots. Additional applications of a water-soluble fertilizer should be given throughout the summer. Remove faded blossoms to encourage more blooms. In early spring, remove dead or diseased canes and prune to maintain outward growing, vase-shaped plants. In warmer areas, cut canes back by about a third; in colder areas cut back a bit more than that. Remove any suckers growing from the roots. 'Betty Prior' will need winter protection in colder zones.

Clusters of single flowers give 'Betty Prior' a simple, old-fashioned charm.

229

'Bonica'

'B onica' is a lovely name for a rose, isn't it? Once you actually meet this deservedly treasured rose, you'll want to have it in your garden. Bred in France, it was an immediate hit when introduced in the United States in 1982. It has double, medium-pink flowers; an imposingly wide girth (it grows up to 6 feet wide, and 4 to 8 feet tall); and a pleasant fragrance.

Like all floribunda roses, 'Bonica' flowers profusely, and is a showstopper at its peak in early summer. With a bit of protection it can withstand our cold midwestern winters; a 6-inch layer of mulch should suffice. As for disease resistance—a practical necessity if you have hot, humid summers—'Bonica' excels there, too. It was named to an elite group of outstanding performers at the Montreal Botanical Garden after scoffing at black spot, powdery mildew, and rust. Don't be confused, by the way, by the other French 'Bonica.' It has red flowers. Go pink.

'Bonica' has a naturally bushy shape, wider than it is tall, and makes a good edging plant.

PEAK SEASON

Best bloom in June then intermittently until frost; bright orange hips form in winter.

GOOD ALTERNATIVES

The following are all profuse bloomers similar to 'Bonica' with a nice growth habit.

'Royal Bonica' is newer (1994) and grows to 5 feet. Flowers are more double, a bit larger, and darker pink.

'Carefree Wonder', also from France, is a low-growing shrub rose (to 4 feet tall) that bears clusters of delicate, semidouble, pink-and-white blooms all summer. It is hardier than 'Bonica' but not quite as floriferous, though it comes close.

'Iceberg' has white flowers.

GARDEN COMPANIONS

Grow 'Bonica' with

- lady's-mantle
- lavender
- catmint
- euphorbia
- clematis
- honeysuckle

When The best time to plant 'Bonica' is early spring. Plant bare-root roses as soon as the soil can be worked. Plant nursery-grown plants after all danger of spring frost has passed.

Where Choose a site in full sun 5 to 6 hours a day with well-drained soil. 'Bonica' is an excellent landscape plant.

How Amend the soil with organic matter to a depth of $1\frac{1}{2}$ to 2 feet. Soak bare-root roses overnight in water before planting. Plant so that the bud union is half-buried in soil, deeper in colder areas. Space plants 5 feet apart, closer for hedges.

'Bonica' bears large clusters of 3-inch-wide double flowers on and off throughout the summer. It is one of America's best-loved roses.

TLC Keep the soil evenly moist throughout the growing season. Deep watering is more effective than frequent sprinkling. After the soil has warmed up in late spring, apply a 3- to 4-inch layer of organic mulch such as shredded leaves or bark around plants. Mulch should come close to but not touch canes. Feed established plants as early as possible in spring, sprinkling a controlled-release 10-10-10 fertilizer or an organic equivalent around the base of each plant. Water immediately to dissolve granules and carry nutrients to the roots. Additional applications of a water-soluble fertilizer should be given throughout the summer. Remove faded blossoms to encourage more blooms. Keep pruning to a minimum, removing dead or diseased canes in early spring. 'Bonica' will need winter protection in colder areas.

'Carefree Beauty'

'Carefree Beauty' is the crowning achievement of Griffith J. Buck, a legendary botanist at Iowa State University who spent much of his life seeking to develop a beautiful, disease-resistant rose that would survive midwestern winters unprotected. Though the two are often confused, 'Carefree Beauty' is no relation to the French floribunda 'Carefree Wonder'. Both roses have long-lasting pink flowers, but Buck's creation is distinguished by a long, pointed bud that opens to a semidouble bloom more than 4 inches across. The flowers grow in clusters.

Like all the roses Buck developed, 'Carefree Beauty' is both cold-hardy and ever-blooming, and an excellent landscape rose. It grows to 5 feet tall and wide, making it

The aptly named 'Carefree Beauty' is a reliable, good-looking, disease-resistant rose that blooms all summer long and needs no winter protection.

the perfect size and shape for an informal hedge. This rose is also effective planted in masses and in a perennial border. 'Carefree Beauty' has a fine record of fending off black spot and other common rose complaints.

PEAK SEASON

Blooms mid-June through July. Orange-red rose hips form in fall.

GOOD ALTERNATIVES

Buck developed several other roses that are also winter-hardy without protection. All have moderate to good disease resistance.

'Aunt Honey' has double, carmine pink buds that open to highly fragrant, pale rose flowers in clusters of ten. It grows to 3 feet tall.

'Brook Song' has lemon yellow buds that open to chrome yellow and age to amber yellow. It has leathery foliage and a bushy habit, and grows to 3 feet tall.

'Bright Melody' has double, ruby red flowers; a lovely fragrance; and a bushy habit. It grows to 3 feet tall.

'Prairie Princess' has long pink buds that open to semidouble, coral flowers. It can be grown as a climber or tall shrub.

GARDEN COMPANIONS

Grow 'Carefree Beauty' with *Nepeta* 'Six Hills Giant' (a tall catmint with dark blue flowers), *Clematis alpina,* and balloon flower *(Platycodon grandiflorus).* Or try pairing it with ornamental grasses such as purple fountain grass, chartreuse hakone grass, or a wispy feather reed grass.

When The best time to plant 'Carefree Beauty' is early spring. Plant bare-root roses as soon as the soil can be worked and nursery-grown plants after all danger of spring frost has passed.

Where Choose a site in full sun 5 to 6 hours a day with well-drained soil. A compact, neat growth habit makes this rose a good landscape plant, especially when planted in groups of three. Its ability to regenerate new shoots quickly makes it suitable for a mixed border, where it can be cut back each spring along with perennials.

How Amend the soil with organic matter to a depth of 1½ to 2 feet. Plant bare-root roses after soaking them overnight in water. Plant so the bud union is half-buried in soil, deeper in colder areas. Space plants 3 to 4 feet apart.

TLC Keep the soil evenly moist throughout the growing season. Deep watering is more effective than frequent sprinkling. After the soil has warmed up in late spring, apply a 3- to 4-inch layer of organic mulch such as shredded leaves or bark around plants. Mulch should come close to but not touch canes. Feed established plants as early as possible in spring, sprinkling a controlled-release 10-10-10 fertilizer or an organic equivalent around the base of each plant. Water immediately to dissolve granules and carry nutrients to the roots. Additional applications of a water-soluble fertilizer should be given throughout the summer. Remove faded blossoms to encourage more blooms. In colder climates, these shrubs may suffer dieback over winter. Because they regenerate shoots quickly, they can simply be cut to the ground each spring. Within a few weeks abundant new shoots will appear.

'Carefree Beauty' has gorgeous semidouble flowers that give off the unmistakable aroma of apples.

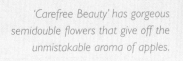

'The Fairy'

The fact that 'The Fairy', introduced in England in 1932, is a polyantha makes it exceptional. Polyanthas are an older class of roses that have largely been shoved aside by the newer, everblooming floribundas. What keeps gardeners coming back to 'The Fairy' is its uniquely dainty flowering habit. The tiny, ruffled, double, pale pink blooms grow in dense clusters on long, arching canes. The canes are thornier than most, but you'll forgive 'The Fairy' its pricklish ways. This rose is a profuse repeat bloomer, disease resistant, and quite hardy; and it has thoroughly modern versatility: it can be trained to climb a support, allowed to ramble as a ground cover, or grafted on a standard as a small specimen tree. I suspect another reason 'The Fairy' sticks in people's minds is that it is one of the few roses whose name really captures its delicate beauty.

With its loose form and small, pale pink flowers that bloom all summer, 'The Fairy' makes an excellent addition to an informal perennial border or cottage garden.

PEAK SEASON

Flowers nonstop from spring to fall in mild climates, profusely in June and sporadically thereafter in colder climates.

GOOD ALTERNATIVES

These roses, like 'The Fairy', feel at home in an informal setting, such as a cottage garden.

'Red Fairy' is the red-flowering twin of 'The Fairy,' with the same habit and long-blooming flower clusters.

'Nearly Wild' is a floribunda with medium-pink flowers that grows to 2 feet wide and 4 feet tall. It's super hardy and, like 'The Fairy', has an old-time feel about it, though its single blooms are less showy.

'Kent' is a low, spreading rose with semidouble white blooms abundantly grown on long trusses. It grows to 2 feet tall and spreads to 10 feet. It's excellent grown in masses or in a flower bed. A single plant makes quite an impact in a small garden. 'Kent' is extremely hardy.

GARDEN COMPANIONS

Grow 'The Fairy' in a cottage garden. It can be trained to share a fence with clematis. It also looks good with catmint, lavender, or Russian sage (Perovskia atriplicifolia).

When The best time to plant 'The Fairy' is early spring. Plant bare-root roses as soon as the soil can be worked and nursery-grown plants after all danger of spring frost has passed.

Where Select a site in full sun with rich, well-drained soil. 'The Fairy' can be used as a climber or ground cover.

How Amend the soil with abundant organic matter before planting. Clay or rocky soil should be replaced with loam soil. Soak bare-root roses overnight in water before planting. Plant so the bud union is half-buried in the soil, deeper in colder areas. Give these spreading plants plenty of room to grow, spacing them at least 3 feet apart.

'The Fairy' is a heavy bloomer, producing dense clusters of dainty flowers. Flowers may fade to white in the heat.

TLC Keep the soil evenly moist throughout the growing season. Deep watering is more effective than frequent sprinkling. Soak the ground thoroughly. After the soil has warmed up in late spring, apply a 3- to 4-inch layer of organic mulch such as shredded leaves or bark around plants. Mulch should come close to but not touch canes. Feed established plants as early as possible in spring, sprinkling a controlled-release 10-10-10 fertilizer or an organic equivalent around the base of each plant. Water immediately to dissolve granules and carry nutrients to the roots. Additional applications of a water-soluble fertilizer should be given throughout the summer. Remove faded blossoms to encourage more blooms. In early spring, remove dead or diseased canes and remove older canes to help keep plants vigorous. Remove any suckers growing from the roots. 'The Fairy' is susceptible to powdery mildew; adequate spacing will help reduce the problem.

'Flower Carpet Pink'

When 'Flower Carpet Pink' arrived in the United States from Germany in the mid-1990s, its marketers predicted an instant sellout. Having read the hype about these hardy, disease-resistant roses, I was curious when I spied a truck unloading hundreds of plants in shocking pink plastic pots at the nearby garden center.

Too bad about those pots, I thought to myself. But I brought some home. I liked the idea of everblooming roses that would hug the ground, spreading cheer where most roses refused to go, and that were absolutely, positively immune to black spot. I noticed a few blemishes on the leaves. They got bigger. Surprise, surprise. No rose is immune to black spot. These particular plants had been shipped with an unrelated rose raging with illness in rainy weather, just what black spot thrives on. I pruned the plants hard, and destroyed the infected leaves. Before long 'Flower Carpet Pink' was back in my garden. It's proving to be a hard-working, long-suffering, and truly garden-worthy rose.

When The best time to plant 'Flower Carpet Pink' is early spring. Plant bare-root roses as soon as the soil can be worked and nursery-grown plants after all danger of spring frost has passed.

Where Choose a site in full sun 5 to 6 hours a day with well-drained soil. Its dense, low-branching habit makes 'Flower Carpet Pink' suitable as a ground cover.

How Amend the soil with organic matter to a depth of 1½ to 2 feet. Soak bare-root roses

ABOVE AND BELOW: *Flower Carpet roses come in white and pink (shown here), as well as red, yellow, and coral. Deadheading stimulates them to bloom all summer.*

overnight in water before planting. Plant so that the bud union is half-buried in soil. Space plants 3 to 4 feet apart.

TLC For best results, keep the soil evenly moist throughout the growing season. Deep watering is more effective than frequent sprinkling. After the soil has warmed up in late spring, apply a 3- to 4-inch layer of organic mulch such as shredded leaves or bark around plants. Mulch should come close to but not touch canes. Feed established plants just as buds appear in spring, sprinkling a controlled-release 10-10-10 fertilizer or an organic equivalent around the base of each plant. Water immediately to dissolve granules and carry nutrients to the roots. 'Flower Carpet Pink' is more disease resistant than most roses and requires very little pruning. Shrubs may suffer some dieback over winter in colder climates.

OPPOSITE PAGE: *'Flower Carpet Pink's' mounding habit makes it a versatile shrub rose, excellent in borders and as a ground cover.*

PEAK SEASON
Blooms mid-June until frost.

GOOD ALTERNATIVES
The Flower Carpet series features dense, low-branching shrub roses that are suitable for use as ground covers and exceptionally hardy and disease resistant. Besides pink, blooms come in red, white, yellow, and coral. You won't find easier roses to grow.

GARDEN COMPANIONS
Grow 'Flower Carpet Pink' with lavender, artemisia, cranesbill geraniums, and dianthus. It looks good in front of taller, blue-flowered plants like catmint and veronica. It also looks good with creeping junipers and creeping cotoneasters.

'Graham Thomas'

This brilliant yellow rose was named after the legendary English rose breeder who brought "old roses" out of obscurity. It was developed by David Austin, another ambitious Englishman, who is attempting to create an alternative to modern roses that he rather sweepingly calls English roses. Austin's mission has been to combine the best

qualities of old roses—delicately ruffled, long-lasting flowers; rich fragrance; good habit and foliage—and features desired by modern gardeners, notably more frequent bloom and improved health and hardiness, traits borrowed from floribundas and hybrid teas.

'Graham Thomas' has red-tinted buds that open to 4-inch cupped flowers of butter yellow. It grows to 4 feet tall and wide, making it ideal in the perennial border or in groups of three as a landscape rose.

'Graham Thomas' has small, glossy green leaves and a fairly compact growth habit.

When The best time to plant 'Graham Thomas' is early spring. Plant bare-root roses as soon as the soil can be worked and nursery-grown plants after all danger of spring frost has passed.

Where Choose a site in full sun 5 to 6 hours a day with well-drained soil. 'Graham Thomas' looks best planted in groups of three. Plants spaced 1½ feet apart look like one dense shrub.

How Amend the soil with organic matter to a depth of 1½ to 2 feet. Soak bare-root roses overnight in water before planting. Plant so that the bud union is half-buried in the soil, deeper in colder areas. Space plants 1½ to 3 feet apart, depending on their use.

With its tightly petaled, peony-like flowers and rich fragrance, 'Graham Thomas' resembles the classic English-style rose. It is among the most popular of the David Austin roses.

TLC Keep the soil evenly moist throughout the growing season. Deep watering is more effective than frequent sprinkling. After the soil has warmed up in late spring, apply a 3- to 4-inch layer of organic mulch such as shredded leaves or bark around plants. Mulch should come close to but not touch canes. Feed established plants as early as possible in spring, sprinkling a controlled-release 10-10-10 fertilizer or an organic equivalent around the base of each plant. Water immediately to dissolve granules and carry nutrients to the roots. Additional applications of a water-soluble fertilizer should be given throughout the summer. Remove faded blossoms to encourage more blooms. In early spring, remove dead or diseased canes and prune to maintain outward growing, vase-shaped plants. Remove any suckers growing from the roots. In colder zones, you will need to use some type of winter protection. The best way to protect tender roses is the "Minnesota tip" method (see page 224).

PEAK SEASON

Best bloom in mid-June followed by less abundant repeat blooms until frost.

GOOD ALTERNATIVES

The following are all good substitutes for 'Graham Thomas' if bright yellow isn't your color.

'L. D. Braithwaite', named by Austin for his father-in-law, is a deep red rose with a more continuous blooming habit than that of most English roses. It grows 3 feet tall and wide and has a strong old-rose fragrance.

'Constance Spry' was introduced by Graham Thomas in 1961 and was, as David Austin puts it, "a stepping-stone toward the true English rose," most of which have been developed by Austin himself. 'Constance Spry' grows to 6 feet tall and wide with rich pink flowers and a perfumy fragrance. Austin recommends training it to a fence or trellis. It blooms heavily but only once, in early summer.

GARDEN COMPANIONS

English roses get along well with other perennials, and 'Graham Thomas' is quite at home in a border with tall foxgloves, veronica, lady's-mantle, lamb's ears, catmint, and other English roses. David Austin warns, however, that modern roses and English roses don't mix well.

'Morden Blush'

This Canadian rose was developed as part of a series at the Morden Research Station in southern Manitoba. While their main claim to fame is cold-hardiness, Morden roses (also called Parkland roses) are more than just tough. What sold me on 'Morden Blush' was its beauty. A truly elegant rose, it has dainty, double, ivory-colored petals with pinkish centers that do make the flower look like it's blushing. I first saw it in a friend's garden. I had never seen such a soft pink flower; it was like the color of a baby's skin, or the first pale but warm rose pink of dawn. I immediately wanted 'Morden Blush' in my garden.

The delicate appearance of 'Morden Blush' belies a tough disposition. It is disease resistant and requires little care.

'Morden Blush' grows 2 to 5 feet tall and is an excellent rose to grow in a container. Lustrous, dark green leaves set off the soft blooms beautifully and seem immune to powdery mildew and black spot. True to its reputation, it sails through subzero winters with little or no protection.

240

When The best time to plant 'Morden Blush' rose is early spring. Plant bare-root roses as soon as the soil can be worked and nursery-grown plants after all danger of spring frost has passed.

Where Select a site in full sun 5 to 6 hours a day with well-drained soil. This plant's compact growth habit makes it suitable for use in a mixed border or a container.

How Amend the soil with organic matter to a depth of 1½ to 2 feet. Soak bare-root roses overnight in water before planting. Plant so the bud union is half-buried in the soil, deeper in colder areas. Space plants 1½ to 2 feet apart.

TLC Keep the soil evenly moist throughout the growing season. Deep watering is more effective than frequent sprinkling. After the soil has warmed up in late spring, apply a 3- to 4-inch layer of organic mulch such as shredded leaves or bark around plants. Mulch should come close to but not touch canes. Feed established plants as early as possible in spring, sprinkling a controlled-release 10-10-10 fertilizer or an organic equivalent around the base of each plant. Water immediately to dissolve granules and carry nutrients to the roots. Additional applications of a water-soluble fertilizer should be given throughout the summer. Remove faded blossoms to encourage more blooms. In early spring, remove dead or diseased canes and prune to maintain outward growing, vase-shaped plants.

PEAK SEASON

Best bloom in mid-June followed by less abundant repeat blooms until frost.

GOOD ALTERNATIVES

All roses in the Morden family survive winter with little or no protection. The following also have lovely blooms.

'Morden Snow Beauty' grows to 3 feet tall and has clusters of lightly fragrant, semidouble white flowers that bloom continuously.

'Morden Sunrise' grows to 4 feet tall and has yellow flowers tinged with orange.

'Morden Ruby' grows to 3 feet tall and has dark red flowers speckled with deeper red. It blooms most profusely in early summer.

'Morden Fireglow' has dark green foliage and red-orange double flowers with scarlet undersides. An upright plant, it resembles a hybrid tea and grows to just over 3 feet tall.

GARDEN COMPANIONS

'Morden Blush' goes with everything. Set off its creamy color with the dark blue flower spikes of *Nepeta* 'Six Hills Giant' or, for a monochrome scheme, tall, creamy foxgloves. Try it behind purple feather reed grass.

Everblooming 'Morden Blush' has pale pink blooms that grow in clusters. The flowers open flat.

'Sea Foam'

This rose was a mystery to me. I really had no idea what to expect when I bought it, except that the flowers would be white. That was the first surprise. They aren't really white. They're more like cream tinged with pink, and the color changes very subtly, growing pinker as summer wears on. That 'Sea Foam' blooms nonstop from early summer into fall was another nice surprise.

This rose is super hardy, and doesn't need cover even in my Minnesota garden. In winter and spring I'm always tempted to cut back its slender, arching canes, but most of the plant comes back to life if I wait long enough, and every year 'Sea Foam' spreads a little farther along the stone wall where I planted it. It's quite lovely draped over the gray stones and dipping

'Sea Foam' grows 2 to 8 feet tall and 4 feet wide with lax and trailing canes that can be trained to climb a support. Its small, creamy white flowers can turn pinkish in summer.

down to mingle with the luridly colored Asiatic lilies on the level below. Its leaves are the leathery, dark green type that go so well with rose blossoms, especially white ones.

'Sea Foam' can be trained to a low fence, but it is happy just creeping slowly along the ground and could be used as a ground cover.

When The best time to plant 'Sea Foam' is early spring. Plant bare-root roses as soon as the soil can be worked and nursery-grown plants after all danger of spring frost has passed.

Where Choose a site in full sun 5 to 6 hours a day with well-drained soil. The trailing canes make 'Sea Foam' suitable as a ground cover. The rose can also be used as a short climber if the canes are supported and tied.

How Amend the soil with organic matter to a depth of 1½ to 2 feet. Soak bare-root roses overnight in water before planting. Plant so the bud union is half-buried in the soil, deeper in colder areas. Space plants 3 to 4 feet apart.

TLC For best results, keep the soil evenly moist throughout the growing season. Deep watering is more effective than frequent sprinkling. After the soil has warmed up in late spring, apply a 3- to 4-inch layer of organic mulch such as shredded leaves or bark around plants. Mulch should come close to but not touch canes. Feed established plants just as buds appear in spring, sprinkling a controlled-release 10-10-10 fertilizer or an organic equivalent around the base of each plant. Water immediately to dissolve granules and carry nutrients to the roots. 'Sea Foam' is more disease resistant than most roses and requires very little pruning, but you may want to cut back the vigorous canes in spring to keep it neater. Shrubs may suffer some dieback over winter in colder climates.

PEAK SEASON
Blooms continuously from mid-June into fall.

GOOD ALTERNATIVES
These roses are all excellent landscape roses and similar either in color or habit to 'Sea Foam'.

'Iceberg' has pure white flowers. A floribunda, it has bushier growth than 'Seafoam', so it won't ramble across the ground. It can also be pruned to a 3-foot-tall shrub or trained as a weeping standard (tree). 'Climbing Iceberg' can be trained to climb a fence.

'Golden Showers' is a yellow-flowered, everblooming climber that, like 'Sea Foam', can be trained to a low support. With its luxurious, disease-resistant foliage, it is an excellent rose for beginners, though it needs winter protection. Gardeners in the far north should use the "Minnesota tip" method (see page 224).

'Pink Sunsation' produces many small, bright pink flowers on a plant that grows horizontally 3 feet out from its center. It can be grown as a ground cover or trained as a weeping standard. It is quite hardy but needs protection in the coldest regions.

GARDEN COMPANIONS
'Sea Foam' is an excellent companion in the garden. Grow small flowers such as chives, dianthus, or creeping veronica up through its canes.

ABOVE: 'Sea Foam' looks great intermingling with the climbing miniature rose 'Red Cascade'. BELOW: Frothy clusters of blooms grow at the ends of the canes.

'William Baffin'

'William Baffin' produces long canes and can be trained to climb an arbor or trellis or grown as a large, arching shrub.

I used to ban climbing roses from my garden. I was simply unwilling to haul the canes off a trellis once a year and bury them in a trench. Then I heard about a new group of roses developed in Canada that were named after North American explorers. These roses were said to be so hardy you didn't have to bury or even cover them in winter. I decided to give the Explorers a try and brought home four, including the vigorous, long-caned climber 'William Baffin'. I planted it in full sun beside a cedar arch over my garden gate. Within 3 or 4 years, my gate was the talk of the neighborhood, and it was even featured in a gardening magazine.

Now I take it for granted that my gate will be as floriferous as any rose-covered cottage in England, festooned with deep pink, semidouble flowers and handsome dark leaves that never show a sign of illness or distress.

244

When The best time to plant 'William Baffin' is early spring. Plant bare-root roses as soon as the soil can be worked and nursery-grown plants after all danger of spring frost has passed.

Where 'William Baffin' thrives in well-drained soil where it gets full sun 5 to 6 hours a day. Its extensive root system needs lots of space to grow freely. Its long canes make it ideal for climbing arbors, fences, trellises, and pergolas.

How Amend the soil with organic matter to a depth of 1½ to 2 feet. Soak bare-root roses overnight in water before planting. Plant so the bud union is half-buried in the soil, deeper in colder areas. Space plants at least 4 feet apart, making sure they have ample room to grow.

TLC For best results, keep the soil evenly moist throughout the growing season, especially during the first year. Deep watering is more effective than frequent sprinkling. Mature plants will tolerate drought better than other roses. After the soil has warmed up in late spring, apply a 3- to 4-inch layer of organic mulch such as shredded leaves or bark around plants. Mulch should come close to but not touch canes. Feed established plants just as buds appear in spring, sprinkling a controlled-release 10-10-10 fertilizer or an organic equivalent around the base of each plant. Water immediately to dissolve granules and carry nutrients to the roots. In early spring, remove dead or diseased canes as well as older canes. Try to restrict plants to three or four main canes, pruning older canes to the ground to promote new growth (and more profuse blooming). Removing faded blossoms throughout the season will also encourage more blooms. Remove any suckers growing from the roots.

Large clusters of flowers bloom on and off throughout the growing season.

PEAK SEASON

Mid-June into July, followed by recurrent bloom into late fall.

GOOD ALTERNATIVES

The following are all excellent super-hardy roses. The first three belong to the Explorer series. 'Dublin Bay' is of unknown origin.

'John Cabot' is a tall shrub rose with double, dark pink flowers and light green leaves.

'Henry Kelsey' has semidouble crimson flowers and can be trained to climb.

'Champlain' is a 3- to 4-foot-tall double rose noted for its flowers' vivid red color and persistent blooming. The plant will suffer some dieback in winter (which can be pruned out).

The climber 'Dublin Bay' has it all: disease resistance, beauty, and exceptional hardiness. Its semidouble flowers are velvety red and grow in clusters. It is considered by some the finest red rose ever developed.

GARDEN COMPANIONS

'William Baffin' can share a trellis with a clematis like the early-blooming, blue-flowered 'Will Goodwin'. Plant cranesbill geraniums, lady's-mantle, lavender, or catmint at the base of the climber to cover up its bare lower canes.

Lawns, Ground Covers, and Prairie Plantings

My yard once consisted of a thin, weedy lawn. Every summer I'd dig up more of the grass for flower beds. I assumed that one day there wouldn't be any grass left in my yard. That was the unspoken objective (unspoken because my practical husband did not share this vision). Then an interesting thing happened. The less of it I had, the more I liked grass.

Now enclosed by curving brick edging, my lawn looks neat and manicured. It is the calming foil for borders densely planted with perennials, annuals, and shrubs of every shape and color. A few clumps of clover and crabgrass don't bother me, because the lawn plays a secondary role in my garden. The eye glides right over it to linger on the roses or the clematis or the blooming crabapple tree.

Sometimes I try to imagine the garden without grass, and just picturing myself trying to steer an overloaded wheelbarrow through the borders makes me tired. My lawn lets me move freely about the garden. It offers easy access to every flower in need of deadheading and every weed that needs pulling. How I used to take lawns for granted!

Because I like my grass better, I don't mind babying it. It's easy to repair dead patches by reseeding or just digging up healthy patches from less visible areas and transplanting them. And because the lawn is so small now, I can easily dispense with unwanted intruders using a long-handled weeder. I even indulge my grass with an occasional feeding of organic fertilizer.

ABOVE: *A tall-grass prairie meadow in late summer.* OPPOSITE PAGE: *A broad, curving grass path leads through perennial beds.*

CHOOSING THE RIGHT GRASS

The critical steps to a healthy lawn, no matter how big, are pretty much the same as for gardens. Choose the right plants for your site and prepare the soil properly before they go in the ground. For lawns in full sun, the grass of choice for most gardeners in the Midwest is bluegrass. Whether you start your lawn from seed or sod, it will contain a blend of grasses, about 80 percent bluegrass with a tougher perennial such as ryegrass blended in. If your lawn gets only partial sun, as mine does, it's a good idea to plant a shade mixture, which is half bluegrass, half a blend of ryegrass and shade-tolerant, fine-leafed fescues. Most lawns have both sunny and shady areas. The blend adapts to these conditions, with the fescues dominating in shady areas and the bluegrass and ryegrass taking over the sunny spots.

A word of caution: Though fescue-heavy grass blends are useful in shady places, don't expect the kind of unblemished turf you see in golf magazines. All grasses grow best with full sun; in shade, weeds may gradually overtake the grass, in which case you'll wish you'd planted a shade-tolerant ground cover instead (see page 254).

There are alternative grasses that are supposedly more ecologically correct. Zoysia grass, for example, is slow growing and drought resistant, thus requiring fewer mowings and waterings, and forms a dense mat that keeps down weeds naturally. Buffalo grass has similar attributes but is finer textured; left unmowed it forms a thick,

BELOW, LEFT: A curving path made of aggregate blocks leads through a ground cover of ivy and myrtle. BELOW, RIGHT: Long, wavy grass sets off an amur maple at its peak of fall color. OPPOSITE PAGE: A sturdy wooden gazebo opens onto a formal lawn and herb garden.

waving sea of grass 6 to 8 inches tall—so don't plan on using it for croquet or touch football. Both require full sun. Unfortunately, both are also slow to green up in spring and quick to turn brown in fall.

SEED OR SOD?

Fall is the best time for starting new grass—and time to ask the age-old question, should I seed or sod? If your yard is shady, you have no choice. Sod is grown on sod farms in full sun only. It won't contain that all-important ingredient for shade: fescue grasses. So seed it is. If your yard is sunny, you should still carefully weigh the pros and cons of seed versus sod. Certainly you'll get immediate results with

sod, but seed is significantly less expensive and eventually will give you a lusher, healthier lawn, especially if you use a high-quality mix that's guaranteed to contain no weed seeds.

Are you doing the work yourself? Seeding probably sounds like more trouble, but it really isn't. The biggest job is preparing the site, and you'll have to do that whether you're seeding or sodding. Any existing turf must be carefully removed, along with weeds and weed seeds. This is going to be hard work, as a thin or weed-infested lawn is usually a sign of compacted soil. Site preparation won't be any easier if you've bought a new home in a suburban housing development with no lawn to remove; most likely the topsoil was hauled away during construction and you'll be dealing with hard-packed clay.

In either case, you'll need to dig to a depth of at least 3 or 4 inches and blend the existing soil, such as it is, with good topsoil and organic matter to lighten the growing medium so that tender, young grass roots won't suffocate. Sprinkle a starter fertilizer over the site after that, using a mechanical spreader, and thoroughly rake it into the soil. Then moisten the soil with water and lay sod or sow seed.

If you're laying sod, it'll be a whole lot simpler if you have a strong back. Those rolls are heavy, especially when they're wet, and you have to keep them moist. Also, when you roll out the strips make sure they fit together tightly. Any

ABOVE: *Tucked into a shady corner of a formal garden, a rattan table and chairs create an inviting, casual sitting area.* OPPOSITE PAGE: *A rustic arbor links perennial beds filled with lamb's ears, rudbeckia, canna, and coleus, and beckons visitors to stroll across the lawn and have a seat beside it.*

openings are invitations to weeds. Overlap ½ inch where the strips meet at the ends, as they'll shrink a bit. Especially on a slope, it's a good idea to stake the strips to hold them in place. This also helps reduce shrinkage. Once the sod is in place, run a heavy roller over it (you can rent one at the hardware store) to help the new sod make a tight

bond with the soil underneath. Using sprinklers or soaker hoses, apply twice-daily waterings (unless it's raining) for the first week or so; water until the soil is moist but not soggy and let it dry out between waterings so the roots don't rot.

If you're seeding your lawn, fill a spreader with seed mix after you've spread the fertilizer and watered. Follow the instructions on the package. Hold the seed in place (and protect it from birds) with a thin layer of straw or light cotton mesh secured with stakes. If you use

straw, take care not to layer on too much or you'll block out sun and water.

At this point in our lesson, you may be wanting to call in the professionals. Here's an idea if you have a large yard and want to hire out the work: hydroseeding. A hydroseeding company will prepare the site and then bring in a tank truck equipped with high-powered hoses that spray a blend of seed and fertilizer over your yard, forcing the mixture deep enough into the soil that it won't wash away or get eaten by birds. Hydroseeding is fast and effective, a cheaper-than-sod route to a lush, healthy lawn. All you have to do, literally, is add water.

ABOVE: *A well-kept lawn sheltered by mature trees appears as a delightful forest glade.* OPPOSITE PAGE: *A rippling expanse of buffalo grass invites wading.*

CARE AND FEEDING

Your new lawn is ready for mowing when it's about 3 inches tall. (Be sure the blade on your mower is sharp. Dull blades damage grass.) Keeping the height between 2 and 3 inches allows grass to develop deeper roots that can compete with weeds. If you mow frequently you won't need to bag the clippings but can leave them on the lawn. They'll decompose and add nitrogen to the soil.

If you have your heart set on a perfect lawn, you'll need to fertilize it four times a year—

twice in spring, once in midsummer, and again in fall. Otherwise, the best month for an annual dose of fertilizer is September. Your lawn will green up more quickly the following spring and put up a stronger defense against weed invasions. For the first couple of years you can apply crabgrass preventer in spring and broad-leafed weed killer in fall. But once your lawn is established, weeds shouldn't be much of a problem. Crabgrass won't get a foothold in a lawn that's kept dense by frequent mowing. Dandelions can be kept to minimum if you snip their flowers before they

go to seed or, better still, if you dig up the plants by the taproot.

Aerating compacted soil does wonders for grass. I spend a lot of time pushing a heavy wheelbarrow across my lawn. Unfortunately, this constant heavy pounding compresses the spaces between soil particles and makes it harder for air and water to reach plant roots. Occasionally I rent an aerating tool to remove small chunks of lawn (called plugs). This gives the roots more breathing room. Mostly, though, I let earthworms do the work of aerating for me, another reason to leave clippings on the grass to decompose: the earthworms bring the nutrients down under, and their tunneling lightens the soil. See, even a lawn can be a healthy ecosystem.

Ideally you won't need to do anything else to your lawn to keep it healthy but mow and water it occasionally. Be forewarned that your lawn may go dormant and turn brown during long dry spells. Don't panic. Lawns almost always come back. Dormancy is their way of

protecting themselves by conserving their energy for better times. In a normal summer, a weekly watering should be plenty for established lawns.

SHADE-LOVING GROUND COVERS

If you want plants that act like grass but will grow where grass won't—that is, in dense shade—consider planting low-growing ground covers. You don't have to mow them. They're surprisingly tough. You can even walk on some without harming them. Okay, you're not going to want to sunbathe on a bed of pachysandra, but you wouldn't sunbathe in the shade anyway. Best of all, the dappled light of a shade garden is ideally suited to bringing out the subtle beauty of plants whose foliage is their best feature.

Technically, ground covers are plants no more than 6 to 8 inches tall that spread by sending out runners. Most of the plants I'll talk about here fit that definition. If you want to cover a shady area in a hurry, a super-aggressive spreader like variegated gout weed *(Aegopodium podagraria* 'Variegatum')* will do the job. I recommend it only for real trouble spots where nothing else will grow, so it'll be unlikely to compromise the health of a prettier plant.

Slower growing but far more refined, if a bit commonplace, are Japanese pachysandra or spurge *(Pachysandra terminalis)*, bugleweed or carpet bugle *(Ajuga reptans)*, English ivy

LEFT: *Ostrich ferns* (Matteuccia struthiopteris) *thrive in a woodland setting with moist, acidic soil.* OPPOSITE PAGE: *A garden nymph plays in dappled shade surrounded by bugleweed, hosta, and Siberian iris.*

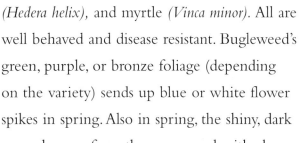

ABOVE: *Masses of blue bugleweed and other vividly colored ground covers spill over old stone walls and spread across the lawn, turning a formal garden romantic.* BELOW, LEFT: *Lily-of-the-valley in bloom.* BELOW, RIGHT: Lamium maculatum *'White Nancy' with white-flowered sweet woodruff.*

(Hedera helix), and myrtle *(Vinca minor).* All are well behaved and disease resistant. Bugleweed's green, purple, or bronze foliage (depending on the variety) sends up blue or white flower spikes in spring. Also in spring, the shiny, dark green leaves of myrtle are covered with charm-ing, light blue flowers. *(Euonymus fortunei* is similar but has a larger leaf and no flowers, and is slightly hardier.) Pachysandra has white flowers, but its dense, green masses of shiny, pointed leaves are its main appeal. It looks good in formal gardens or under trees.

European wild ginger *(Asarum europaeum)* takes a bit longer to get established, but it will eventually cover a large shady area with lovely, glossy green leaves that are a little like small lily pads. It blooms in spring, but its flowers are shy and hide under the foliage. Dead nettle *(Lamium)* has variegated leaves and either pink, white, or lavender flowers all summer. It also grows in sunny spots. Though dead nettle may die back in a hard winter, come spring it will spread at an accelerating pace. I grow it to fill spaces between ferns and hostas, along with sweet woodruff *(Galium odoratum),* a more delicate plant with white flowers in spring and nice fragrance.

Most of these plants like a fairly moist soil. Unfortunately, dry shade is more common. This came as a surprise to me. I'd always figured the leafy trees that shaded my garden also kept the soil moist. Luckily, some ground covers prefer, or at least tolerate, the dry, infertile soil found beneath birch, beech, and maple trees. Ground covers generally grow a bit more slowly in these conditions, but they will survive. My favorites are barrenwort or bishop's hat *(Epimedium),* barren strawberry *(Waldsteinia ternata),* Serbian bellflower *(Campanula poscharskyana),* creeping Veronica or speedwell *(Veronica peduncularis* 'Georgia Blue'), and big-root geranium *(Geranium macrorrhizum).* All have interesting foliage and pretty flowers. 'Georgia Blue' has amazingly clear blue flowers and dark green, rounded leaves that form a low mat. Bellflower has lavender flowers in May and is quite vigorous. Barren strawberry has evergreen foliage and yellow flowers in April and May and grows almost anywhere. Big-root geranium is a bit taller

than the classic ground covers, growing to about 1 foot, and has fragrant magenta flowers, and leaves that turn flaming red in fall.

Some other taller ground covers that are useful for filling large shady spaces are hosta, lily-of-the-valley, lady's-mantle, foamflower *(Tiarella cordifolia),* ferns, pulmonaria, forget-me-nots (a vigorously self-sowing biennial), and astilbe.

Barrenwort, 'Blue Umbrella' hosta, and sensitive fern (Onoclea sensibilis) *make an enticing green border along a stone path to a wooden bridge in this Japanese-influenced shade garden.*

GROUND COVERS FOR SUN

I introduced ground covers as plants that will grow where grass won't. However, once you develop a taste for ground covers, you're going to want to grow them in sunny places, too.

Probably the most popular ground covers for sun (or shade) are the English ivies. Creeping Jenny *(Lysimachia nummularia)* and the creeping sedums *(Sedum kamtschaticum* and *S. sempervivoides)* are good choices for full sun. Sedum isn't quite as aggressive as creeping Jenny. It comes in many leaf colors, from gray-green to purplish pink, and its small yellow, orange, or red flowers are long lasting.

Perennial herbs add something else to the list of ground-cover virtues: they smell good and you can use them in cooking. Plant creeping thyme in the sunniest, hottest, driest spot, in well-drained soil, and it will take off. Lavender is too tall to be considered a ground cover, but it's excellent for mass plantings. Catmint *(Nepeta)* is an herblike, very fragrant, clumping perennial that looks like lavender but is much hardier. It is a vigorous self-sower, but if it gets too aggressive you can easily pull it up by the roots or shear it back to the ground.

A few of the ground covers I've mentioned are evergreen, meaning they keep their leaves all winter, which is nice if you live somewhere warm enough to enjoy them. I don't. My evergreen ground covers (dead nettle, ivy, and myrtle) look pretty ratty after a long winter under mulch and snow. I usually cut back most of each plant in spring and wait for it to sprout fresh leaves. You won't have this problem with ground-hugging conifers like creeping juniper (for sun) and yew (for shade). Their needles hold up well in winter and, unless they've suffered from overexposure to sun and wind, they'll look just as good next spring as they did when you planted them. Find out more about using evergreen conifers as ground covers in "Evergreen Conifers," beginning on page 128.

A PRAIRIE LANDSCAPE

More and more homeowners in the Midwest are paying homage to their ancestors by planting a prairie or meadow in their own back (or front) yards. The original prairie landscape was a virtual ocean of tall grasses and flowering plants extending in all directions as far as the eye could see. Lewis and Clark found it beautiful. The pioneers found it daunting. The earth was so thick with roots, early settlers broke their plows tilling it. But they prevailed and eventually replaced the prairie plants with crops that thrived in the fertile soils left behind.

Restoring the native landscape isn't as easy as you might think. Weeds must be entirely eliminated by hand-pulling and tilling before they set seed or by applying an herbicide. Then you have to know your plants. The most successful prairie gardens use tall plants with deep roots that pull up water and nutrients, along with short plants with shallow roots and a matlike habit that cover the soil and keep down weeds. That takes research. The payoff is that once established, prairie plants require little care and are impervious to drought and disease. They were survivors in their natural habitat and if conditions are

LEFT: Helianthus 'Summer Sun' welcomes visitors to a farmhouse entry garden. OPPOSITE PAGE: A weathered fence and a stone path set the right mood for an easygoing planting of Coreopsis 'Zagreb', poppies, bee balm, and other perennials.

right in your yard—if the soil is rich but drains well, and if the weeds are controlled from the outset—your summertime chores will be limited to deadheading and bringing in bouquets for the dinner table.

Prairie plants come in all shapes and sizes. There are flowering perennials and annuals, as well as tall, short, feathery, and clumping grasses. Most require full sun. You can buy seed mixes that come with detailed directions for soil preparation, seed sowing, fertilizing, and so on. If you buy plants, you will have more control over the design. But there is no one right way to design a prairie. The original prairie differed from region to region. In some places tall grasses predominated. In others it

ABOVE, LEFT: *The reliable, late bloomer goldenrod.* ABOVE, RIGHT: *Prairie dropseed, a short, clumping native grass, makes an excellent edging plant.*

was a mix of grasses and flowering plants. For those of you who picture a prairie as a daisy-filled meadow, a wildflower mix may be the place to start.

Prairie plantings are almost by definition natural and wild, but there are always exceptions. Some garden designers create formal borders by massing native plants in "blocks" of the same variety or alternating two or more different plant types. Ornamental grasses, purple cone-flower *(Echinacea purpurea),* and rudbeckia, as well as nonnative plants like Russian sage *(Perovskia atriplicifolia),* everblooming daylilies, and upright sedums, are effective when planted this way, especially in large spaces.

Your first step in creating a prairie garden is to get to know native plants. Some of the most popular and easy-to-grow flowering perennials are rudbeckia, liatris, purple coneflower, lupine *(Lupinus),* sunflowers *(Helianthus),* asters, goldenrod *(Solidago),* yarrow *(Achillea),* spiderwort *(Tradescantia),* bee balm *(Monarda),* and Joe Pye

ABOVE: *Black-eyed Susan and purple coneflower edge a lawn, with tall feather reed grass serving as a vertical backdrop.* BELOW, LEFT: Liatris spicata. BELOW, RIGHT: *A meadow planting of orange California poppies, scarlet flax* (Linum grandiflorum 'Rubrum'), *baby blue eyes* (Nemophila menziesii), *and red Flanders Field poppies.*

weed *(Eupatorium).* Some annuals that reseed themselves are poppies, zinnias, cosmos, wallflower *(Erysimum),* and cornflower or bachelor's

button *(Centaurea cyanus)*. Prairie dropseed *(Spor-obolus heterolepis)* is a short, clumping grass, equally effective in masses and as an edging. For taller grasses see "Ornamental Grasses," beginning on page 186. Remember that your prairie landscape will be dense with plants and not suitable for long strolls unless you're prepared to cut paths through it with a lawn mower.

Remember, too, that your neighbors may not appreciate your prairie garden at first, especially if their taste runs to perfect lawns and sculpted conifers. Be sensitive to the look and feel of your neighborhood when designing a "wild" garden. My favorite examples of this style are planted at some distance from the house—in a field or on a hillside—where their sweeping grandeur can be admired from afar, offering a hint of what "prairie" meant a century ago.

In a sunny herb garden, a stone path meanders through soft-textured clumps of thyme, dianthus (in foreground), and low grasses, passing under an arbor made of tree saplings and in front of a stone bench.

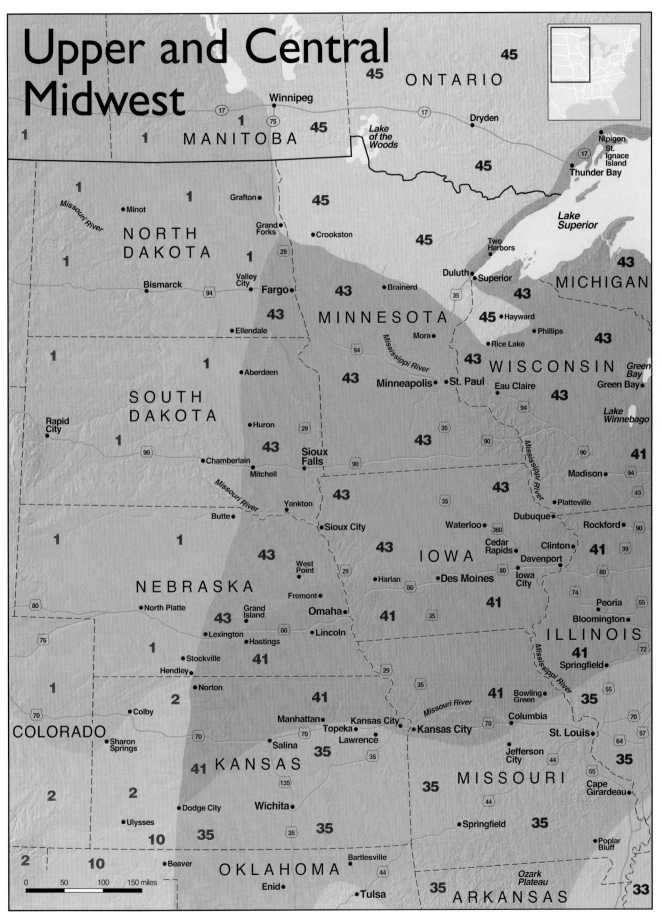

Upper and Central
Midwest

ONTARIO

45

45

Winnipeg

17

Dryden

1

75

45

1

1

MANITOBA

Lake of the Woods

17

Nipigon

St. Ignace Island

17

Thunder Bay

45

45

45

1

1

Grafton

Minot

Missouri River

45

Crookston

45

Lake Superior

NORTH DAKOTA

Grand Forks

29

Two Harbors

1

Duluth

Superior

43

MICHIGAN

1

Bismarck

94

Valley City

Fargo

43

Brainerd

35

43

Hayward

45

Ellendale

43

MINNESOTA

Mora

Phillips

43

94

Rice Lake

43

WISCONSIN

1

1

Aberdeen

43

Minneapolis

St. Paul

43

Eau Claire

Green Bay

Green Bay

SOUTH DAKOTA

94

43

Lake Winnebago

Rapid City

1

Huron

29

35

90

43

41

90

Chamberlain

Mitchell

43

Sioux Falls

90

43

Madison

94

43

Missouri River

Yankton

35

43

Platteville

Dubuque

Rockford

90

Butte

1

1

Sioux City

43

Waterloo

380

Cedar Rapids

Clinton

Davenport

41

39

IOWA

West Point

29

Harlan

80

Des Moines

Iowa City

80

80

Peoria

55

North Platte

Fremont

41

74

NEBRASKA

43

Grand Island

Omaha

35

Bloomington

76

Lexington

80

Lincoln

ILLINOIS

72

1

Hastings

41

Springfield

Stockville

41

Hendley

29

35

1

Norton

35

41

Bowling Green

35

70

2

41

Manhattan

Kansas City

Missouri River

Columbia

70

Colby

70

Topeka

Kansas City

St. Louis

70

COLORADO

Sharon Springs

70

Salina

Lawrence

35

57

41

KANSAS

135

Jefferson City

44

35

64

2

2

Dodge City

Wichita

MISSOURI

55

Cape Girardeau

Ulysses

35

44

35

10

35

35

Springfield

Poplar Bluff

2

10

Beaver

OKLAHOMA

Bartlesville

Ozark Plateau

33

0 50 100 150 miles

Enid

44

Tulsa

35

ARKANSAS

The Great Lakes

Lake
Superior

45   45   43

43

43   MINNESOTA   • Two Harbors

45   43

45   Duluth

• Superior   • Houghton

• Ashland   • Marquette   Newberry •

• Ironwood   • Ishpeming

43   43   43   MICHIGAN   43

45   • Drummond

• Manistique

43   • Hayward   51

• Radisson   • Kingsford   • Escanaba

Mora •   45   • Phillips   • Rhinelander

35   43

43

• New   43   • Merill   Marinette •   43

Richmond

Minneapolis •   • Holcombe   • Wausau   Green   41

St.   94   Bay   • Sturgeon   Travers

Paul   Bay   City

51   • Shawano   43

• Eau Claire   43   Green

Bay

• Marshfield

43   WISCONSIN   • Manistee

• Appleton   41   41

35   Osh Kosh   Lake   • Ludington

• •   Winnebago   • Manitowoc

90   Fond du Lac •   43   Sheboygan

• La Crosse   Lake

90   43   94   Michigan

43   90

• Reedsburg   • Portage   • Beaver

43   Dam

• Prairie   41   • Watertown

43   du Chien   • Madison   94   Muskegon •   Grand

Rapids

IOWA   Milwaukee   41

90   • Elkhorn   43   • Racine   Holland •

43   • Platteville   41   196

• Waterloo   • Dubuque   Janesville •   41   94   39

380   • Rockford   94   South

Haven   • Kalama

43   • Rockford   90   39   94   Three

Cedar   Clinton •   ILLINOIS   39   • Evanston   Rivers

• Rapids   41   41   • Chicago   39

0   30   60   90 miles   Aurora   Gary   80   90   41

• Davenport   55   • Harvey   39   South

• Hammond   41   Bend

43

45 **45**

ONTARIO

45

17

17 Sault Ste. Marie

• Eliot
Lake **45**

75 **43** **45**

17 • Sudbury • North
Bay

43 **43**

75

Mackinac
Island **69** **45**

31 **41** • Parry
Sound

• Petoskey Georgian
Bay **43** • Huntsville

131 • Wolverine • Alpena **43**

39

Lake **43**

75 Huron **400** **40**

41 Owen
Sound • Barrie • Peterborough

• Grayling Port
Elgin **40**

27 **43** • Newmarket **401** • Newcastle

Illac Port
Austin **39** • Hanover ONTARIO **40** York Scarborough Lake
Ontario
• Toronto
Brampton • • Mississauga

Saginaw **41** **43** • Kitchener **QEW** **39**

41 Bay

Midland • **401**

MICHIGAN **39** • Hamilton **39**

75 Stratford QEW • Niagara
Saginaw • • Marlette **40** • Brantford **40** Falls **90**
27 London • **401** St.
Catharines • Buffalo
Port
Huron **402**

• Alma **39** **40**

41 • Flint **41** **90** **39** NEW
YORK
96 **69** Port
Huron • Sarnia **17** **42**
• Lansing **75** • Pontiac Lake • Jamestown
96 St. Clair

Battle • Jackson Ann **94** Detroit **39** **401** Lake **42**
Creek Arbor • Windsor Erie Erie
94 **41** **39** • Monroe **39**

69 **40**

41 • Adrian **90** **79**

• Toledo **39** PENNSYLVANIA

80 **90** **75** Cleveland • **90**

41 **39** OHIO **90** **71** **77** **41** **40** **80** **40**

Ohio River Valley

Lake Michigan

MICHIGAN

IOWA

Cedar Rapids
Clinton
Iowa City
Davenport
Kewanee
Galesburg
Peoria
Bloomington
Quincy
Jacksonville
Decatur
Springfield

ILLINOIS

Rockford
Aurora
Joliet
Harvey

Evanston
Chicago
Gary
Hammond

Lansing
South Haven
Kalamazoo
Defiance

South Bend
Plymouth
Fort Wayne
Logansport

INDIANA

Lafayette
Tipton
Muncie
Crawfordsville
Greenville
Indianapolis

Urbana
Champaign

Terre Haute

Bowling Green
Effingham
Bloomington
Scottsburg
Cincinnati

St. Louis

Salem
Jasper
Louisville
Lexington

MISSOURI

Carbondale
Marion
Anna
Cape Girardeau

Evansville
Owensboro

Ohio River

Elizabethtown

KENTUCKY

Madisonville
Bowling Green

Paducah
Poplar Bluff
Hopkinsville
Albany

Clarksville

Martin

TENNESSEE

Mississippi River
Missouri River
Mississippi River

43
41
41
39
41
41
39
41
41
41
41
41
41
35
35
35
35
35
35
35
35
35
35
35
35
35
33
33
33
33
33
33

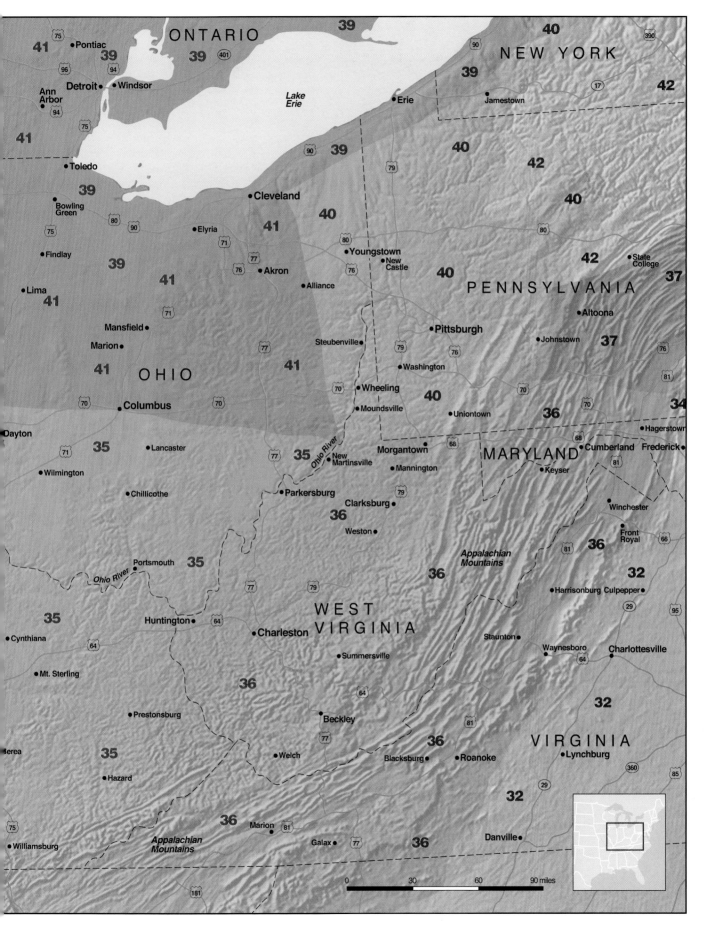

ONTARIO

39

40

NEW YORK

41 • Pontiac

39
94

39
401

90

Ann
Arbor
• Detroit • Windsor

Lake
Erie

• Erie

39

17
• Jamestown

42

94

75

41

• Toledo

90

39

• Cleveland

90

40

40

79

80

42

39

• Bowling
Green

80

• Elyria

71

41

77

80
• Youngstown
• New
Castle

76

80

40

• State
College

42

37

75

• Findlay

90

39

76

• Akron

• Alliance

PENNSYLVANIA

• Altoona

• Lima

41

71

41

• Pittsburgh
• Johnstown

37

76

• Mansfield

77

• Steubenville

79

76

81

• Marion

41

OHIO

41

• Washington

70

• Wheeling

70

40

70

36

34

70

• Columbus

70

• Moundsville
• Uniontown

68

MARYLAND

• Hagerstown

Dayton

35

71
• Lancaster

77

35

Ohio River
• New
Martinsville

Morgantown
68
• Cumberland Frederick

• Wilmington

• Chillicothe

• Parkersburg

• Mannington

• Keyser

81

• Winchester

Clarksburg •

79

36

• Weston

Appalachian
Mountains

81

36

Front
Royal

66

• Portsmouth

35

Ohio River

36

32

• Harrisonburg Culpepper •

29

95

35

Huntington •
64

77

79

• Charleston

WEST
VIRGINIA

• Staunton

• Waynesboro • Charlottesville
64

• Cynthiana

64

• Summersville

36

32

• Mt. Sterling

36

64

• Prestonsburg

• Beckley
77

81

VIRGINIA

Berea

35

• Welch

36
• Blacksburg • Roanoke

• Lynchburg

• Hazard

75

36

Marion •

81

Galax •

77

36

360

85

29

32

• Danville

• Williamsburg

Appalachian
Mountains

0   30   60   90 miles

181

Index Pages listed in *italics* include photographs.